BETTY & VERONICA

BY ADAM HUGHES

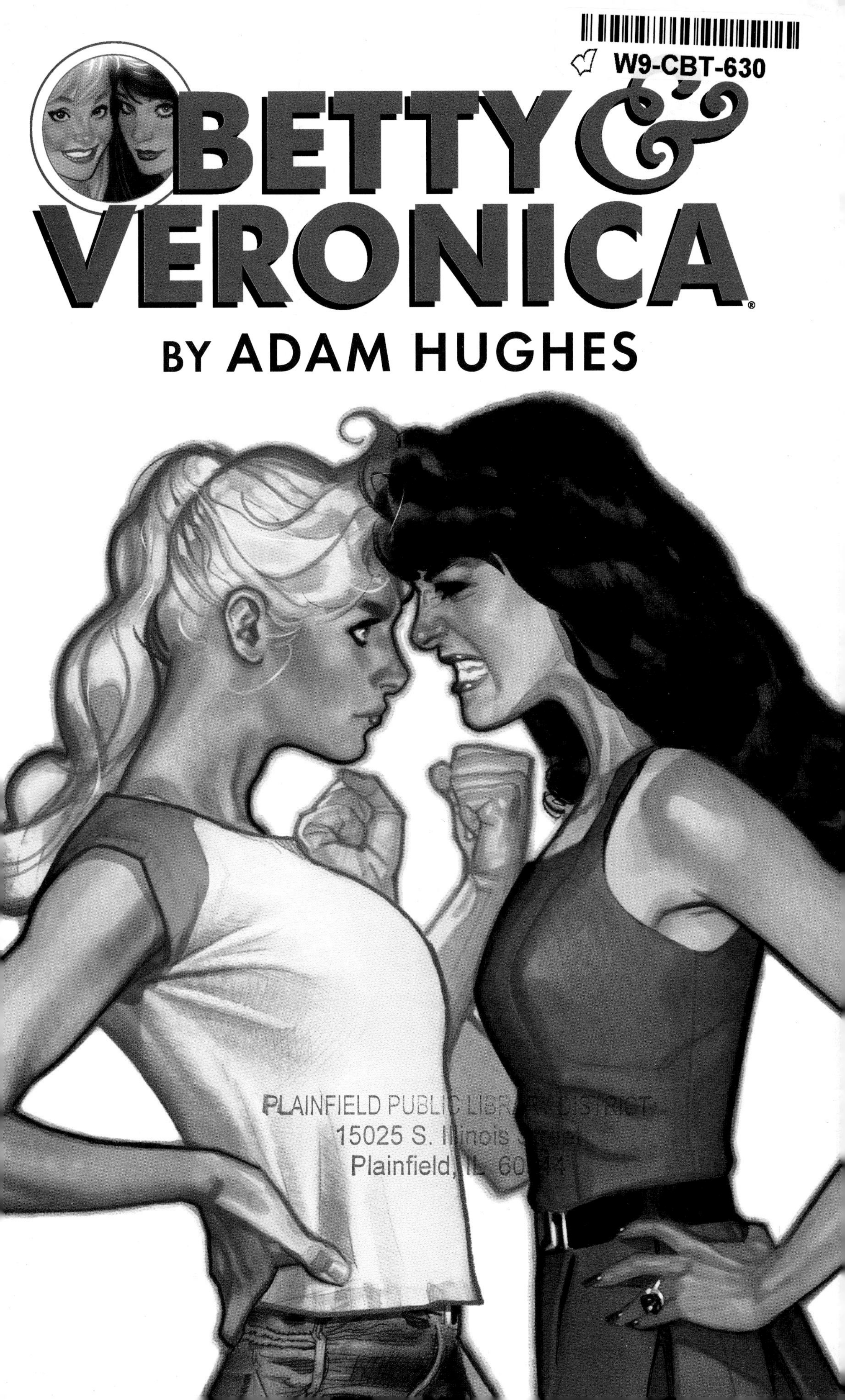

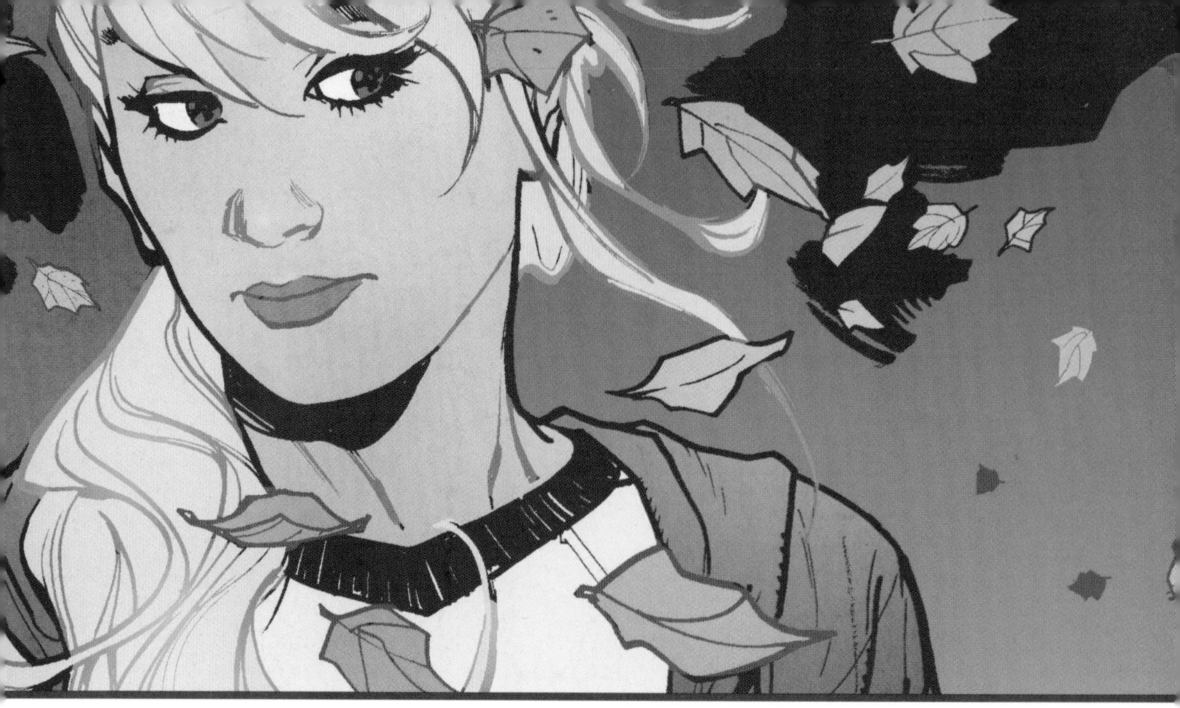

STORY & ART:

ADAM HUGHES

COLORING:

JOSÉ VILLARRUBIA

LETTERING:

JACK MORELLI

EDITOR:

MIKE PELLERITO

ASSOCIATE EDITOR:

STEPHEN OSWALD

ASSISTANT EDITOR:

JAMIE LEE ROTANTE

GRAPHIC DESIGN:

KARI McLACHLAN

PUBLISHER:

JON GOLDWATER

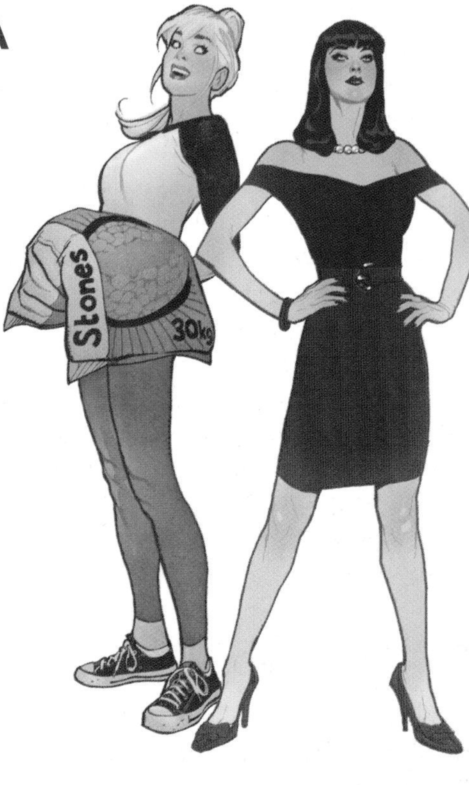
Stones
30kg

BETTY AND VERONICA
BEST FRIENDS FOREVER

Welcome to the collected edition of *Betty & Veronica*, the special mini-series written and drawn by legendary comic artist Adam Hughes. Betty Cooper and Veronica Lodge have been icons for over 75 years and, while things have changed over time for everyone's favorite BFFs, much of what we know and love about them still hold true: they have strong personalities, they can turn everything into a hilarious adventure, they speak up for what they believe in and their friendship stands the tests of time, even against seemingly insurmountable odds.

Betty and Veronica are fun, sexy and intelligent—that's something that will never change and is expertly demonstrated in Hughes' witty writing and gorgeous art.

Pair that with José Villarrubia's masterful coloring and you have a recipe for success. Also featured in this graphic novel are the numerous covers that accompanied the series, showcasing the various beautiful artistic renderings of the two teenagers.

We hope you enjoy this special collection all about America's sweethearts, Betty and Veronica!

ISSUE ONE

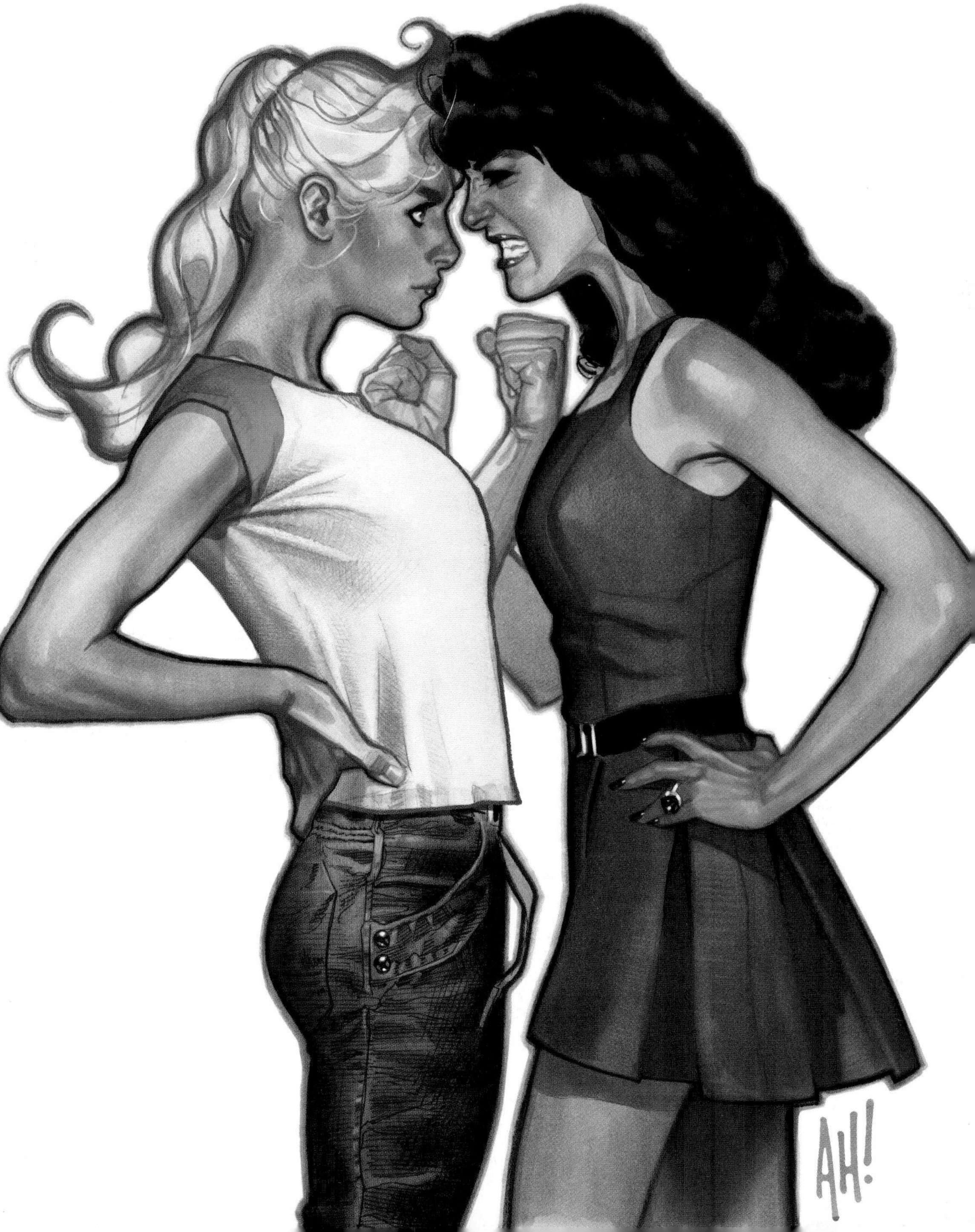
AH!

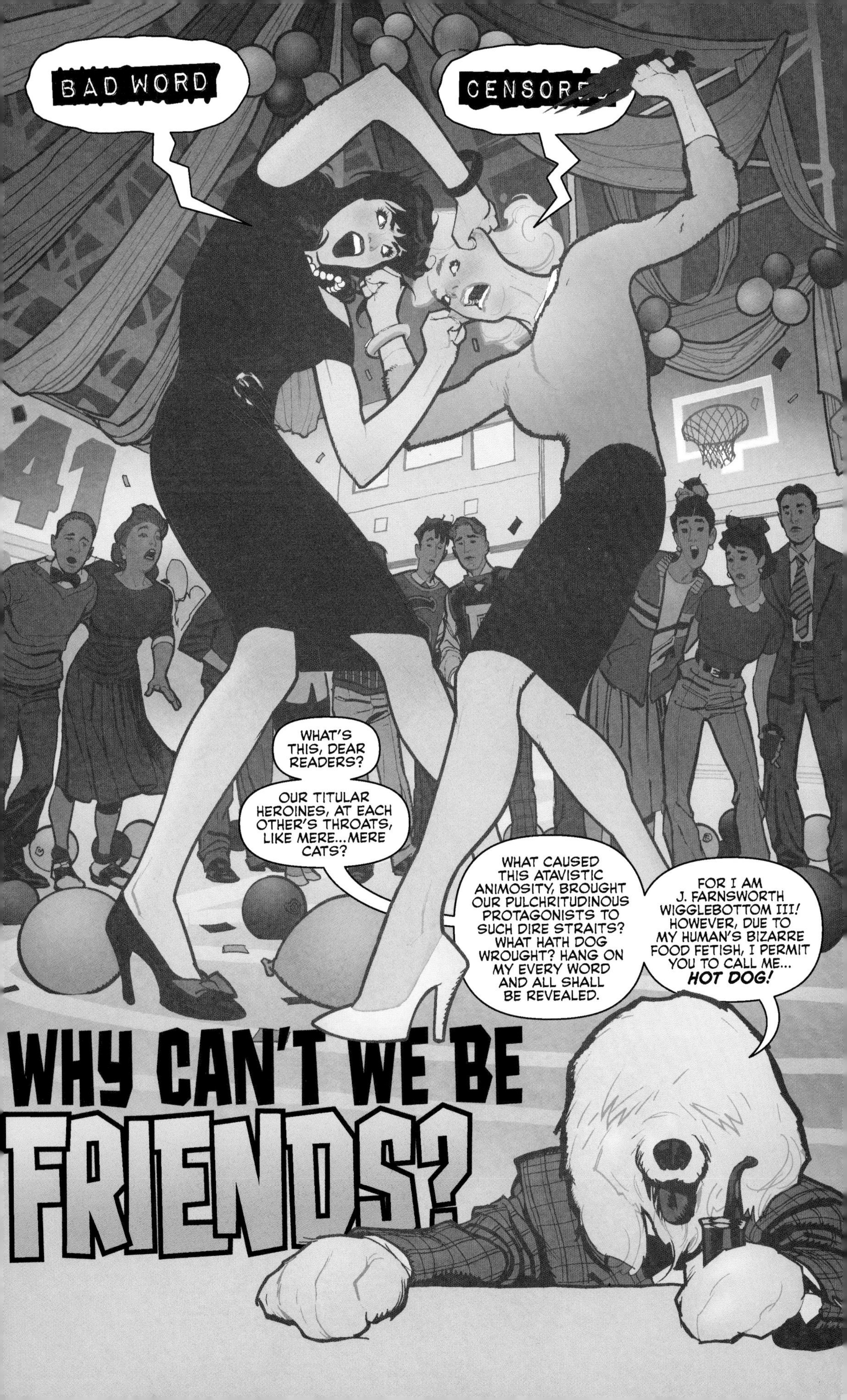
BAD WORD
CENSORED
WHAT'S THIS, DEAR READERS?
OUR TITULAR HEROINES, AT EACH OTHER'S THROATS, LIKE MERE...MERE CATS?
WHAT CAUSED THIS ATAVISTIC ANIMOSITY, BROUGHT OUR PULCHRITUDINOUS PROTAGONISTS TO SUCH DIRE STRAITS? WHAT HATH DOG WROUGHT? HANG ON MY EVERY WORD AND ALL SHALL BE REVEALED.
FOR I AM J. FARNSWORTH WIGGLEBOTTOM III! HOWEVER, DUE TO MY HUMAN'S BIZARRE FOOD FETISH, I PERMIT YOU TO CALL ME... ***HOT DOG!***
WHY CAN'T WE BE FRIENDS?

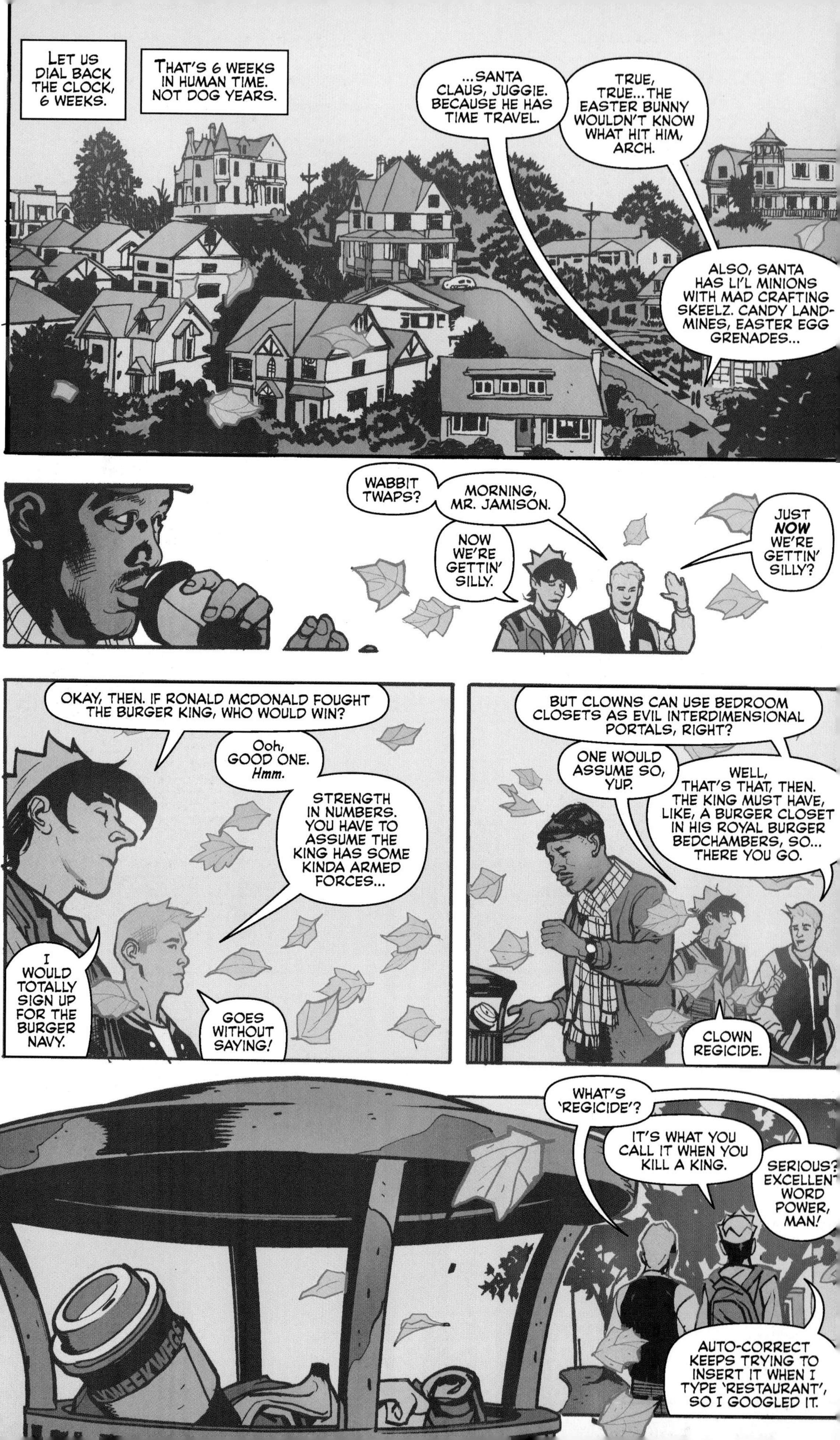
LET US DIAL BACK THE CLOCK, 6 WEEKS.
THAT'S 6 WEEKS IN HUMAN TIME. NOT DOG YEARS.
...SANTA CLAUS, JUGGIE. BECAUSE HE HAS TIME TRAVEL.
TRUE, TRUE...THE EASTER BUNNY WOULDN'T KNOW WHAT HIT HIM, ARCH.
ALSO, SANTA HAS LI'L MINIONS WITH MAD CRAFTING SKEELZ. CANDY LAND-MINES, EASTER EGG GRENADES...
WABBIT TWAPS?
NOW WE'RE GETTIN' SILLY.
MORNING, MR. JAMISON.
JUST NOW WE'RE GETTIN' SILLY?
OKAY, THEN. IF RONALD MCDONALD FOUGHT THE BURGER KING, WHO WOULD WIN?
Ooh, GOOD ONE. Hmm.
STRENGTH IN NUMBERS. YOU HAVE TO ASSUME THE KING HAS SOME KINDA ARMED FORCES...
I WOULD TOTALLY SIGN UP FOR THE BURGER NAVY.
GOES WITHOUT SAYING!
BUT CLOWNS CAN USE BEDROOM CLOSETS AS EVIL INTERDIMENSIONAL PORTALS, RIGHT?
ONE WOULD ASSUME SO, YUP.
WELL, THAT'S THAT, THEN. THE KING MUST HAVE, LIKE, A BURGER CLOSET IN HIS ROYAL BURGER BEDCHAMBERS, SO... THERE YOU GO.
CLOWN REGICIDE.
WHAT'S 'REGICIDE'?
IT'S WHAT YOU CALL IT WHEN YOU KILL A KING.
SERIOUS? EXCELLENT WORD POWER, MAN!
AUTO-CORRECT KEEPS TRYING TO INSERT IT WHEN I TYPE 'RESTAURANT', SO I GOOGLED IT.

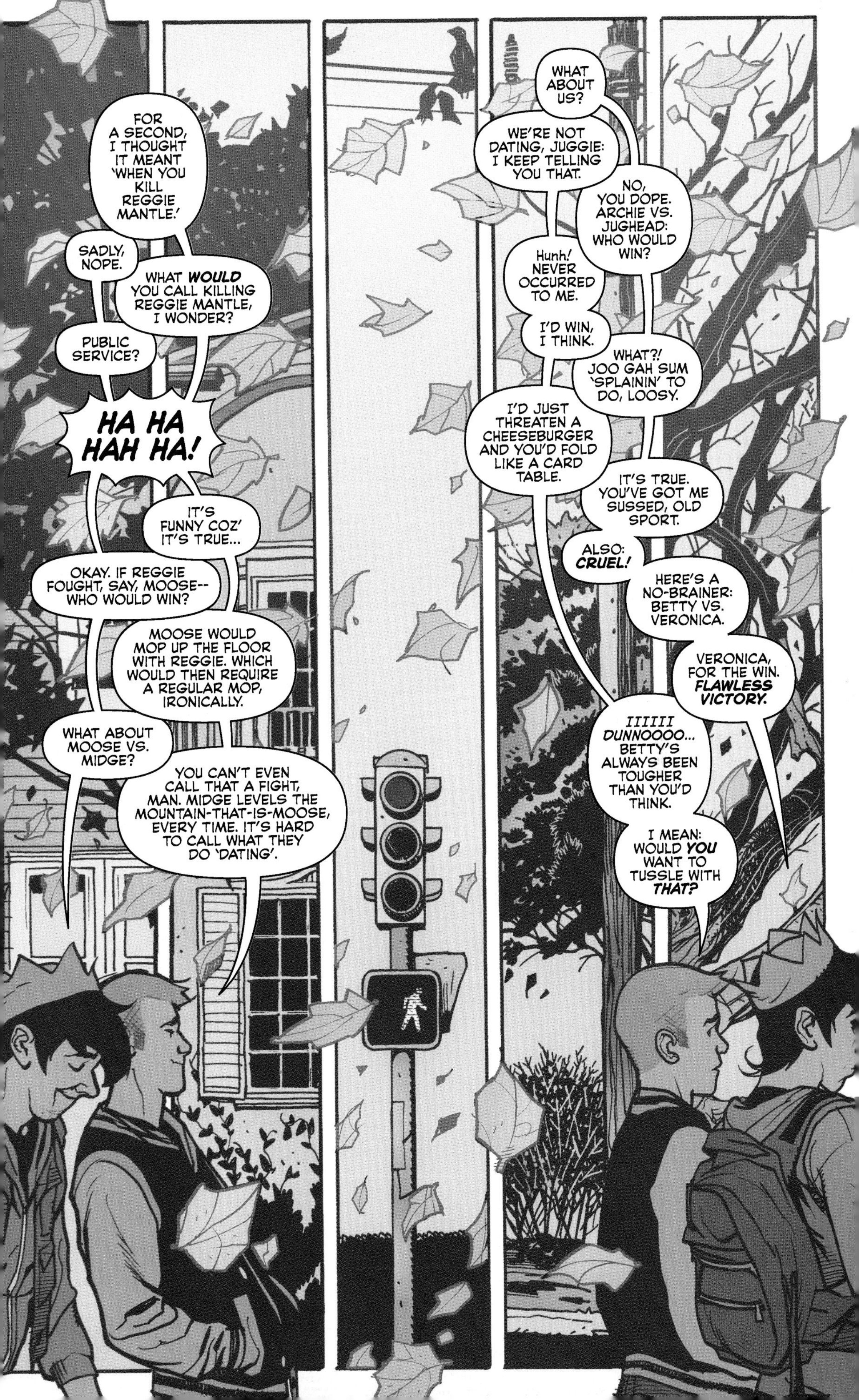
FOR A SECOND, I THOUGHT IT MEANT 'WHEN YOU KILL REGGIE MANTLE.'
SADLY, NOPE.
WHAT **WOULD** YOU CALL KILLING REGGIE MANTLE, I WONDER?
PUBLIC SERVICE?
HA HA HAH HA!
IT'S FUNNY COZ' IT'S TRUE...
OKAY. IF REGGIE FOUGHT, SAY, MOOSE-- WHO WOULD WIN?
MOOSE WOULD MOP UP THE FLOOR WITH REGGIE. WHICH WOULD THEN REQUIRE A REGULAR MOP, IRONICALLY.
WHAT ABOUT MOOSE VS. MIDGE?
YOU CAN'T EVEN CALL THAT A FIGHT, MAN. MIDGE LEVELS THE MOUNTAIN-THAT-IS-MOOSE, EVERY TIME. IT'S HARD TO CALL WHAT THEY DO 'DATING'.
WHAT ABOUT US?
WE'RE NOT DATING, JUGGIE: I KEEP TELLING YOU THAT.
NO, YOU DOPE. ARCHIE VS. JUGHEAD: WHO WOULD WIN?
Hunh! NEVER OCCURRED TO ME.
I'D WIN, I THINK.
WHAT?! JOO GAH SUM 'SPLAININ' TO DO, LOOSY.
I'D JUST THREATEN A CHEESEBURGER AND YOU'D FOLD LIKE A CARD TABLE.
IT'S TRUE. YOU'VE GOT ME SUSSED, OLD SPORT.
ALSO: **CRUEL!**
HERE'S A NO-BRAINER: BETTY VS. VERONICA.
VERONICA, FOR THE WIN. **FLAWLESS VICTORY.**
IIIIII DUNNOOOO... BETTY'S ALWAYS BEEN TOUGHER THAN YOU'D THINK.
I MEAN: WOULD **YOU** WANT TO TUSSLE WITH **THAT?**

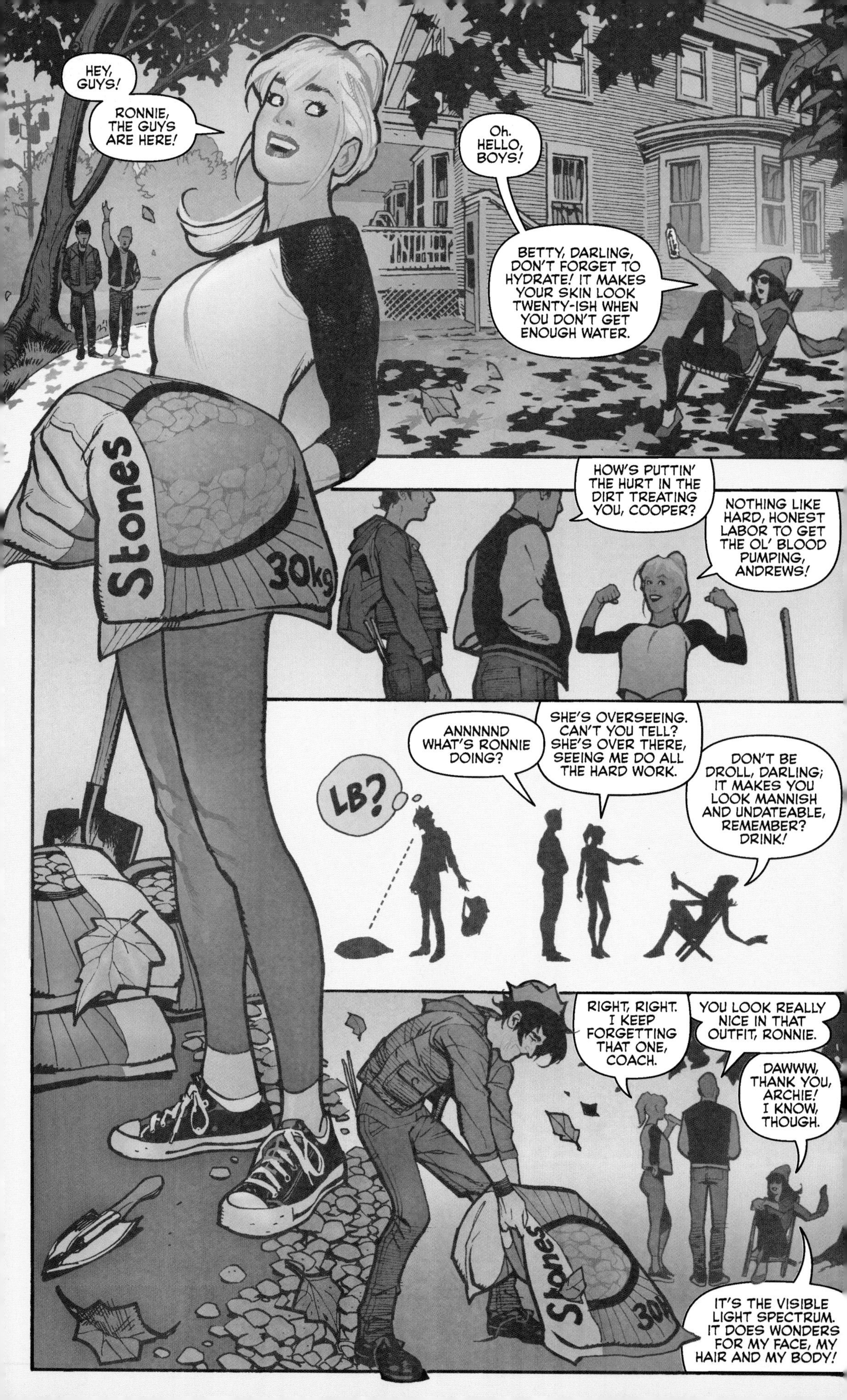
HEY, GUYS!
RONNIE, THE GUYS ARE HERE!
Oh. HELLO, BOYS!
BETTY, DARLING, DON'T FORGET TO HYDRATE! IT MAKES YOUR SKIN LOOK TWENTY-ISH WHEN YOU DON'T GET ENOUGH WATER.
Stones
30kg
HOW'S PUTTIN' THE HURT IN THE DIRT TREATING YOU, COOPER?
NOTHING LIKE HARD, HONEST LABOR TO GET THE OL' BLOOD PUMPING, ANDREWS!
LB?
ANNNNND WHAT'S RONNIE DOING?
SHE'S OVERSEEING. CAN'T YOU TELL? SHE'S OVER THERE, SEEING ME DO ALL THE HARD WORK.
DON'T BE DROLL, DARLING; IT MAKES YOU LOOK MANNISH AND UNDATEABLE, REMEMBER? DRINK!
RIGHT, RIGHT. I KEEP FORGETTING THAT ONE, COACH.
YOU LOOK REALLY NICE IN THAT OUTFIT, RONNIE.
DAWWW, THANK YOU, ARCHIE! I KNOW, THOUGH.
Stones
IT'S THE VISIBLE LIGHT SPECTRUM. IT DOES WONDERS FOR MY FACE, MY HAIR AND MY BODY!

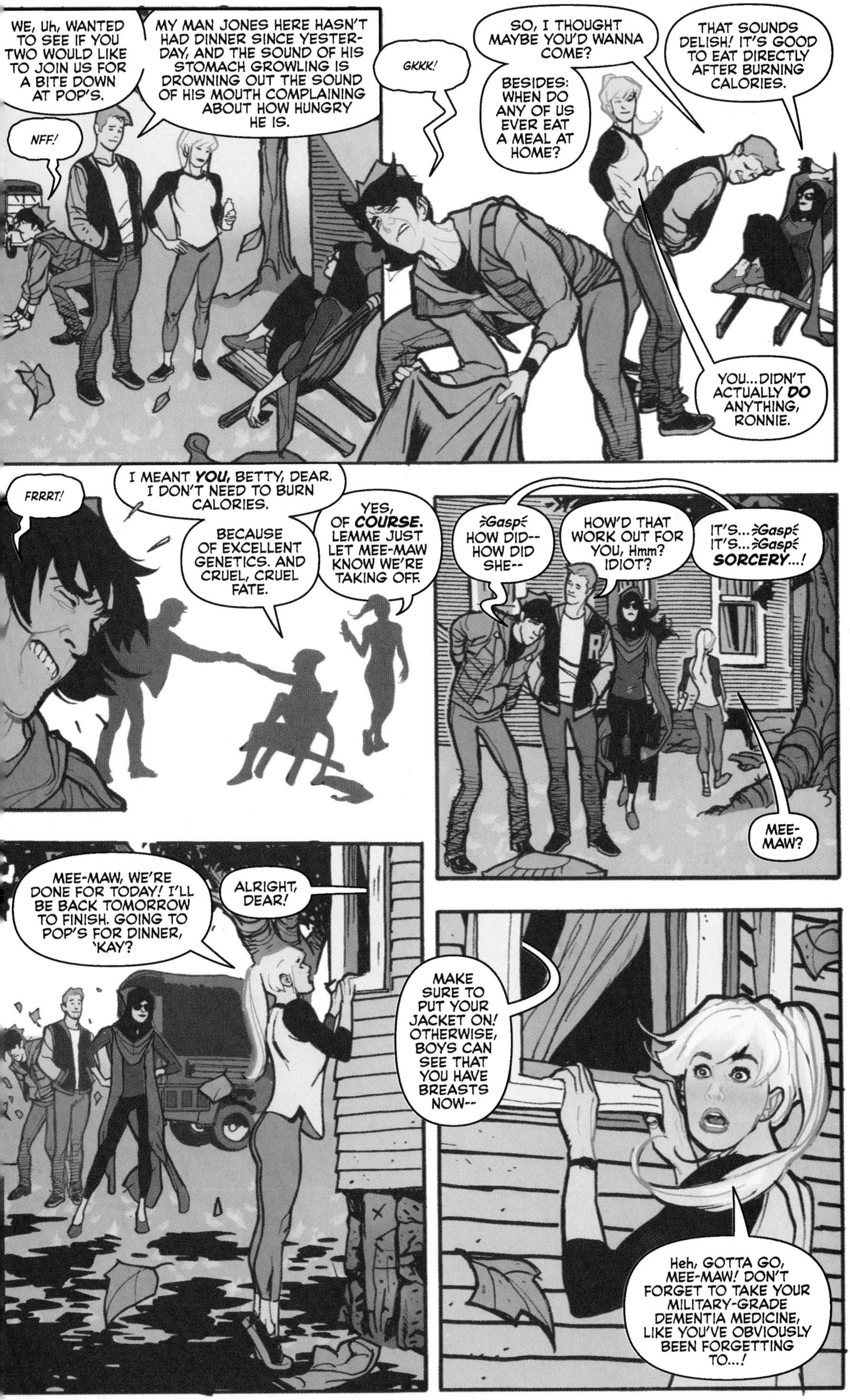
WE, Uh, WANTED TO SEE IF YOU TWO WOULD LIKE TO JOIN US FOR A BITE DOWN AT POP'S.
MY MAN JONES HERE HASN'T HAD DINNER SINCE YESTERDAY, AND THE SOUND OF HIS STOMACH GROWLING IS DROWNING OUT THE SOUND OF HIS MOUTH COMPLAINING ABOUT HOW HUNGRY HE IS.
NFF!
GKKK!
SO, I THOUGHT MAYBE YOU'D WANNA COME?
BESIDES: WHEN DO ANY OF US EVER EAT A MEAL AT HOME?
THAT SOUNDS DELISH! IT'S GOOD TO EAT DIRECTLY AFTER BURNING CALORIES.
YOU...DIDN'T ACTUALLY DO ANYTHING, RONNIE.
FRRRT!
I MEANT YOU, BETTY, DEAR. I DON'T NEED TO BURN CALORIES.
BECAUSE OF EXCELLENT GENETICS. AND CRUEL, CRUEL FATE.
YES, OF COURSE. LEMME JUST LET MEE-MAW KNOW WE'RE TAKING OFF.
Gasp HOW DID-- HOW DID SHE--
HOW'D THAT WORK OUT FOR YOU, Hmm? IDIOT?
IT'S...Gasp IT'S...Gasp SORCERY...!
MEE-MAW?
MEE-MAW, WE'RE DONE FOR TODAY! I'LL BE BACK TOMORROW TO FINISH. GOING TO POP'S FOR DINNER, 'KAY?
ALRIGHT, DEAR!
MAKE SURE TO PUT YOUR JACKET ON! OTHERWISE, BOYS CAN SEE THAT YOU HAVE BREASTS NOW--
Heh, GOTTA GO, MEE-MAW! DON'T FORGET TO TAKE YOUR MILITARY-GRADE DEMENTIA MEDICINE, LIKE YOU'VE OBVIOUSLY BEEN FORGETTING TO...!

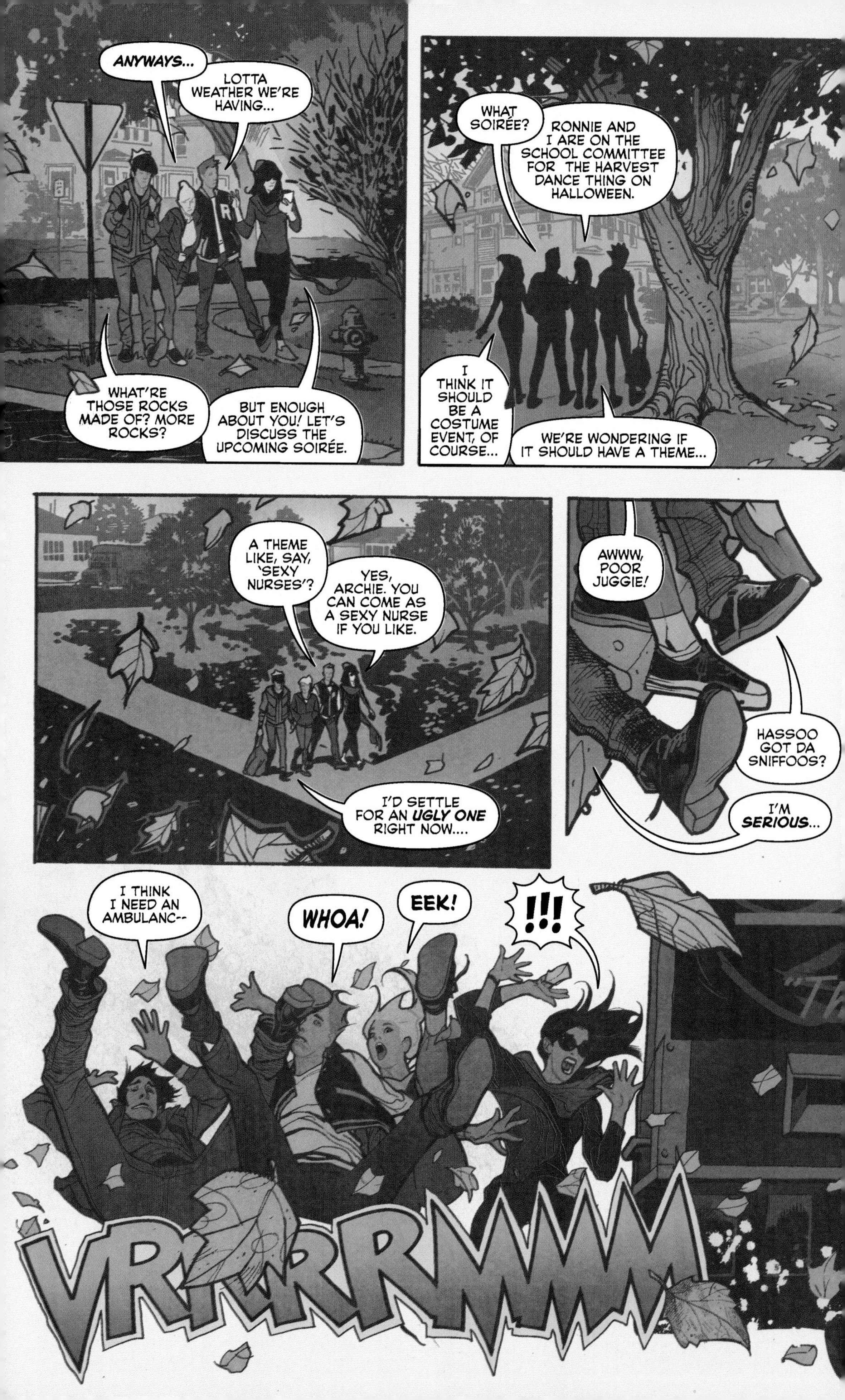
ANYWAYS...
LOTTA WEATHER WE'RE HAVING...
WHAT'RE THOSE ROCKS MADE OF? MORE ROCKS?
BUT ENOUGH ABOUT YOU! LET'S DISCUSS THE UPCOMING SOIRÉE.
WHAT SOIRÉE?
RONNIE AND I ARE ON THE SCHOOL COMMITTEE FOR THE HARVEST DANCE THING ON HALLOWEEN.
I THINK IT SHOULD BE A COSTUME EVENT, OF COURSE...
WE'RE WONDERING IF IT SHOULD HAVE A THEME...
A THEME LIKE, SAY, 'SEXY NURSES'?
YES, ARCHIE. YOU CAN COME AS A SEXY NURSE IF YOU LIKE.
I'D SETTLE FOR AN UGLY ONE RIGHT NOW....
AWWW, POOR JUGGIE!
HASSOO GOT DA SNIFFOOS?
I'M SERIOUS...
I THINK I NEED AN AMBULANC--
WHOA!
EEK!
!!!
VRRRRWWWM

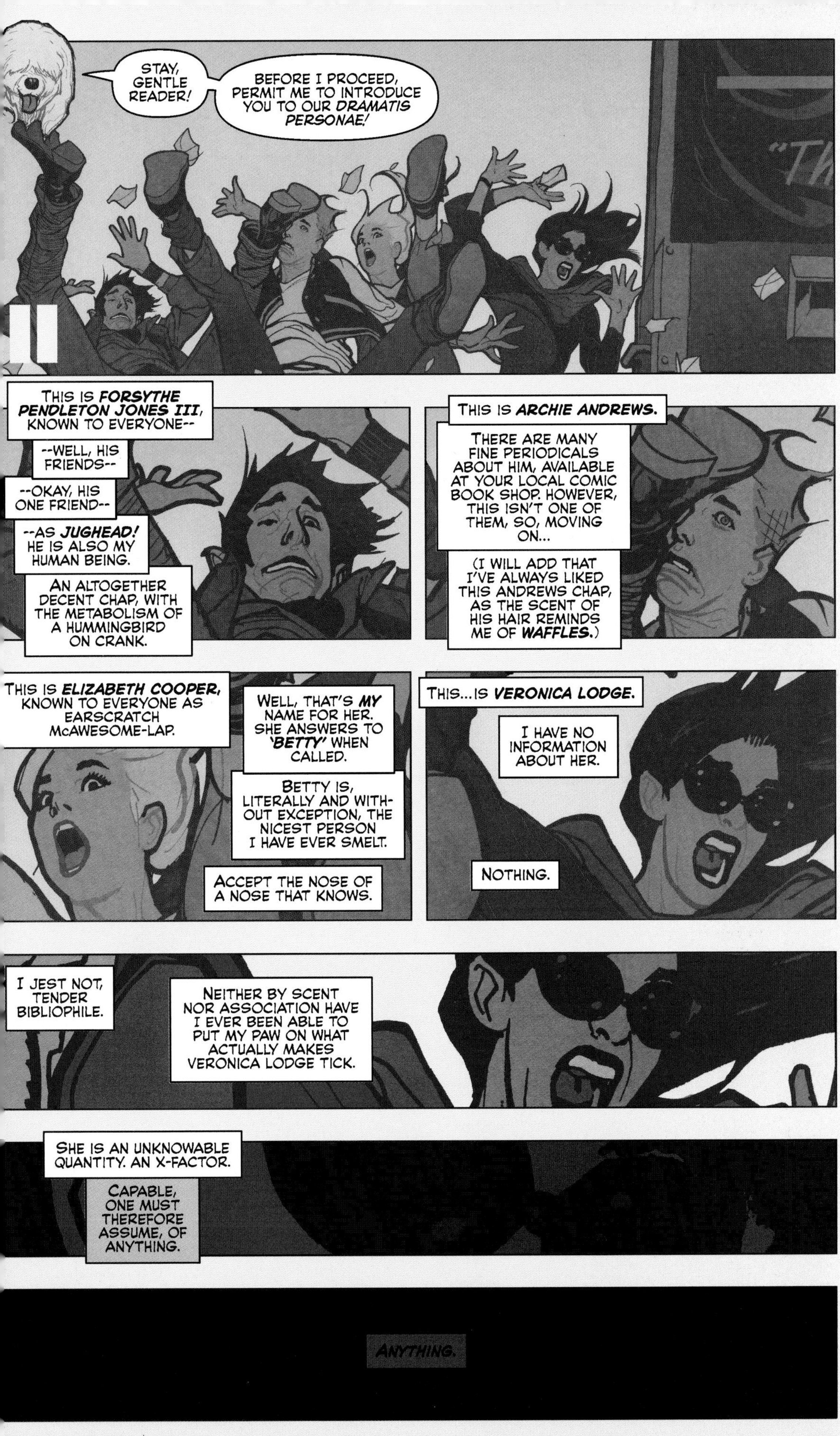
STAY, GENTLE READER!
BEFORE I PROCEED, PERMIT ME TO INTRODUCE YOU TO OUR DRAMATIS PERSONAE!
THIS IS FORSYTHE PENDLETON JONES III, KNOWN TO EVERYONE--
--WELL, HIS FRIENDS--
--OKAY, HIS ONE FRIEND--
--AS JUGHEAD! HE IS ALSO MY HUMAN BEING.
AN ALTOGETHER DECENT CHAP, WITH THE METABOLISM OF A HUMMINGBIRD ON CRANK.
THIS IS ARCHIE ANDREWS.
THERE ARE MANY FINE PERIODICALS ABOUT HIM, AVAILABLE AT YOUR LOCAL COMIC BOOK SHOP. HOWEVER, THIS ISN'T ONE OF THEM, SO, MOVING ON...
(I WILL ADD THAT I'VE ALWAYS LIKED THIS ANDREWS CHAP, AS THE SCENT OF HIS HAIR REMINDS ME OF WAFFLES.)
THIS IS ELIZABETH COOPER, KNOWN TO EVERYONE AS EARSCRATCH McAWESOME-LAP.
WELL, THAT'S MY NAME FOR HER. SHE ANSWERS TO 'BETTY' WHEN CALLED.
BETTY IS, LITERALLY AND WITHOUT EXCEPTION, THE NICEST PERSON I HAVE EVER SMELT.
ACCEPT THE NOSE OF A NOSE THAT KNOWS.
THIS...IS VERONICA LODGE.
I HAVE NO INFORMATION ABOUT HER.
NOTHING.
I JEST NOT, TENDER BIBLIOPHILE.
NEITHER BY SCENT NOR ASSOCIATION HAVE I EVER BEEN ABLE TO PUT MY PAW ON WHAT ACTUALLY MAKES VERONICA LODGE TICK.
SHE IS AN UNKNOWABLE QUANTITY. AN X-FACTOR.
CAPABLE, ONE MUST THEREFORE ASSUME, OF ANYTHING.
ANYTHING.

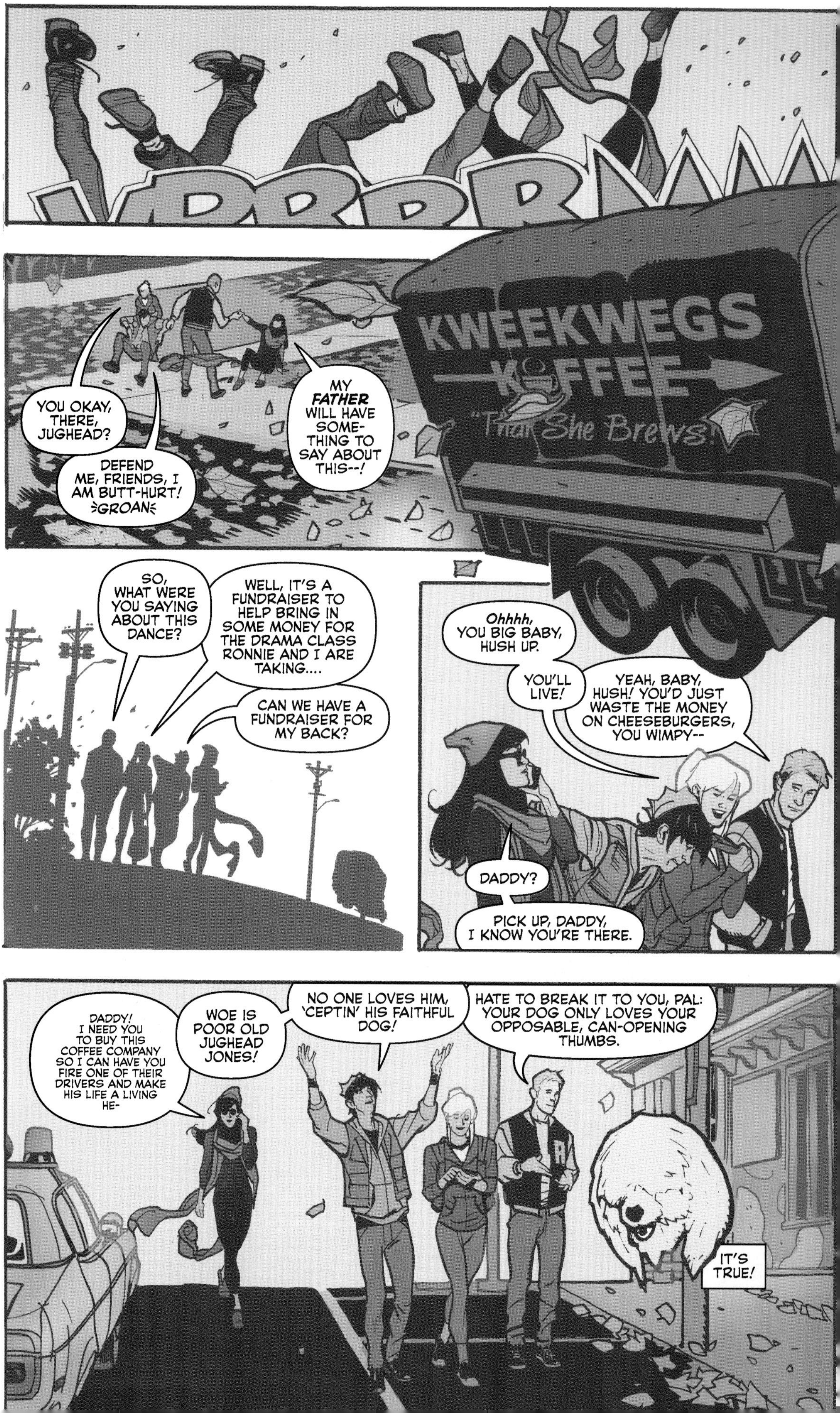
VRRR
KWEEKWEGS
KOFFEE
"That She Brews!"
YOU OKAY, THERE, JUGHEAD?
DEFEND ME, FRIENDS, I AM BUTT-HURT! GROAN
MY FATHER WILL HAVE SOME-THING TO SAY ABOUT THIS--!
SO, WHAT WERE YOU SAYING ABOUT THIS DANCE?
WELL, IT'S A FUNDRAISER TO HELP BRING IN SOME MONEY FOR THE DRAMA CLASS RONNIE AND I ARE TAKING....
CAN WE HAVE A FUNDRAISER FOR MY BACK?
Ohhhh, YOU BIG BABY, HUSH UP.
YOU'LL LIVE!
YEAH, BABY, HUSH! YOU'D JUST WASTE THE MONEY ON CHEESEBURGERS, YOU WIMPY--
DADDY?
PICK UP, DADDY, I KNOW YOU'RE THERE.
DADDY! I NEED YOU TO BUY THIS COFFEE COMPANY SO I CAN HAVE YOU FIRE ONE OF THEIR DRIVERS AND MAKE HIS LIFE A LIVING HE-
WOE IS POOR OLD JUGHEAD JONES!
NO ONE LOVES HIM, 'CEPTIN' HIS FAITHFUL DOG!
HATE TO BREAK IT TO YOU, PAL: YOUR DOG ONLY LOVES YOUR OPPOSABLE, CAN-OPENING THUMBS.
IT'S TRUE!

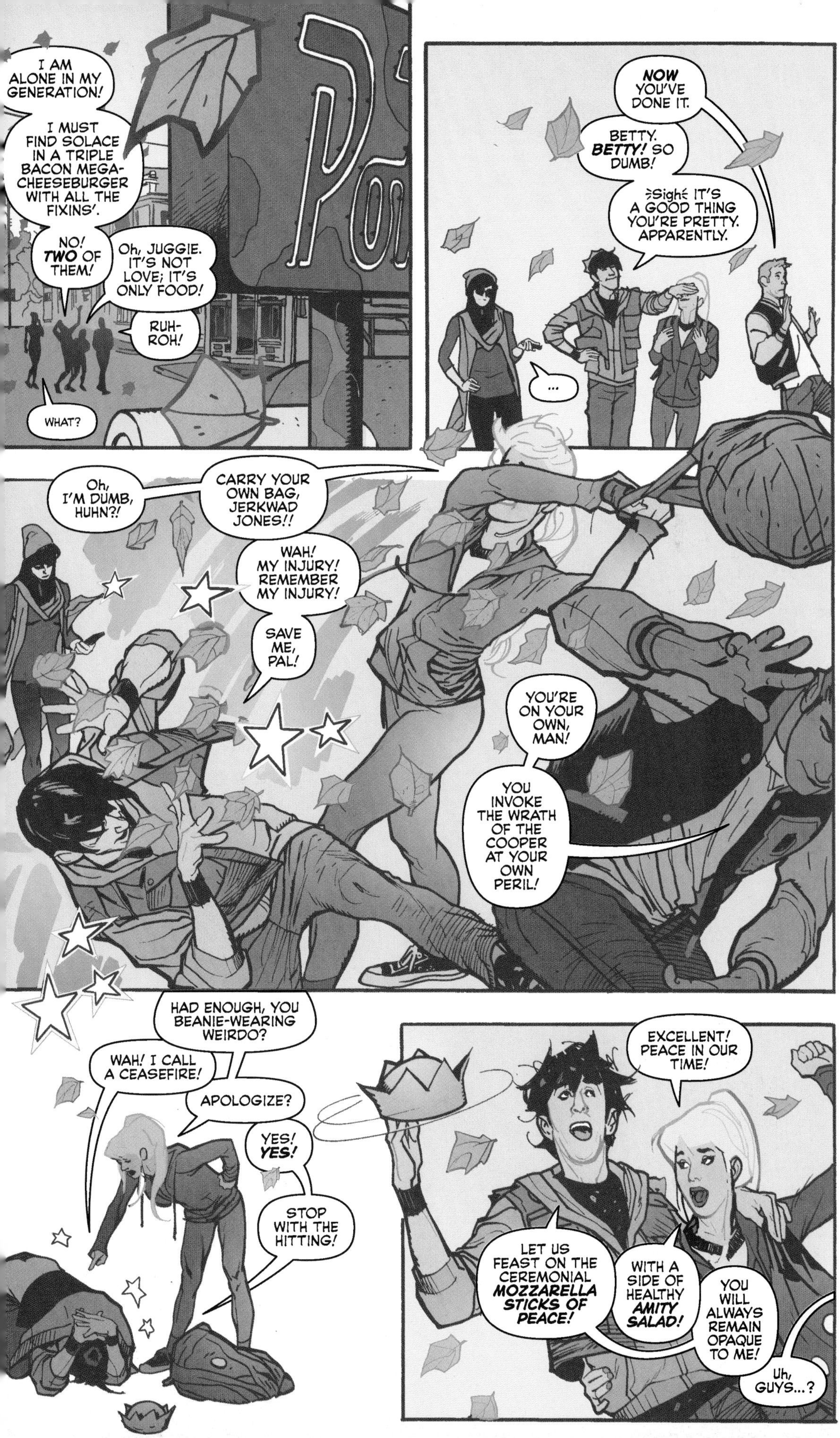

I AM ALONE IN MY GENERATION!
I MUST FIND SOLACE IN A TRIPLE BACON MEGA-CHEESEBURGER WITH ALL THE FIXINS'.
NO! TWO OF THEM!
Oh, JUGGIE. IT'S NOT LOVE; IT'S ONLY FOOD!
RUH-ROH!
WHAT?
NOW YOU'VE DONE IT.
BETTY. BETTY! SO DUMB!
≷Sigh≶ IT'S A GOOD THING YOU'RE PRETTY. APPARENTLY.
...
Oh, I'M DUMB, HUHN?!
CARRY YOUR OWN BAG, JERKWAD JONES!!
WAH! MY INJURY! REMEMBER MY INJURY!
SAVE ME, PAL!
YOU'RE ON YOUR OWN, MAN!
YOU INVOKE THE WRATH OF THE COOPER AT YOUR OWN PERIL!
HAD ENOUGH, YOU BEANIE-WEARING WEIRDO?
WAH! I CALL A CEASEFIRE!
APOLOGIZE?
YES! YES!
STOP WITH THE HITTING!
EXCELLENT! PEACE IN OUR TIME!
LET US FEAST ON THE CEREMONIAL MOZZARELLA STICKS OF PEACE!
WITH A SIDE OF HEALTHY AMITY SALAD!
YOU WILL ALWAYS REMAIN OPAQUE TO ME!
Uh, GUYS...?

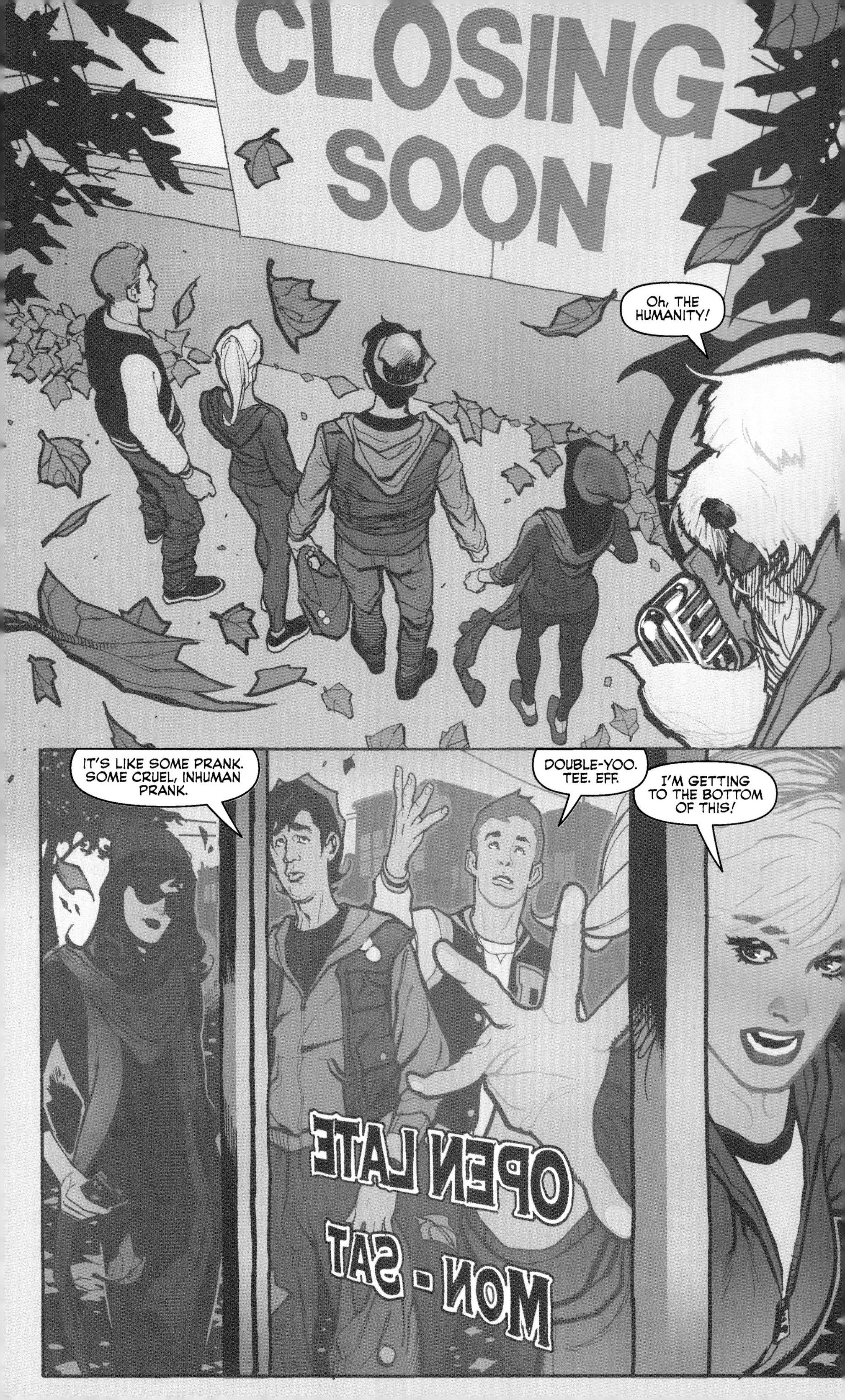
CLOSING SOON
Oh, THE HUMANITY!
IT'S LIKE SOME PRANK. SOME CRUEL, INHUMAN PRANK.
DOUBLE-YOO. TEE. EFF.
I'M GETTING TO THE BOTTOM OF THIS!
OPEN LATE
MON - SAT

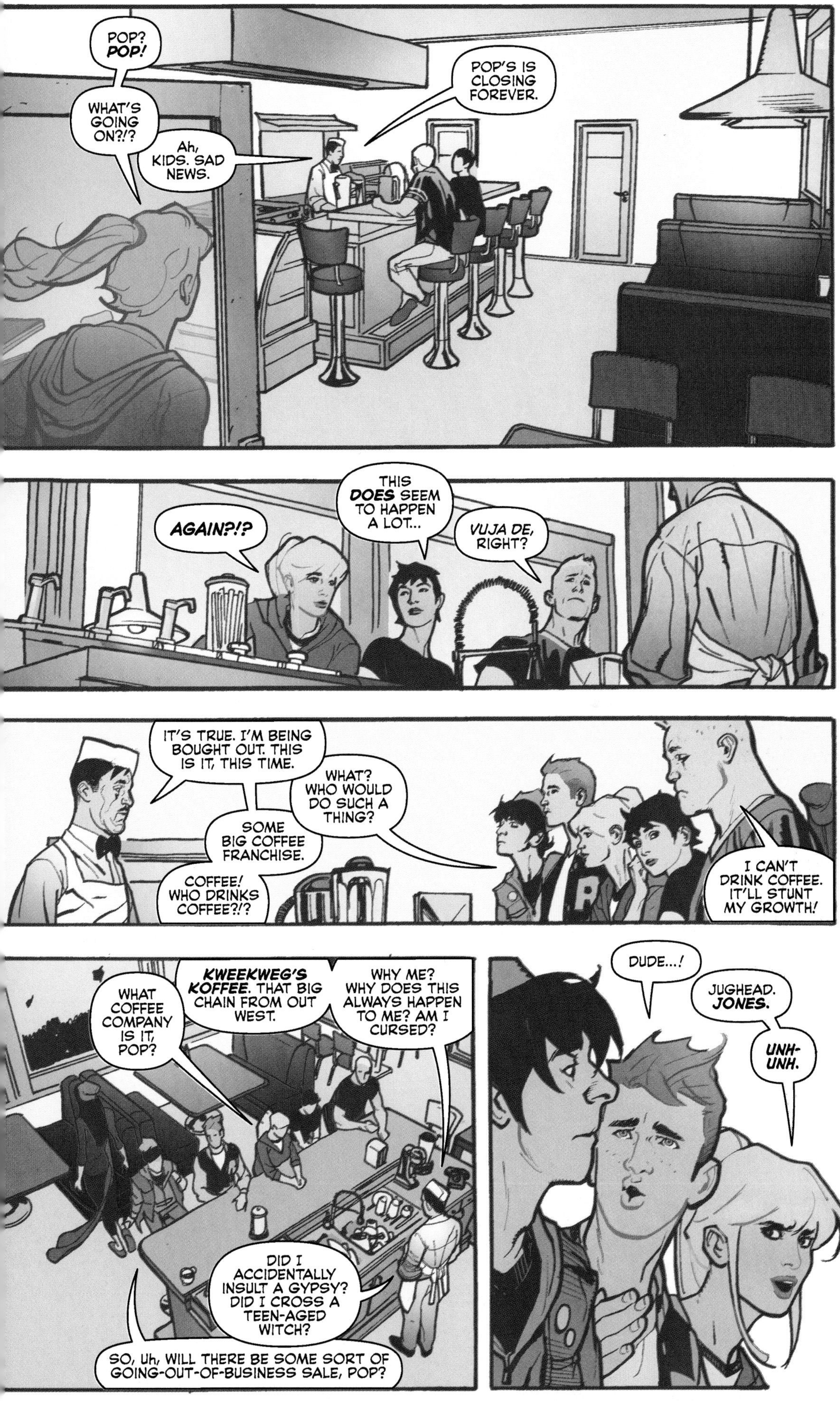
POP? **POP!**
WHAT'S GOING ON?!?
Ah, KIDS. SAD NEWS.
POP'S IS CLOSING FOREVER.
AGAIN?!?
THIS **DOES** SEEM TO HAPPEN A LOT...
VUJA DE, RIGHT?
IT'S TRUE. I'M BEING BOUGHT OUT. THIS IS IT, THIS TIME.
WHAT? WHO WOULD DO SUCH A THING?
SOME BIG COFFEE FRANCHISE.
COFFEE! WHO DRINKS COFFEE?!?
I CAN'T DRINK COFFEE. IT'LL STUNT MY GROWTH!
WHAT COFFEE COMPANY IS IT, POP?
KWEEKWEG'S KOFFEE. THAT BIG CHAIN FROM OUT WEST.
WHY ME? WHY DOES THIS ALWAYS HAPPEN TO ME? AM I CURSED?
DID I ACCIDENTALLY INSULT A GYPSY? DID I CROSS A TEEN-AGED WITCH?
SO, Uh, WILL THERE BE SOME SORT OF GOING-OUT-OF-BUSINESS SALE, POP?
DUDE...!
JUGHEAD. **JONES.**
UNH-UNH.

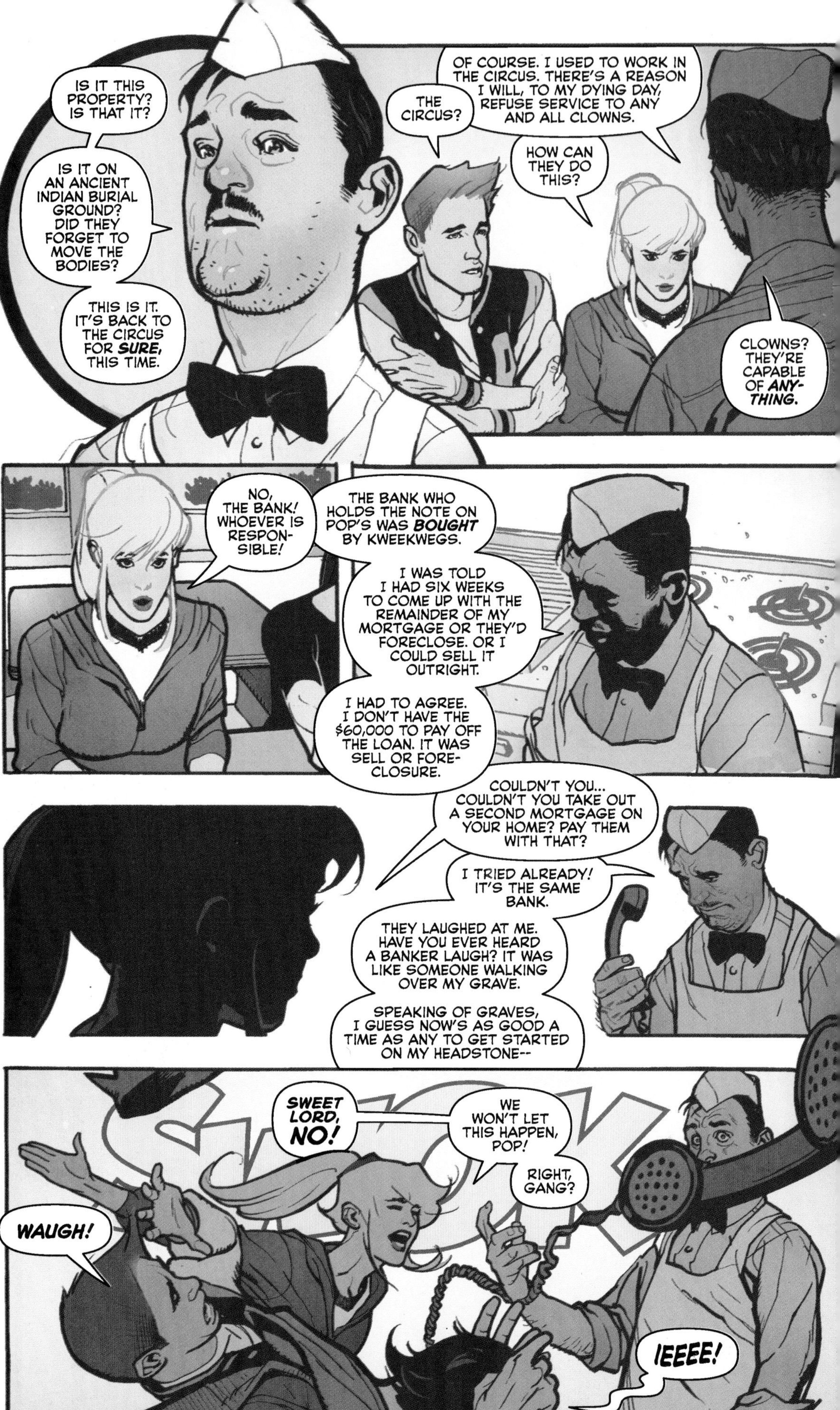
IS IT THIS PROPERTY? IS THAT IT?
IS IT ON AN ANCIENT INDIAN BURIAL GROUND? DID THEY FORGET TO MOVE THE BODIES?
THIS IS IT. IT'S BACK TO THE CIRCUS FOR SURE, THIS TIME.
THE CIRCUS?
OF COURSE. I USED TO WORK IN THE CIRCUS. THERE'S A REASON I WILL, TO MY DYING DAY, REFUSE SERVICE TO ANY AND ALL CLOWNS.
HOW CAN THEY DO THIS?
CLOWNS? THEY'RE CAPABLE OF ANY-THING.
NO, THE BANK! WHOEVER IS RESPON-SIBLE!
THE BANK WHO HOLDS THE NOTE ON POP'S WAS BOUGHT BY KWEEKWEGS.
I WAS TOLD I HAD SIX WEEKS TO COME UP WITH THE REMAINDER OF MY MORTGAGE OR THEY'D FORECLOSE. OR I COULD SELL IT OUTRIGHT.
I HAD TO AGREE. I DON'T HAVE THE $60,000 TO PAY OFF THE LOAN. IT WAS SELL OR FORE-CLOSURE.
COULDN'T YOU... COULDN'T YOU TAKE OUT A SECOND MORTGAGE ON YOUR HOME? PAY THEM WITH THAT?
I TRIED ALREADY! IT'S THE SAME BANK.
THEY LAUGHED AT ME. HAVE YOU EVER HEARD A BANKER LAUGH? IT WAS LIKE SOMEONE WALKING OVER MY GRAVE.
SPEAKING OF GRAVES, I GUESS NOW'S AS GOOD A TIME AS ANY TO GET STARTED ON MY HEADSTONE--
SWEET LORD, NO!
WE WON'T LET THIS HAPPEN, POP!
RIGHT, GANG?
WAUGH!
IEEEE!

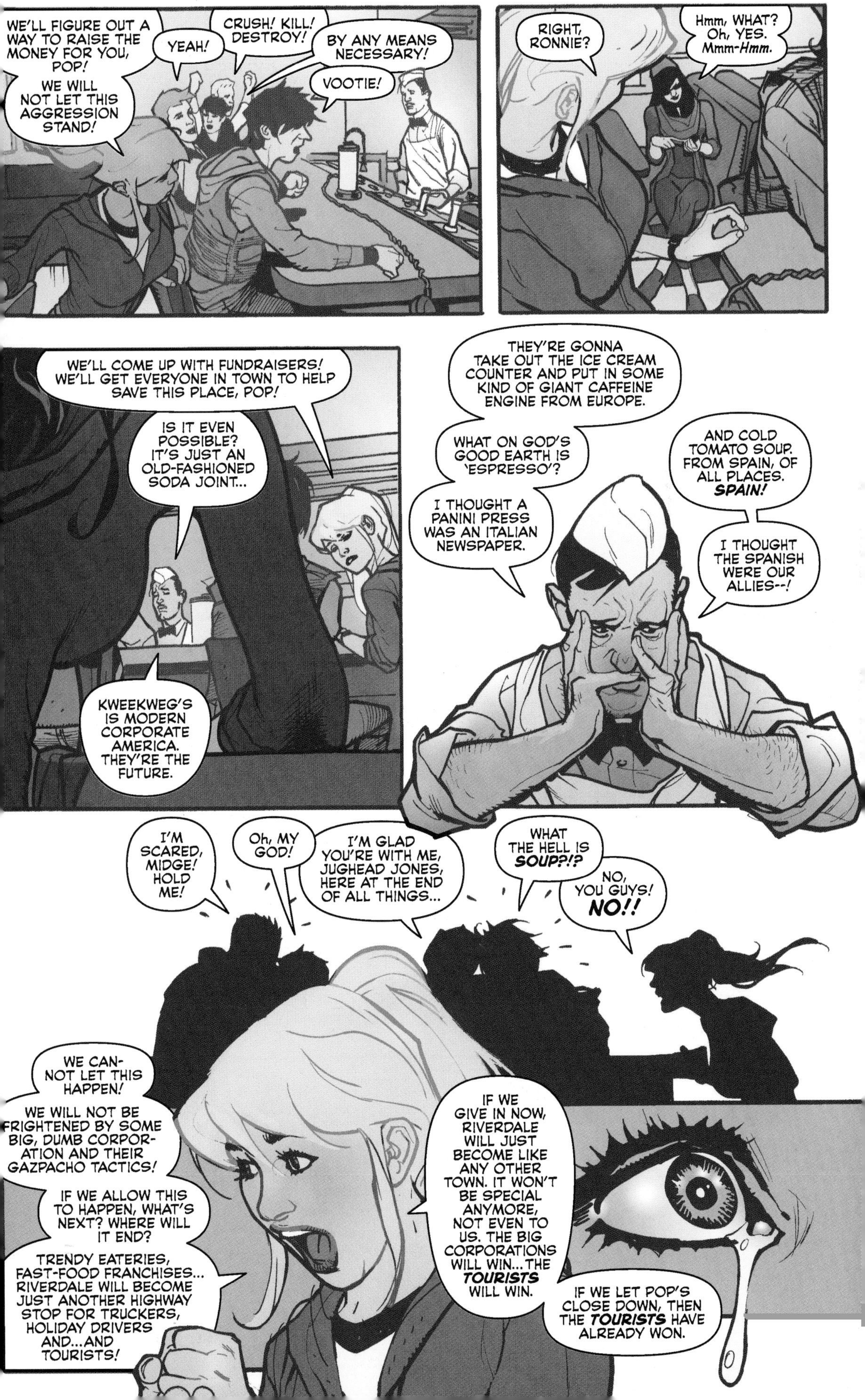
WE'LL FIGURE OUT A WAY TO RAISE THE MONEY FOR YOU, POP!
WE WILL NOT LET THIS AGGRESSION STAND!
YEAH!
CRUSH! KILL! DESTROY!
BY ANY MEANS NECESSARY!
VOOTIE!
RIGHT, RONNIE?
Hmm, WHAT? Oh, YES. Mmm-Hmm.
WE'LL COME UP WITH FUNDRAISERS! WE'LL GET EVERYONE IN TOWN TO HELP SAVE THIS PLACE, POP!
IS IT EVEN POSSIBLE? IT'S JUST AN OLD-FASHIONED SODA JOINT...
KWEEKWEG'S IS MODERN CORPORATE AMERICA. THEY'RE THE FUTURE.
THEY'RE GONNA TAKE OUT THE ICE CREAM COUNTER AND PUT IN SOME KIND OF GIANT CAFFEINE ENGINE FROM EUROPE.
WHAT ON GOD'S GOOD EARTH IS 'ESPRESSO'?
I THOUGHT A PANINI PRESS WAS AN ITALIAN NEWSPAPER.
AND COLD TOMATO SOUP. FROM SPAIN, OF ALL PLACES. SPAIN!
I THOUGHT THE SPANISH WERE OUR ALLIES--!
I'M SCARED, MIDGE! HOLD ME!
Oh, MY GOD!
I'M GLAD YOU'RE WITH ME, JUGHEAD JONES, HERE AT THE END OF ALL THINGS...
WHAT THE HELL IS SOUP?!?
NO, YOU GUYS! NO!!
WE CAN-NOT LET THIS HAPPEN!
WE WILL NOT BE FRIGHTENED BY SOME BIG, DUMB CORPOR-ATION AND THEIR GAZPACHO TACTICS!
IF WE ALLOW THIS TO HAPPEN, WHAT'S NEXT? WHERE WILL IT END?
TRENDY EATERIES, FAST-FOOD FRANCHISES... RIVERDALE WILL BECOME JUST ANOTHER HIGHWAY STOP FOR TRUCKERS, HOLIDAY DRIVERS AND...AND TOURISTS!
IF WE GIVE IN NOW, RIVERDALE WILL JUST BECOME LIKE ANY OTHER TOWN. IT WON'T BE SPECIAL ANYMORE, NOT EVEN TO US. THE BIG CORPORATIONS WILL WIN... THE TOURISTS WILL WIN.
IF WE LET POP'S CLOSE DOWN, THEN THE TOURISTS HAVE ALREADY WON.

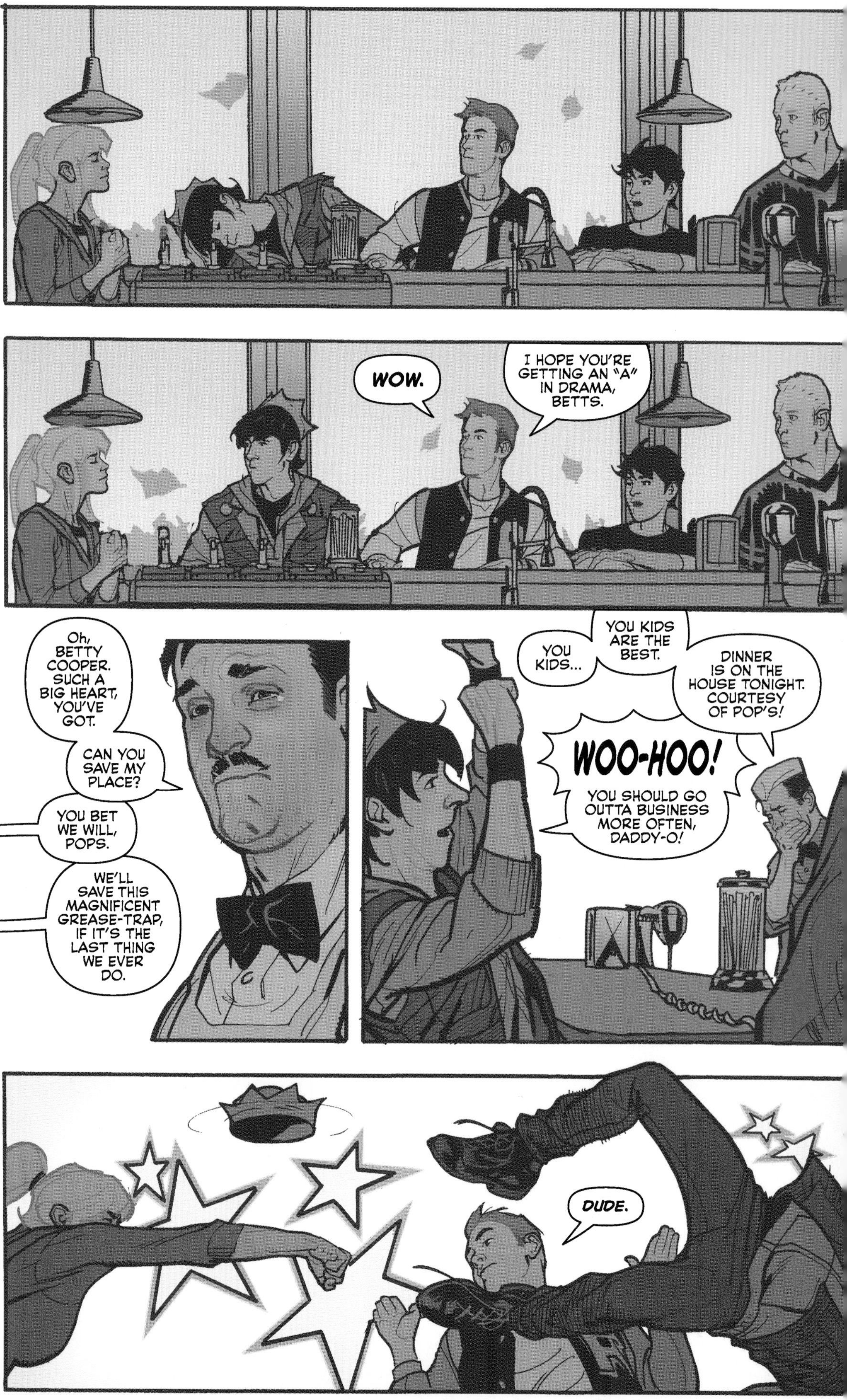
WOW.
I HOPE YOU'RE GETTING AN "A" IN DRAMA, BETTS.
Oh, BETTY COOPER. SUCH A BIG HEART, YOU'VE GOT.
CAN YOU SAVE MY PLACE?
YOU BET WE WILL, POPS.
WE'LL SAVE THIS MAGNIFICENT GREASE-TRAP, IF IT'S THE LAST THING WE EVER DO.
YOU KIDS...
YOU KIDS ARE THE BEST.
DINNER IS ON THE HOUSE TONIGHT. COURTESY OF POP'S!
WOO-HOO!
YOU SHOULD GO OUTTA BUSINESS MORE OFTEN, DADDY-O!
DUDE.

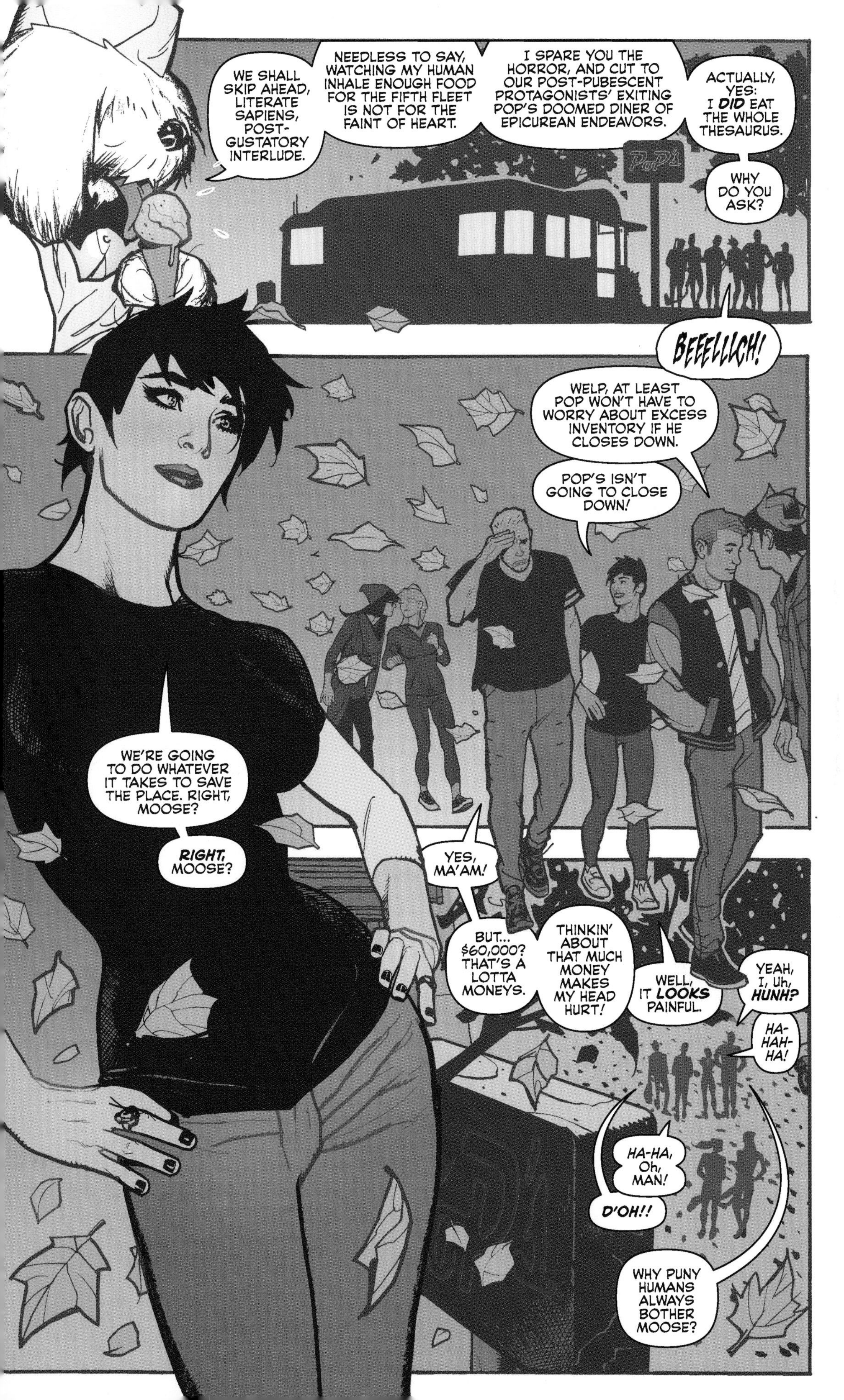

WE SHALL SKIP AHEAD, LITERATE SAPIENS, POST-GUSTATORY INTERLUDE.
NEEDLESS TO SAY, WATCHING MY HUMAN INHALE ENOUGH FOOD FOR THE FIFTH FLEET IS NOT FOR THE FAINT OF HEART.
I SPARE YOU THE HORROR, AND CUT TO OUR POST-PUBESCENT PROTAGONISTS' EXITING POP'S DOOMED DINER OF EPICUREAN ENDEAVORS.
ACTUALLY, YES: I DID EAT THE WHOLE THESAURUS.
WHY DO YOU ASK?
Pop's
BEEELLLCH!
WELP, AT LEAST POP WON'T HAVE TO WORRY ABOUT EXCESS INVENTORY IF HE CLOSES DOWN.
POP'S ISN'T GOING TO CLOSE DOWN!
WE'RE GOING TO DO WHATEVER IT TAKES TO SAVE THE PLACE. RIGHT, MOOSE?
RIGHT, MOOSE?
YES, MA'AM!
BUT... $60,000? THAT'S A LOTTA MONEYS.
THINKIN' ABOUT THAT MUCH MONEY MAKES MY HEAD HURT!
WELL, IT LOOKS PAINFUL.
YEAH, I, UH, HUNH?
HA-HAH-HA!
HA-HA, OH, MAN!
D'OH!!
WHY PUNY HUMANS ALWAYS BOTHER MOOSE?

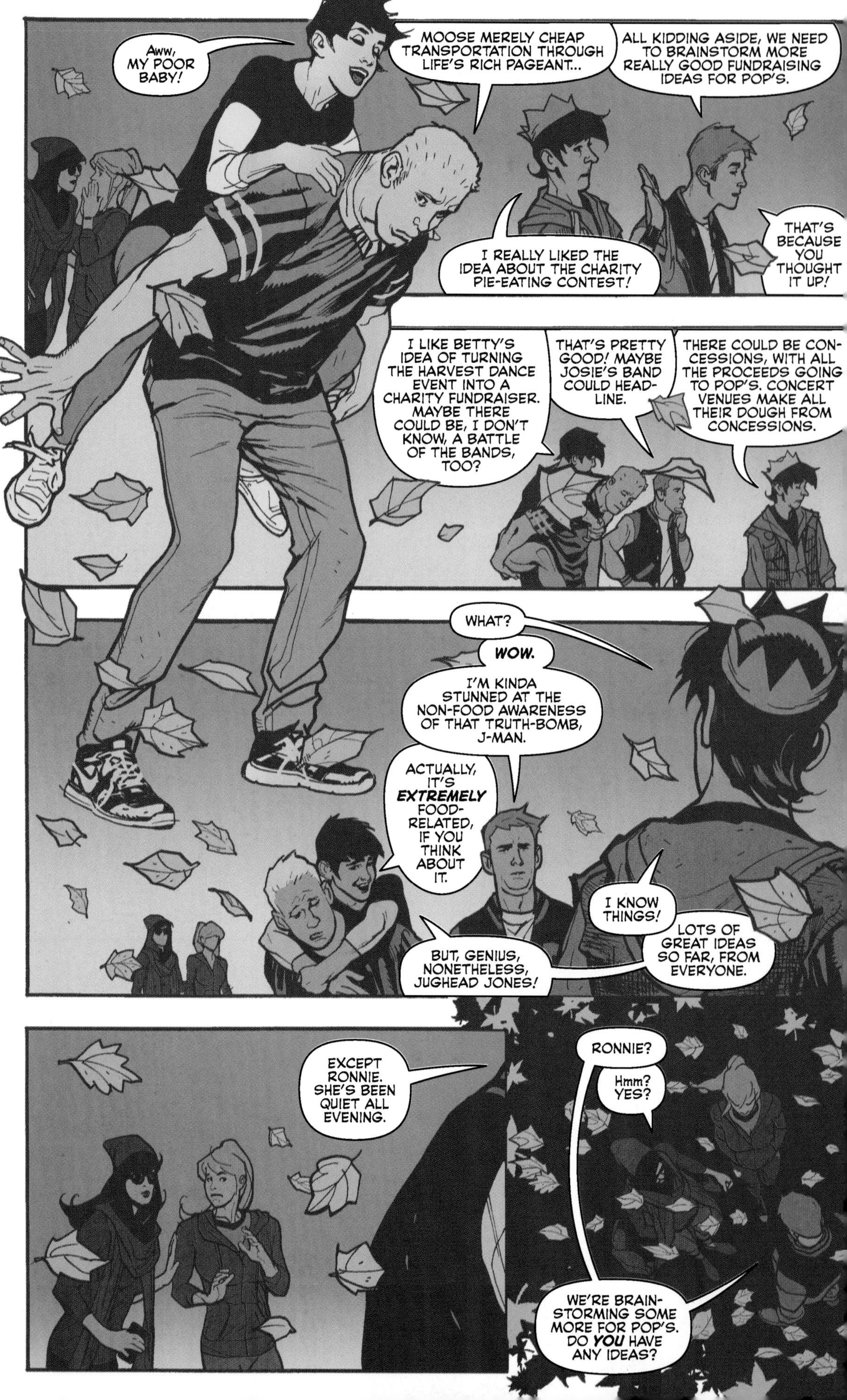
Aww, MY POOR BABY!
MOOSE MERELY CHEAP TRANSPORTATION THROUGH LIFE'S RICH PAGEANT...
ALL KIDDING ASIDE, WE NEED TO BRAINSTORM MORE REALLY GOOD FUNDRAISING IDEAS FOR POP'S.
I REALLY LIKED THE IDEA ABOUT THE CHARITY PIE-EATING CONTEST!
THAT'S BECAUSE YOU THOUGHT IT UP!
I LIKE BETTY'S IDEA OF TURNING THE HARVEST DANCE EVENT INTO A CHARITY FUNDRAISER. MAYBE THERE COULD BE, I DON'T KNOW, A BATTLE OF THE BANDS, TOO?
THAT'S PRETTY GOOD! MAYBE JOSIE'S BAND COULD HEAD-LINE.
THERE COULD BE CON-CESSIONS, WITH ALL THE PROCEEDS GOING TO POP'S. CONCERT VENUES MAKE ALL THEIR DOUGH FROM CONCESSIONS.
WHAT?
WOW.
I'M KINDA STUNNED AT THE NON-FOOD AWARENESS OF THAT TRUTH-BOMB, J-MAN.
ACTUALLY, IT'S EXTREMELY FOOD-RELATED, IF YOU THINK ABOUT IT.
I KNOW THINGS!
BUT, GENIUS, NONETHELESS, JUGHEAD JONES!
LOTS OF GREAT IDEAS SO FAR, FROM EVERYONE.
EXCEPT RONNIE. SHE'S BEEN QUIET ALL EVENING.
RONNIE?
Hmm? YES?
WE'RE BRAIN-STORMING SOME MORE FOR POP'S. DO YOU HAVE ANY IDEAS?

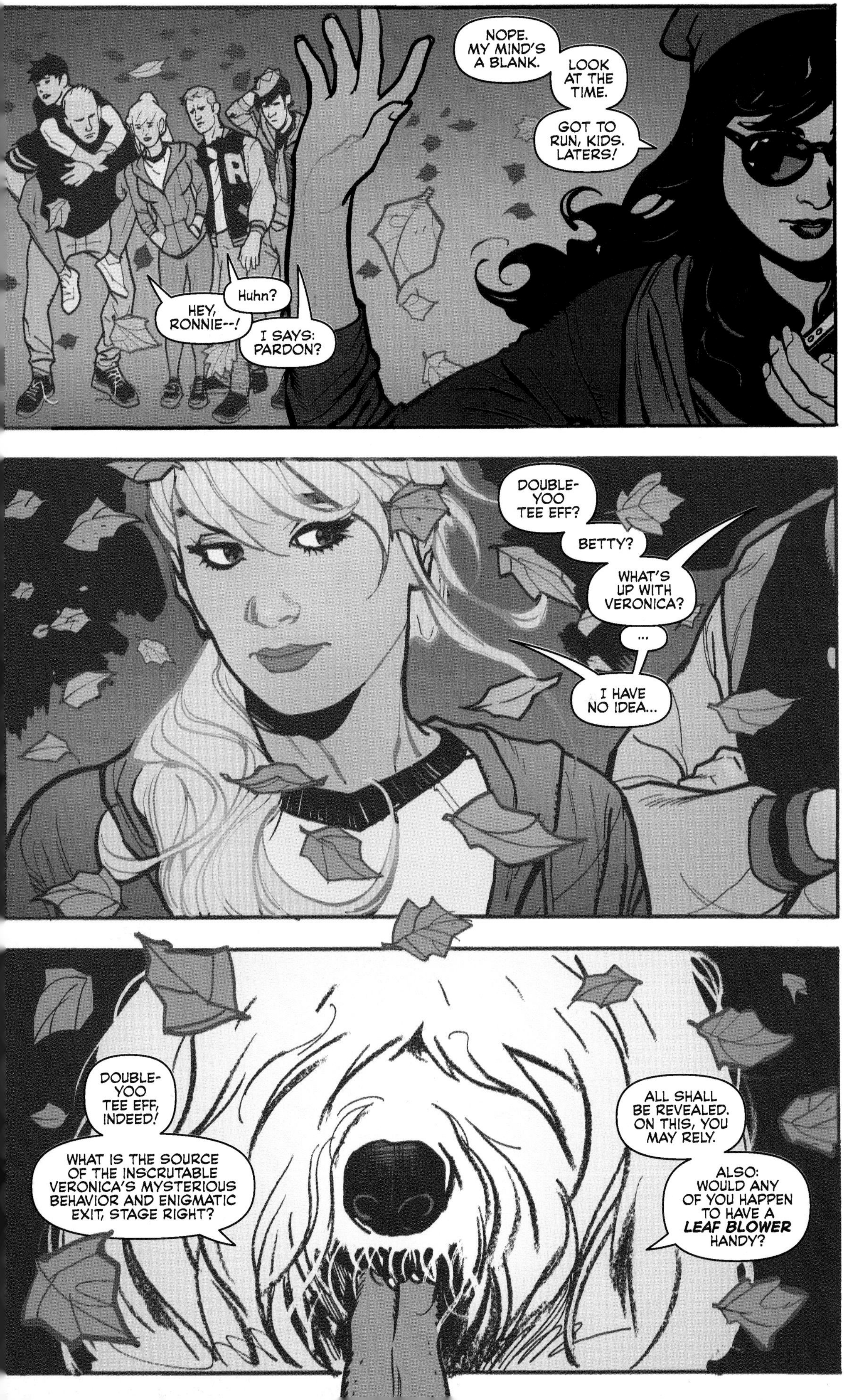

NOPE. MY MIND'S A BLANK.
LOOK AT THE TIME.
GOT TO RUN, KIDS. LATERS!
HEY, RONNIE--!
Huhn?
I SAYS: PARDON?
DOUBLE-YOO TEE EFF?
BETTY?
WHAT'S UP WITH VERONICA?
...
I HAVE NO IDEA...
DOUBLE-YOO TEE EFF, INDEED!
WHAT IS THE SOURCE OF THE INSCRUTABLE VERONICA'S MYSTERIOUS BEHAVIOR AND ENIGMATIC EXIT, STAGE RIGHT?
ALL SHALL BE REVEALED. ON THIS, YOU MAY RELY.
ALSO: WOULD ANY OF YOU HAPPEN TO HAVE A ***LEAF BLOWER*** HANDY?

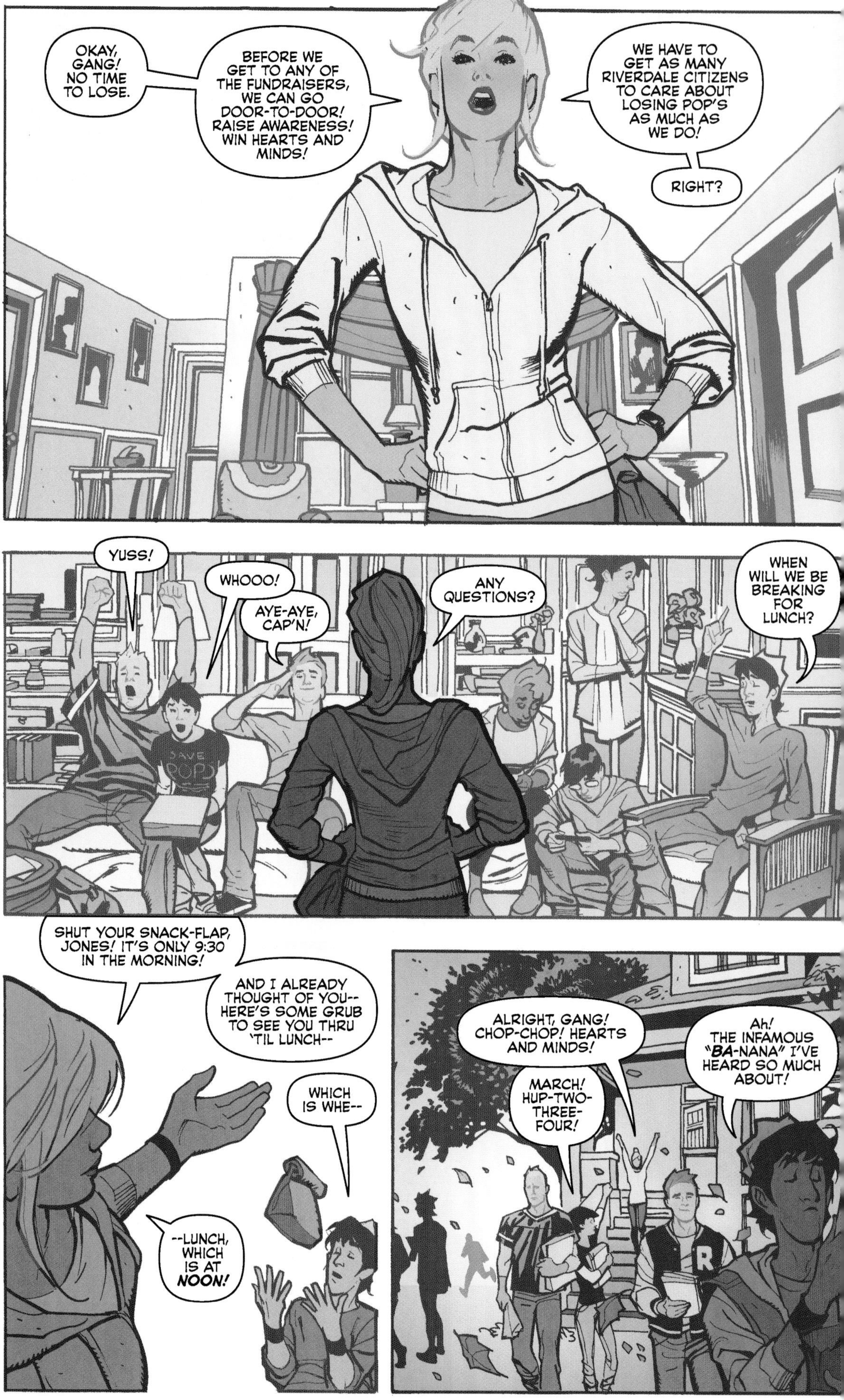

OKAY, GANG! NO TIME TO LOSE.
BEFORE WE GET TO ANY OF THE FUNDRAISERS, WE CAN GO DOOR-TO-DOOR! RAISE AWARENESS! WIN HEARTS AND MINDS!
WE HAVE TO GET AS MANY RIVERDALE CITIZENS TO CARE ABOUT LOSING POP'S AS MUCH AS WE DO!
RIGHT?
YUSS!
WHOOO!
AYE-AYE, CAP'N!
ANY QUESTIONS?
WHEN WILL WE BE BREAKING FOR LUNCH?
SAVE POP'S
SHUT YOUR SNACK-FLAP, JONES! IT'S ONLY 9:30 IN THE MORNING!
AND I ALREADY THOUGHT OF YOU-- HERE'S SOME GRUB TO SEE YOU THRU 'TIL LUNCH--
WHICH IS WHE--
--LUNCH, WHICH IS AT ***NOON!***
ALRIGHT, GANG! CHOP-CHOP! HEARTS AND MINDS!
MARCH! HUP-TWO-THREE-FOUR!
AH! THE INFAMOUS "***BA***-NANA" I'VE HEARD SO MUCH ABOUT!
R

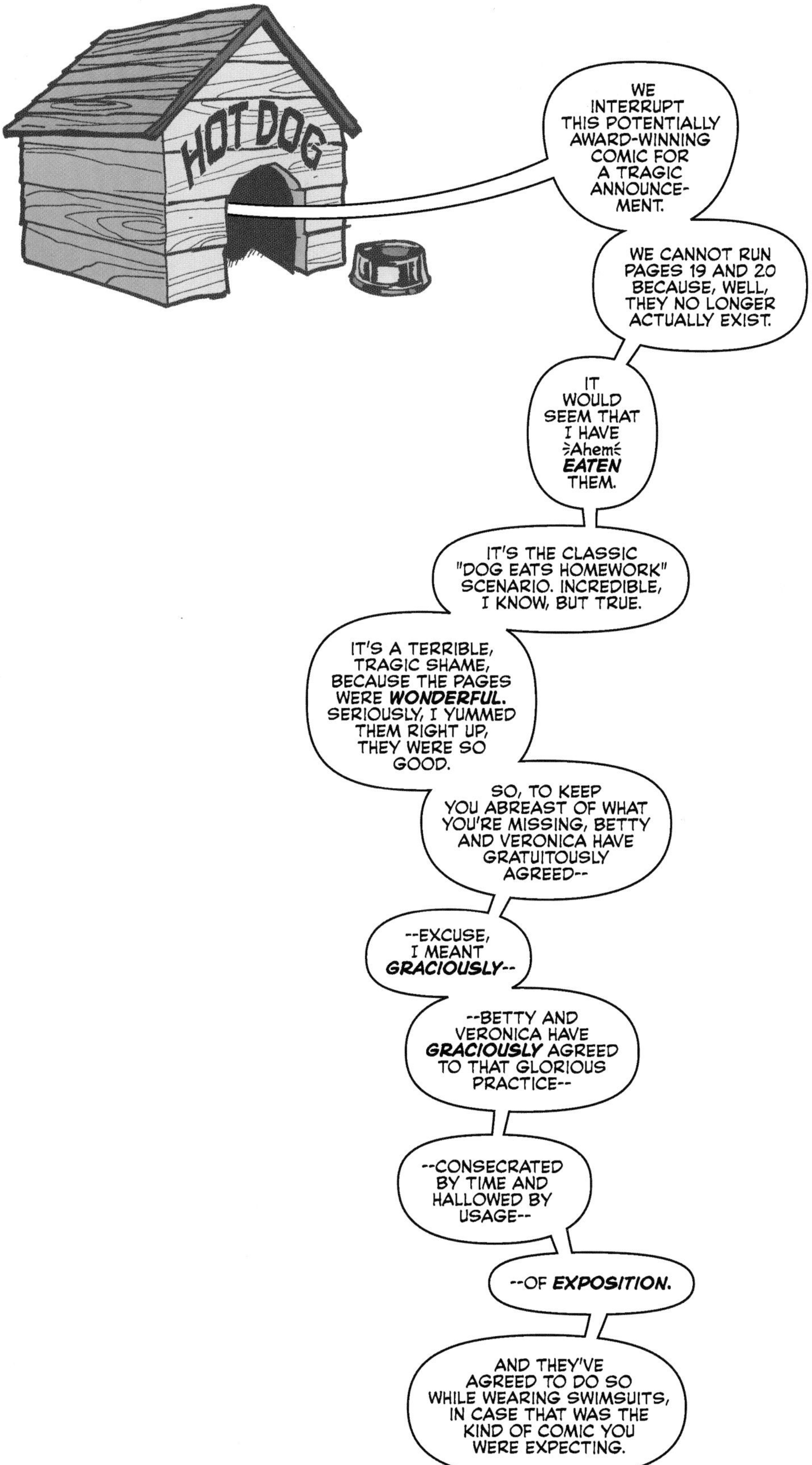
HOT DOG
WE INTERRUPT THIS POTENTIALLY AWARD-WINNING COMIC FOR A TRAGIC ANNOUNCE-MENT.
WE CANNOT RUN PAGES 19 AND 20 BECAUSE, WELL, THEY NO LONGER ACTUALLY EXIST.
IT WOULD SEEM THAT I HAVE *Ahem* ***EATEN*** THEM.
IT'S THE CLASSIC "DOG EATS HOMEWORK" SCENARIO. INCREDIBLE, I KNOW, BUT TRUE.
IT'S A TERRIBLE, TRAGIC SHAME, BECAUSE THE PAGES WERE ***WONDERFUL.*** SERIOUSLY, I YUMMED THEM RIGHT UP, THEY WERE SO GOOD.
SO, TO KEEP YOU ABREAST OF WHAT YOU'RE MISSING, BETTY AND VERONICA HAVE GRATUITOUSLY AGREED--
--EXCUSE, I MEANT ***GRACIOUSLY***--
--BETTY AND VERONICA HAVE ***GRACIOUSLY*** AGREED TO THAT GLORIOUS PRACTICE--
--CONSECRATED BY TIME AND HALLOWED BY USAGE--
--OF ***EXPOSITION.***
AND THEY'VE AGREED TO DO SO WHILE WEARING SWIMSUITS, IN CASE THAT WAS THE KIND OF COMIC YOU WERE EXPECTING.

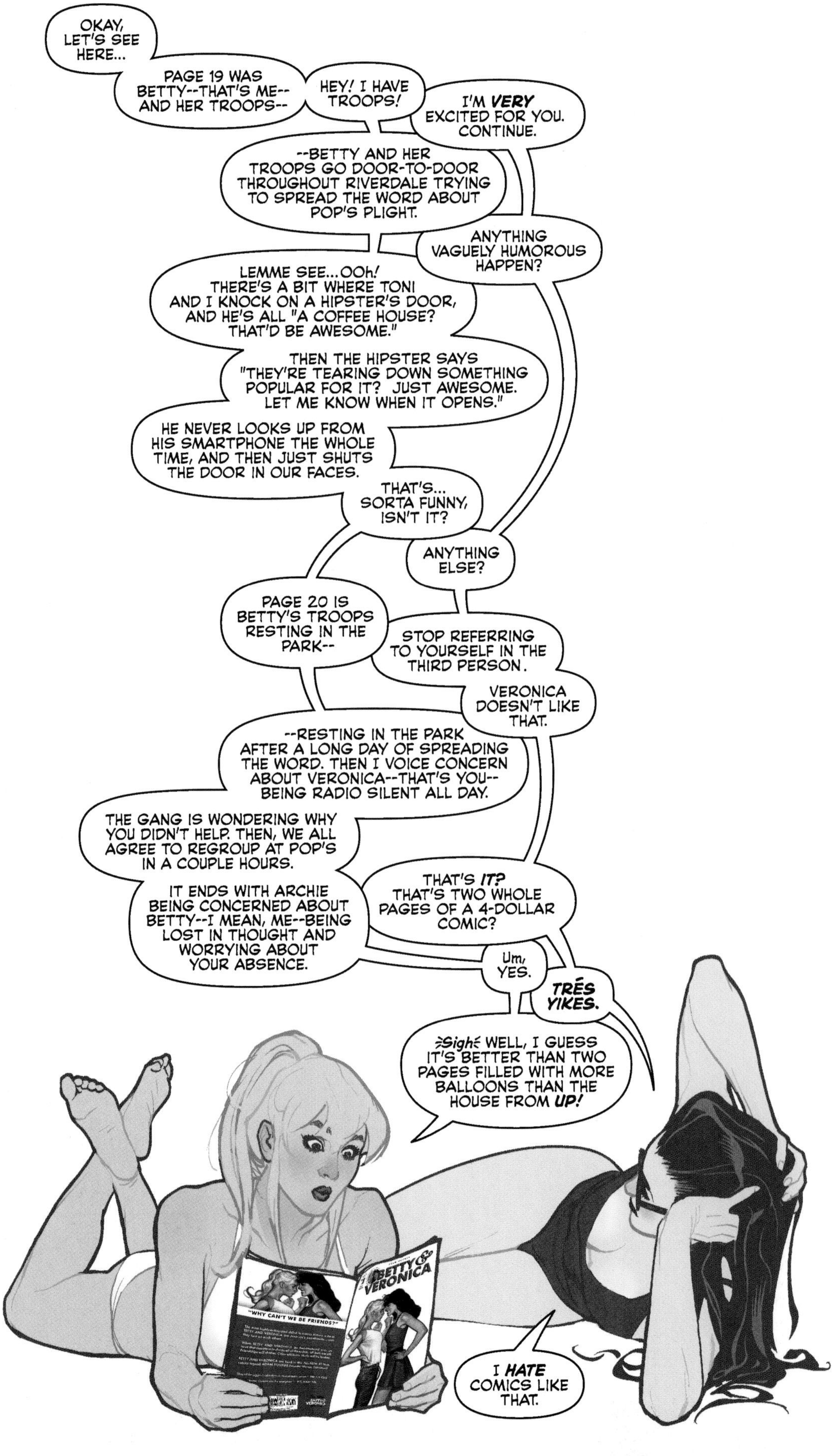

OKAY, LET'S SEE HERE...
PAGE 19 WAS BETTY--THAT'S ME--AND HER TROOPS--
HEY! I HAVE TROOPS!
I'M ***VERY*** EXCITED FOR YOU. CONTINUE.
--BETTY AND HER TROOPS GO DOOR-TO-DOOR THROUGHOUT RIVERDALE TRYING TO SPREAD THE WORD ABOUT POP'S PLIGHT.
ANYTHING VAGUELY HUMOROUS HAPPEN?
LEMME SEE...OOh! THERE'S A BIT WHERE TONI AND I KNOCK ON A HIPSTER'S DOOR, AND HE'S ALL "A COFFEE HOUSE? THAT'D BE AWESOME."
THEN THE HIPSTER SAYS "THEY'RE TEARING DOWN SOMETHING POPULAR FOR IT? JUST AWESOME. LET ME KNOW WHEN IT OPENS."
HE NEVER LOOKS UP FROM HIS SMARTPHONE THE WHOLE TIME, AND THEN JUST SHUTS THE DOOR IN OUR FACES.
THAT'S... SORTA FUNNY, ISN'T IT?
ANYTHING ELSE?
PAGE 20 IS BETTY'S TROOPS RESTING IN THE PARK--
STOP REFERRING TO YOURSELF IN THE THIRD PERSON.
VERONICA DOESN'T LIKE THAT.
--RESTING IN THE PARK AFTER A LONG DAY OF SPREADING THE WORD. THEN I VOICE CONCERN ABOUT VERONICA--THAT'S YOU--BEING RADIO SILENT ALL DAY.
THE GANG IS WONDERING WHY YOU DIDN'T HELP. THEN, WE ALL AGREE TO REGROUP AT POP'S IN A COUPLE HOURS.
IT ENDS WITH ARCHIE BEING CONCERNED ABOUT BETTY--I MEAN, ME--BEING LOST IN THOUGHT AND WORRYING ABOUT YOUR ABSENCE.
THAT'S ***IT?*** THAT'S TWO WHOLE PAGES OF A 4-DOLLAR COMIC?
Um, YES.
TRÉS YIKES.
Sigh WELL, I GUESS IT'S BETTER THAN TWO PAGES FILLED WITH MORE BALLOONS THAN THE HOUSE FROM ***UP!***
I ***HATE*** COMICS LIKE THAT.
"WHY CAN'T WE BE FRIENDS?"
BETTY & VERONICA

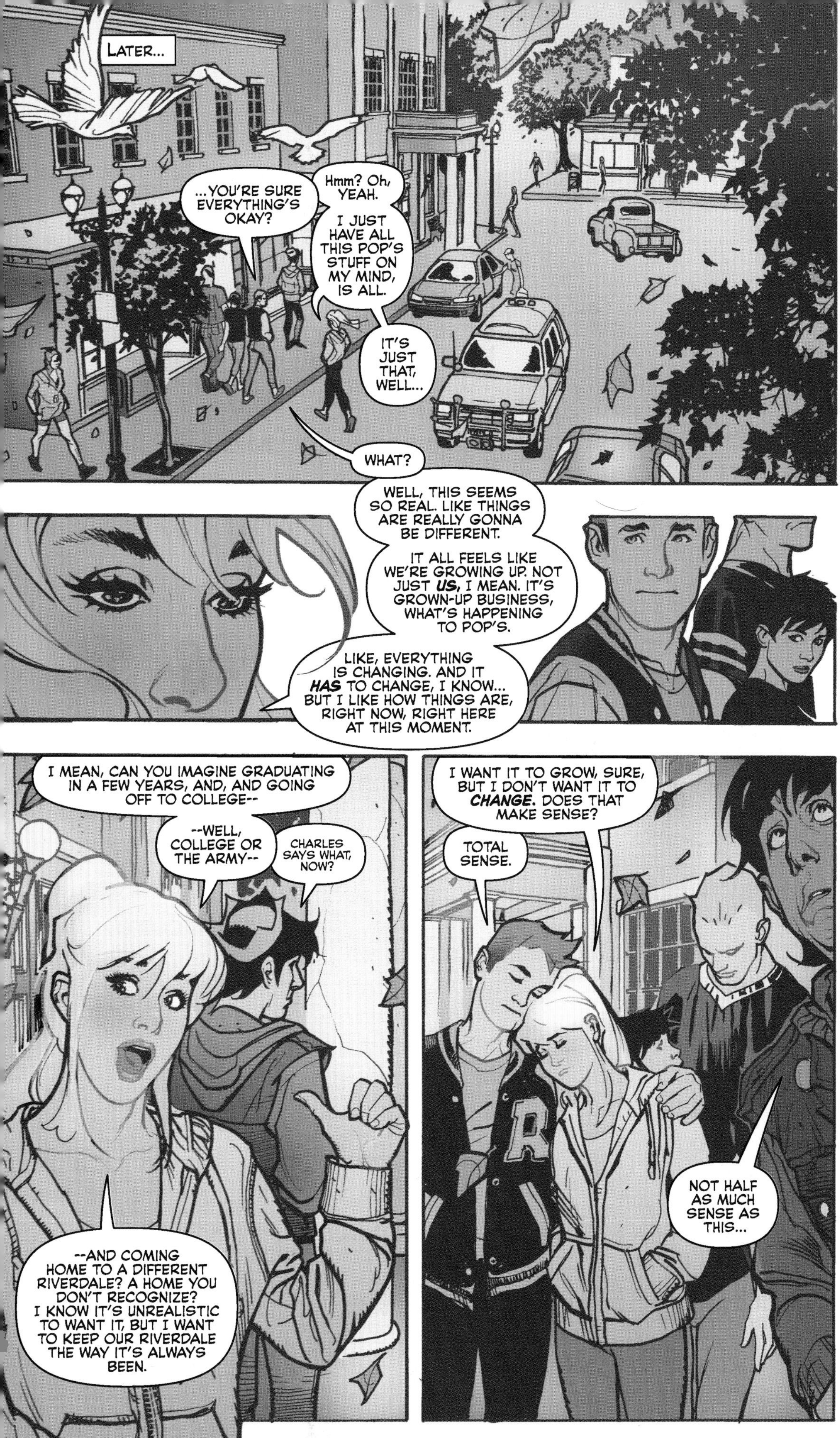
LATER...
...YOU'RE SURE EVERYTHING'S OKAY?
Hmm? Oh, YEAH.
I JUST HAVE ALL THIS POP'S STUFF ON MY MIND, IS ALL.
IT'S JUST THAT, WELL...
WHAT?
WELL, THIS SEEMS SO REAL. LIKE THINGS ARE REALLY GONNA BE DIFFERENT.
IT ALL FEELS LIKE WE'RE GROWING UP. NOT JUST US, I MEAN. IT'S GROWN-UP BUSINESS, WHAT'S HAPPENING TO POP'S.
LIKE, EVERYTHING IS CHANGING. AND IT HAS TO CHANGE, I KNOW... BUT I LIKE HOW THINGS ARE, RIGHT NOW, RIGHT HERE AT THIS MOMENT.
I MEAN, CAN YOU IMAGINE GRADUATING IN A FEW YEARS, AND, AND GOING OFF TO COLLEGE--
--WELL, COLLEGE OR THE ARMY--
CHARLES SAYS WHAT, NOW?
--AND COMING HOME TO A DIFFERENT RIVERDALE? A HOME YOU DON'T RECOGNIZE? I KNOW IT'S UNREALISTIC TO WANT IT, BUT I WANT TO KEEP OUR RIVERDALE THE WAY IT'S ALWAYS BEEN.
I WANT IT TO GROW, SURE, BUT I DON'T WANT IT TO CHANGE. DOES THAT MAKE SENSE?
TOTAL SENSE.
NOT HALF AS MUCH SENSE AS THIS...

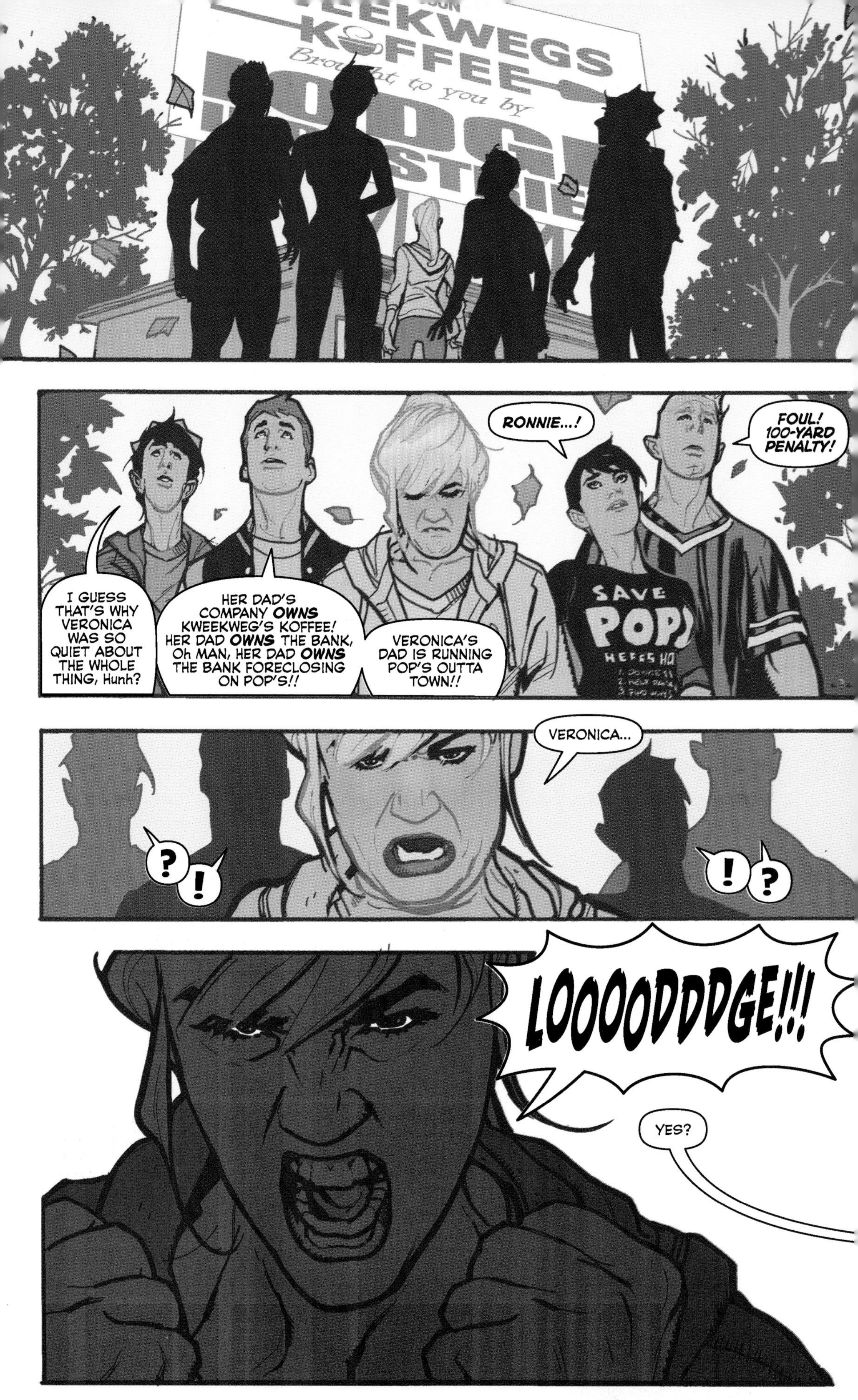
RONNIE...!
FOUL! 100-YARD PENALTY!
I GUESS THAT'S WHY VERONICA WAS SO QUIET ABOUT THE WHOLE THING, Hunh?
HER DAD'S COMPANY OWNS KWEEKWEG'S KOFFEE! HER DAD OWNS THE BANK, Oh MAN, HER DAD OWNS THE BANK FORECLOSING ON POP'S!!
VERONICA'S DAD IS RUNNING POP'S OUTTA TOWN!!
SAVE POP'S
VERONICA...
?
!
!
?
LOOOODDDGE!!!
YES?

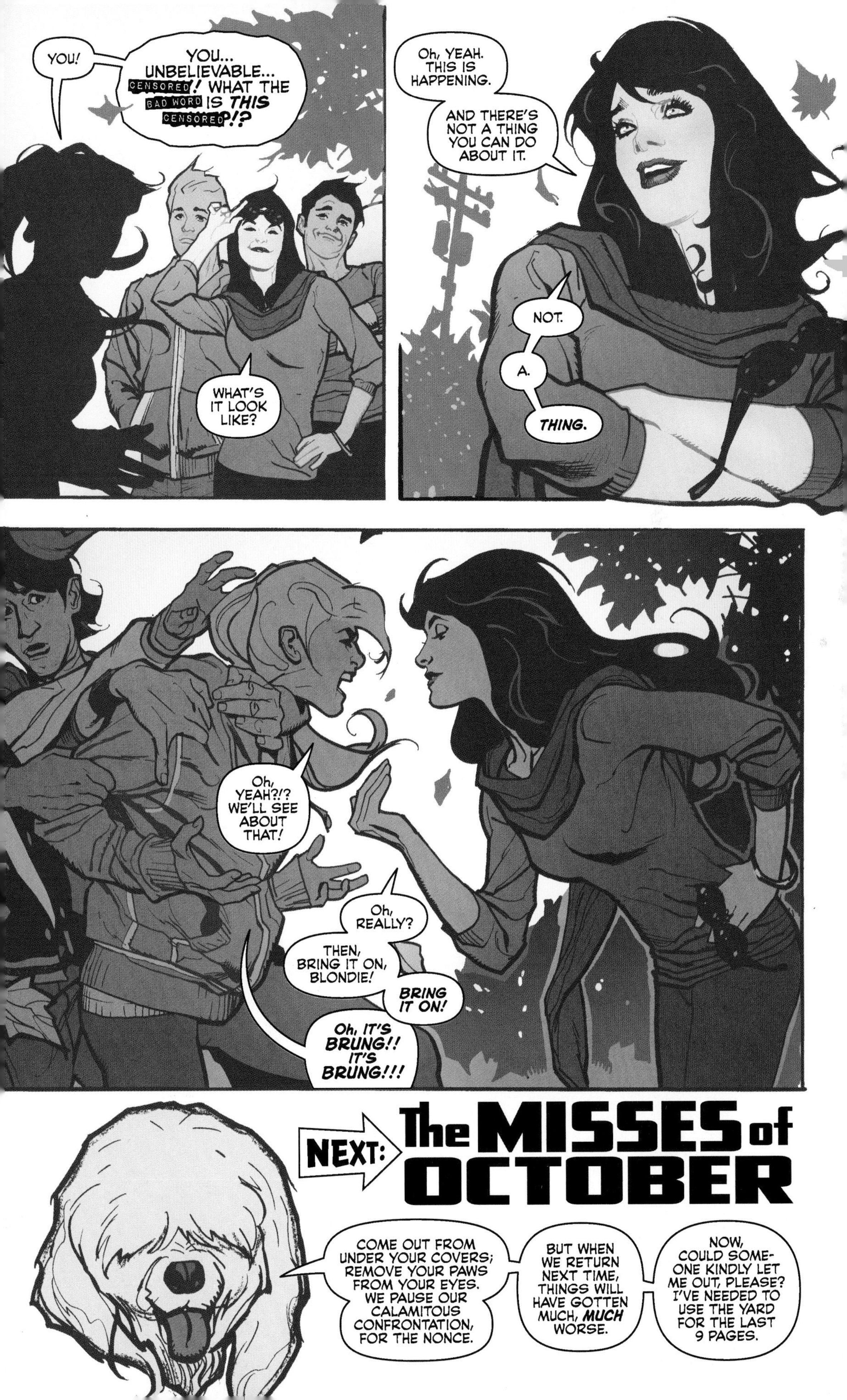
YOU!
YOU... UNBELIEVABLE... CENSORED! WHAT THE BAD WORD IS THIS CENSORED?!?
WHAT'S IT LOOK LIKE?
Oh, YEAH. THIS IS HAPPENING.
AND THERE'S NOT A THING YOU CAN DO ABOUT IT.
NOT.
A.
THING.
Oh, YEAH?!? WE'LL SEE ABOUT THAT!
Oh, REALLY?
THEN, BRING IT ON, BLONDIE!
BRING IT ON!
Oh, IT'S BRUNG!! IT'S BRUNG!!!
NEXT: The MISSES of OCTOBER
COME OUT FROM UNDER YOUR COVERS; REMOVE YOUR PAWS FROM YOUR EYES. WE PAUSE OUR CALAMITOUS CONFRONTATION, FOR THE NONCE.
BUT WHEN WE RETURN NEXT TIME, THINGS WILL HAVE GOTTEN MUCH, MUCH WORSE.
NOW, COULD SOME-ONE KINDLY LET ME OUT, PLEASE? I'VE NEEDED TO USE THE YARD FOR THE LAST 9 PAGES.

ISSUE TWO

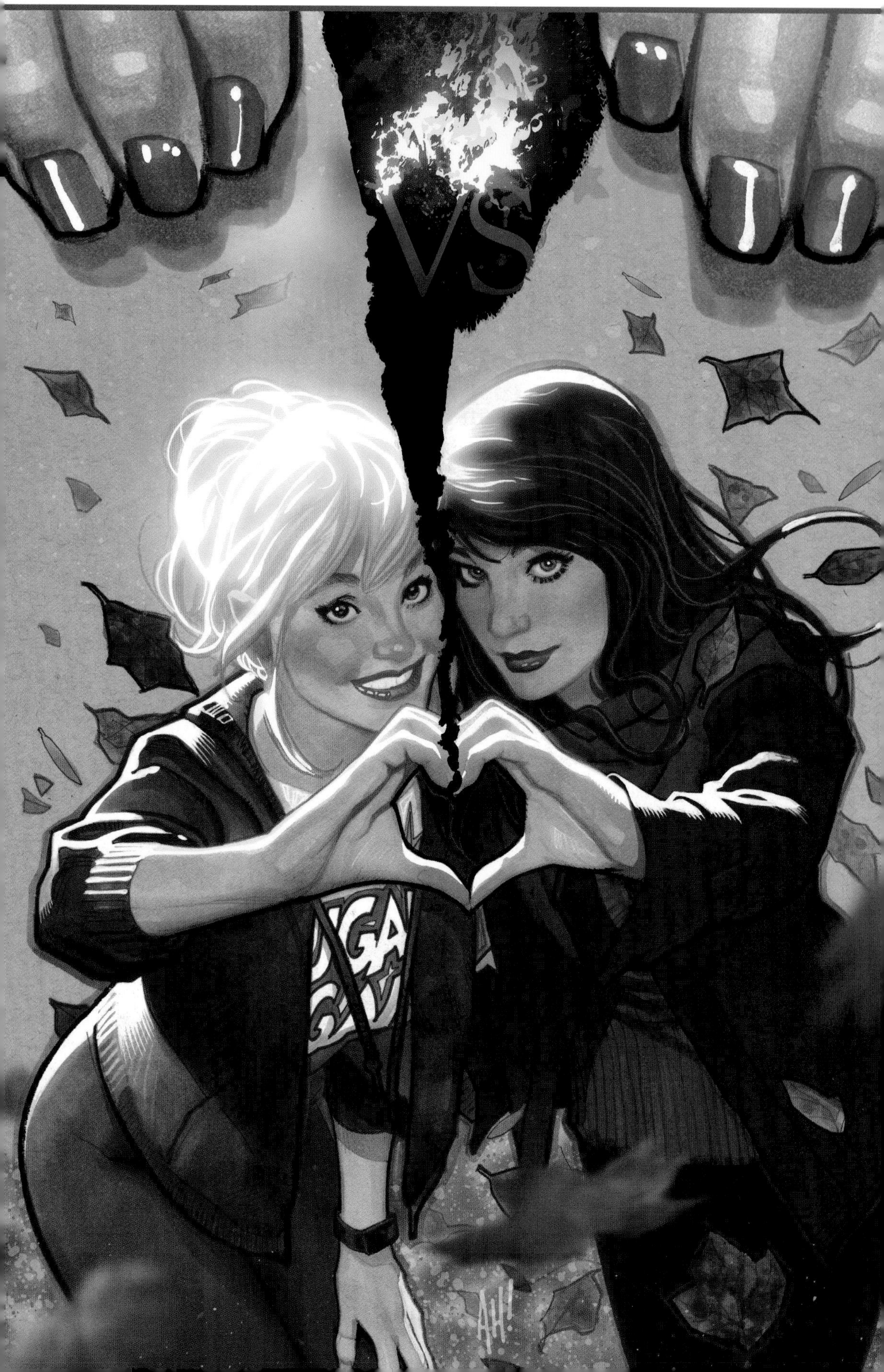
VS

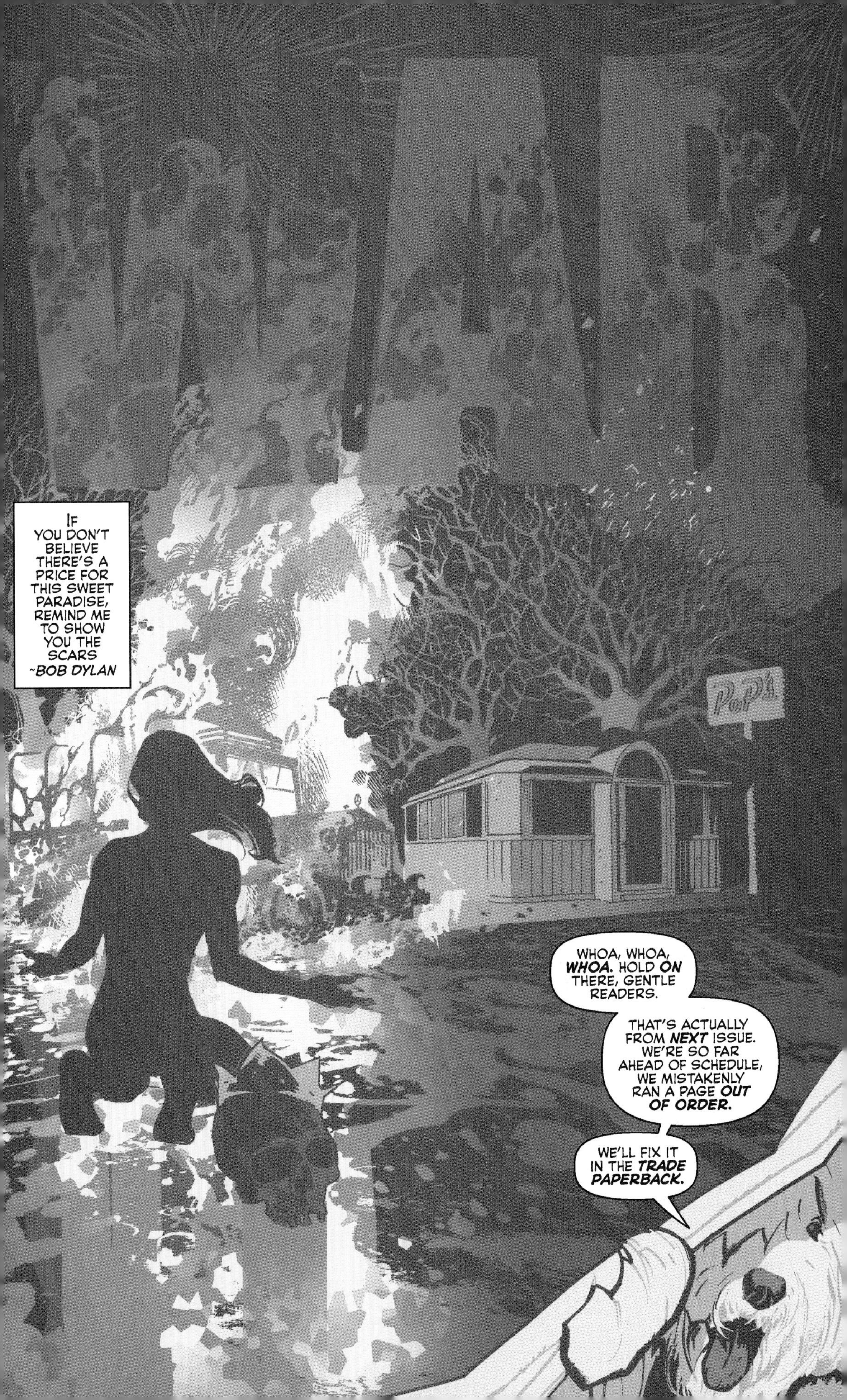
IF YOU DON'T BELIEVE THERE'S A PRICE FOR THIS SWEET PARADISE, REMIND ME TO SHOW YOU THE SCARS
~BOB DYLAN
POP'S
WHOA, WHOA, WHOA. HOLD ON THERE, GENTLE READERS.
THAT'S ACTUALLY FROM NEXT ISSUE. WE'RE SO FAR AHEAD OF SCHEDULE, WE MISTAKENLY RAN A PAGE OUT OF ORDER.
WE'LL FIX IT IN THE TRADE PAPERBACK.

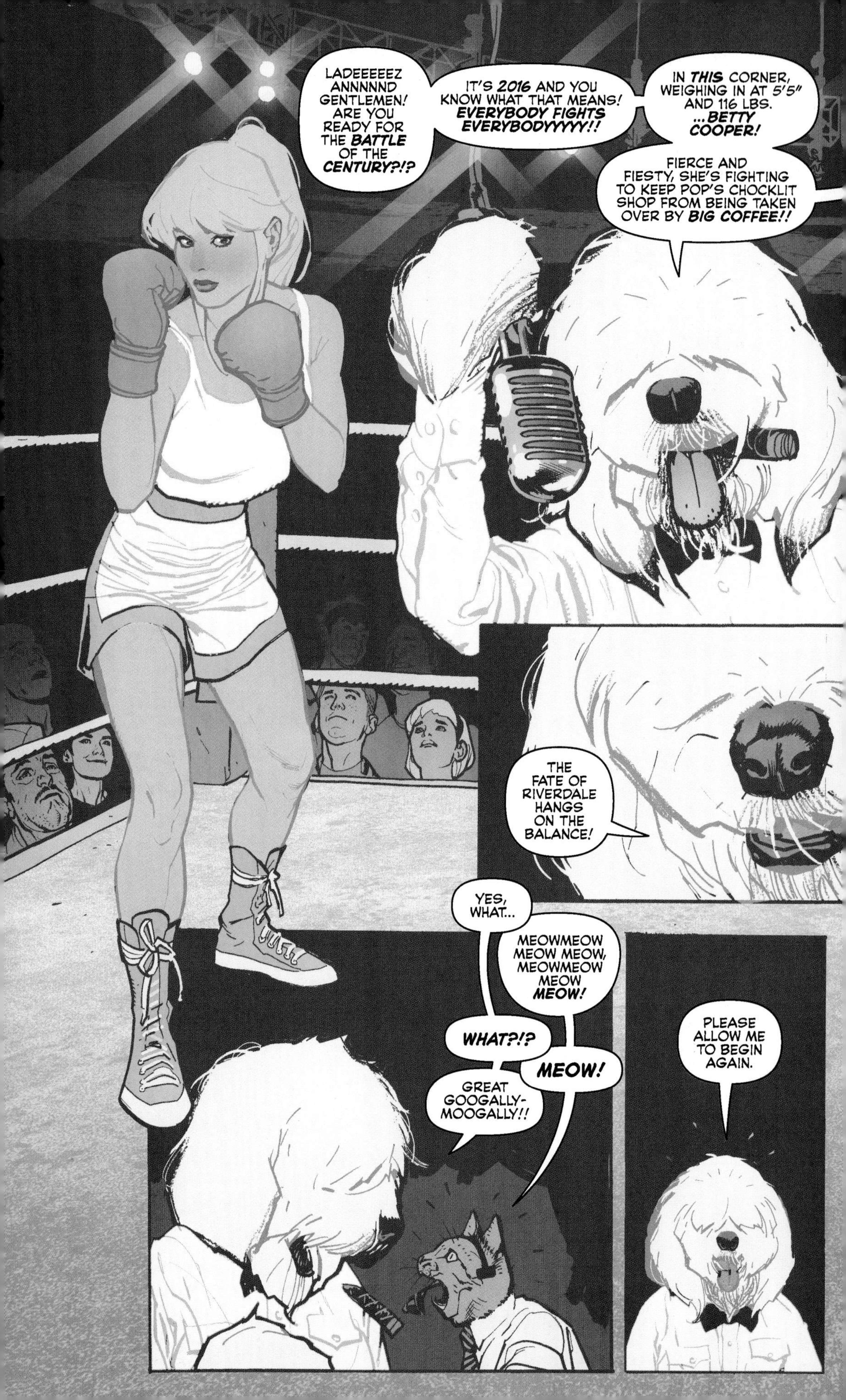

LADEEEEEZ ANNNNND GENTLEMEN! ARE YOU READY FOR THE BATTLE OF THE CENTURY?!?
IT'S 2016 AND YOU KNOW WHAT THAT MEANS! EVERYBODY FIGHTS EVERYBODYYYYY!!
IN THIS CORNER, WEIGHING IN AT 5'5" AND 116 LBS. ...BETTY COOPER!
FIERCE AND FIESTY, SHE'S FIGHTING TO KEEP POP'S CHOCKLIT SHOP FROM BEING TAKEN OVER BY BIG COFFEE!!
THE FATE OF RIVERDALE HANGS ON THE BALANCE!
YES, WHAT...
MEOWMEOW MEOW MEOW, MEOWMEOW MEOW MEOW!
WHAT?!?
MEOW!
GREAT GOOGALLY-MOOGALLY!!
PLEASE ALLOW ME TO BEGIN AGAIN.

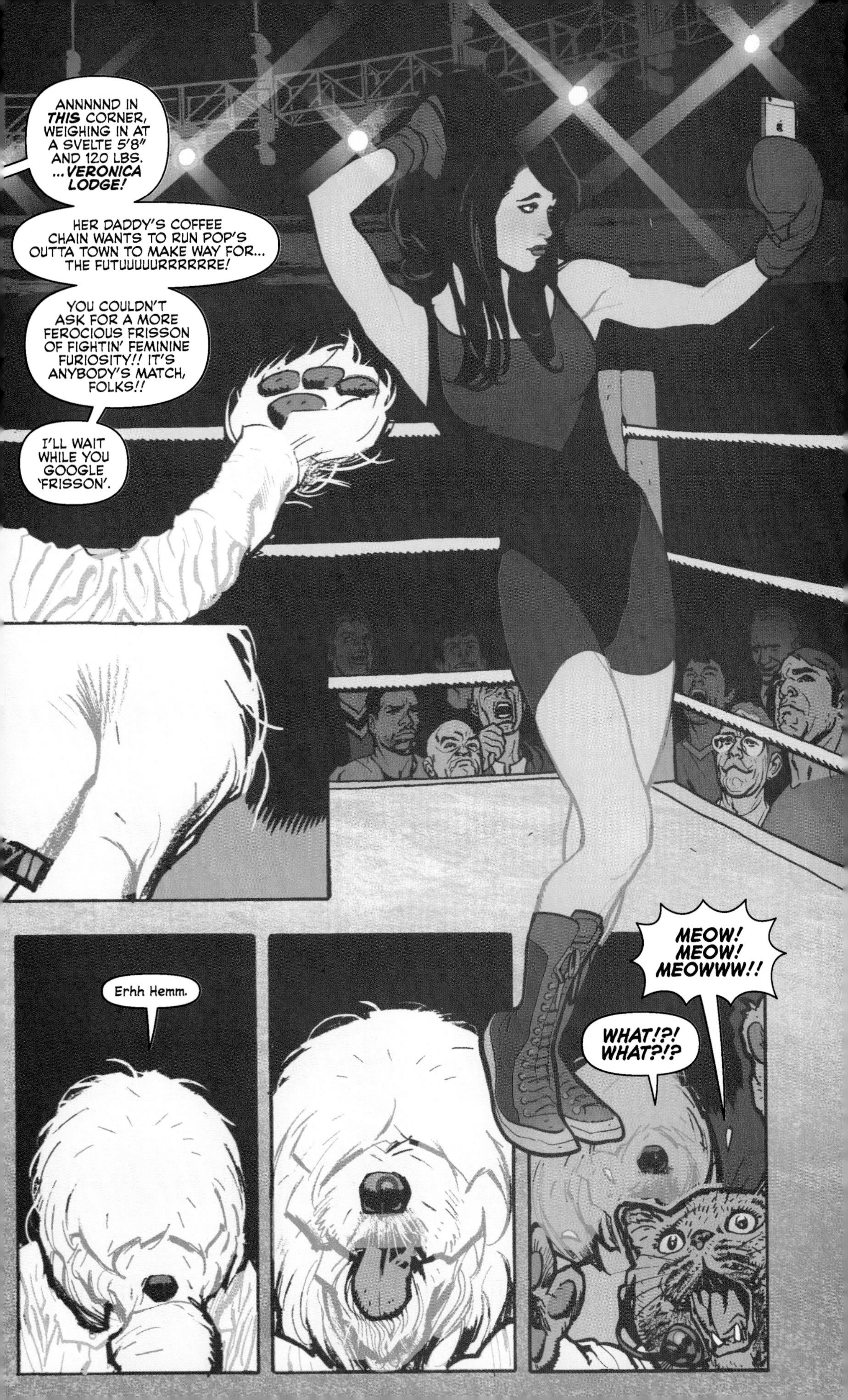
ANNNNND IN THIS CORNER, WEIGHING IN AT A SVELTE 5'8" AND 120 LBS. ...VERONICA LODGE!
HER DADDY'S COFFEE CHAIN WANTS TO RUN POP'S OUTTA TOWN TO MAKE WAY FOR... THE FUTUUUUURRRRRE!
YOU COULDN'T ASK FOR A MORE FEROCIOUS FRISSON OF FIGHTIN' FEMININE FURIOSITY!! IT'S ANYBODY'S MATCH, FOLKS!!
I'LL WAIT WHILE YOU GOOGLE 'FRISSON'.
Erhh Hemm.
MEOW! MEOW! MEOWWW!!
WHAT!?! WHAT?!?

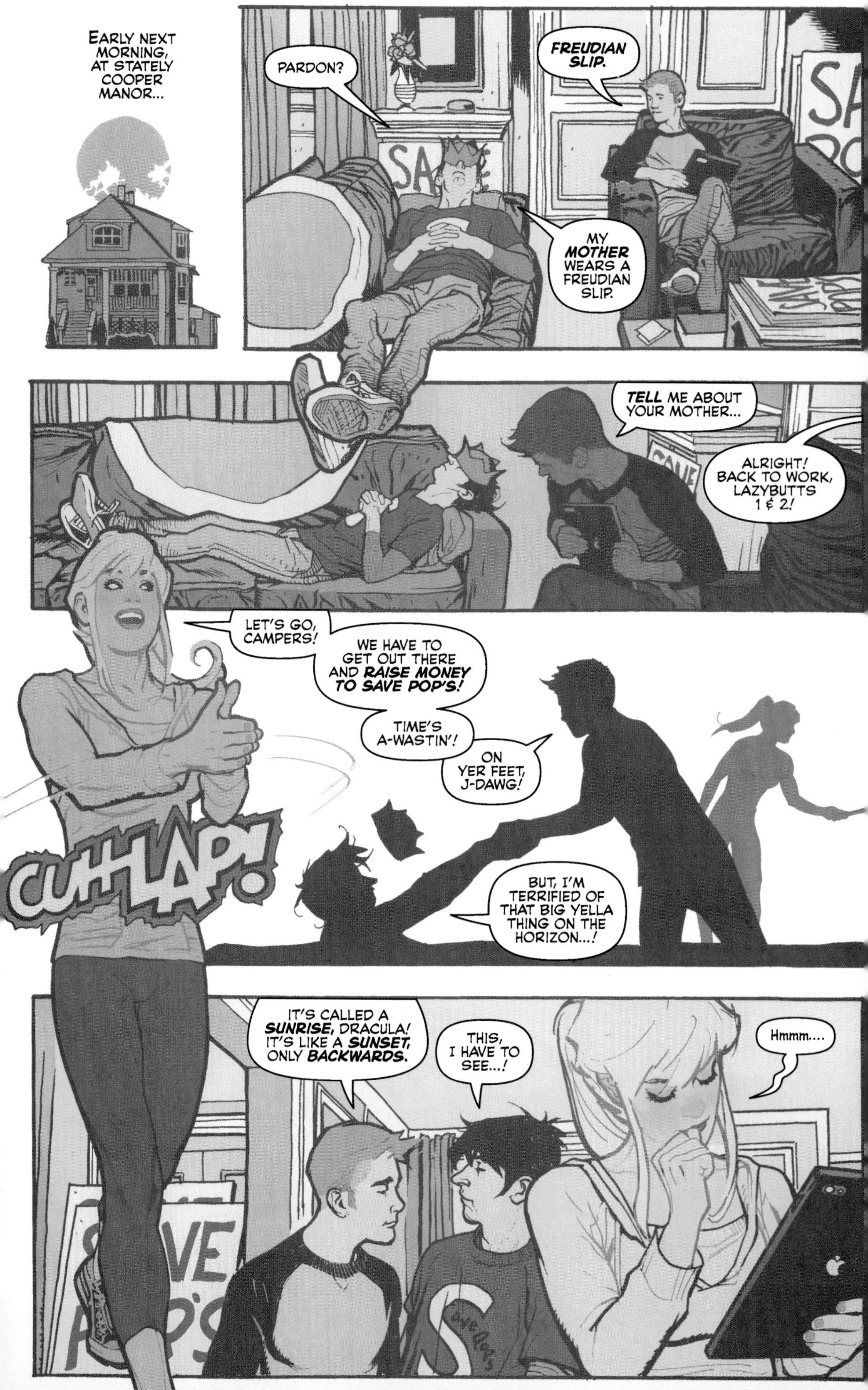

EARLY NEXT MORNING, AT STATELY COOPER MANOR...
PARDON?
FREUDIAN SLIP.
MY MOTHER WEARS A FREUDIAN SLIP.
TELL ME ABOUT YOUR MOTHER...
ALRIGHT! BACK TO WORK, LAZYBUTTS 1 & 2!
LET'S GO, CAMPERS!
WE HAVE TO GET OUT THERE AND RAISE MONEY TO SAVE POP'S!
TIME'S A-WASTIN'!
ON YER FEET, J-DAWG!
CUHLAP!
BUT, I'M TERRIFIED OF THAT BIG YELLA THING ON THE HORIZON...!
IT'S CALLED A SUNRISE, DRACULA! IT'S LIKE A SUNSET, ONLY BACKWARDS.
THIS, I HAVE TO SEE...!
Hmmm....

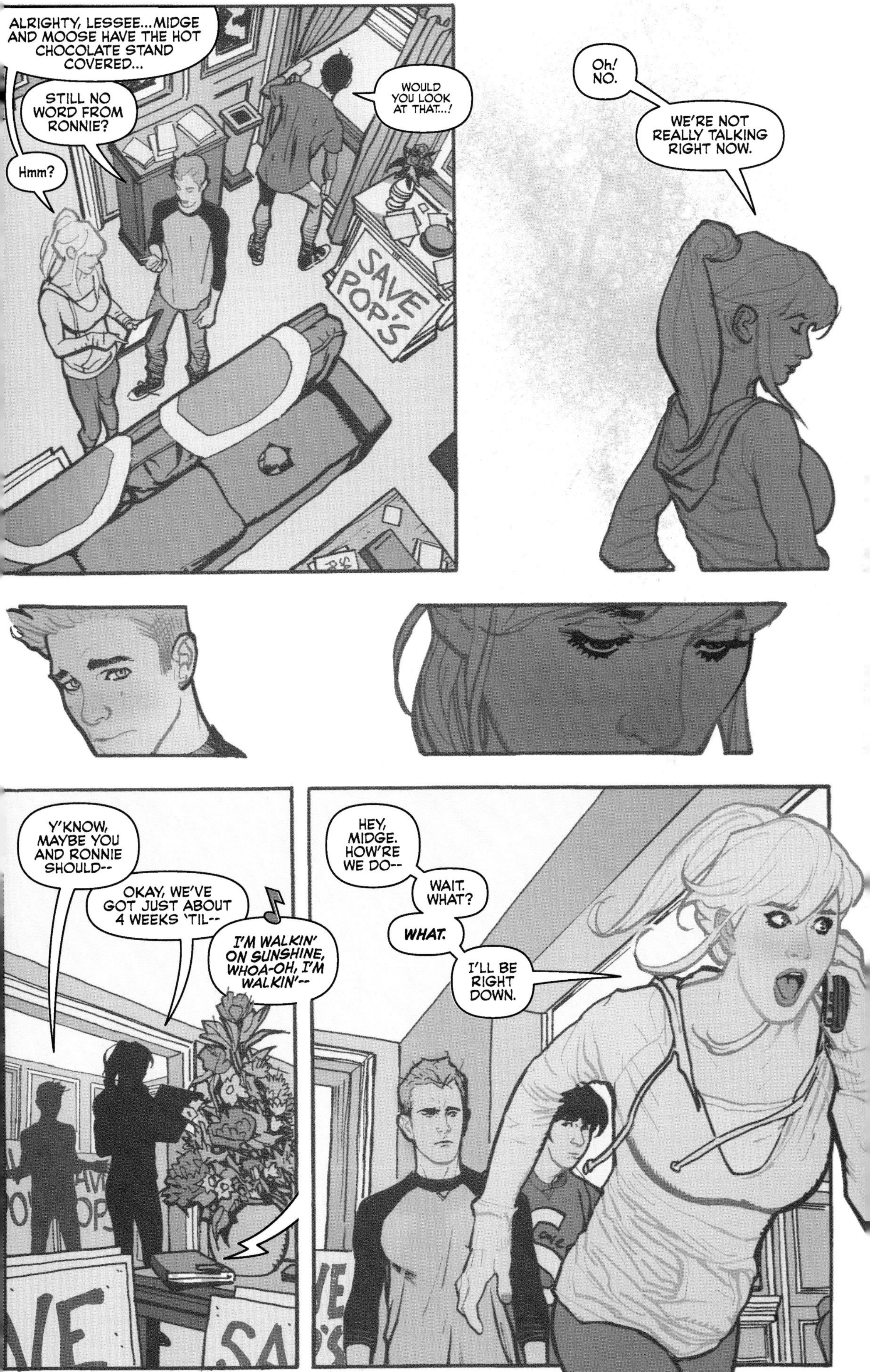
ALRIGHTY, LESSEE...MIDGE AND MOOSE HAVE THE HOT CHOCOLATE STAND COVERED...
STILL NO WORD FROM RONNIE?
Hmm?
WOULD YOU LOOK AT THAT...!
SAVE POP'S
Oh! NO.
WE'RE NOT REALLY TALKING RIGHT NOW.
Y'KNOW, MAYBE YOU AND RONNIE SHOULD--
OKAY, WE'VE GOT JUST ABOUT 4 WEEKS 'TIL--
I'M WALKIN' ON SUNSHINE, WHOA-OH, I'M WALKIN'--
HEY, MIDGE. HOW'RE WE DO--
WAIT. WHAT?
WHAT.
I'LL BE RIGHT DOWN.

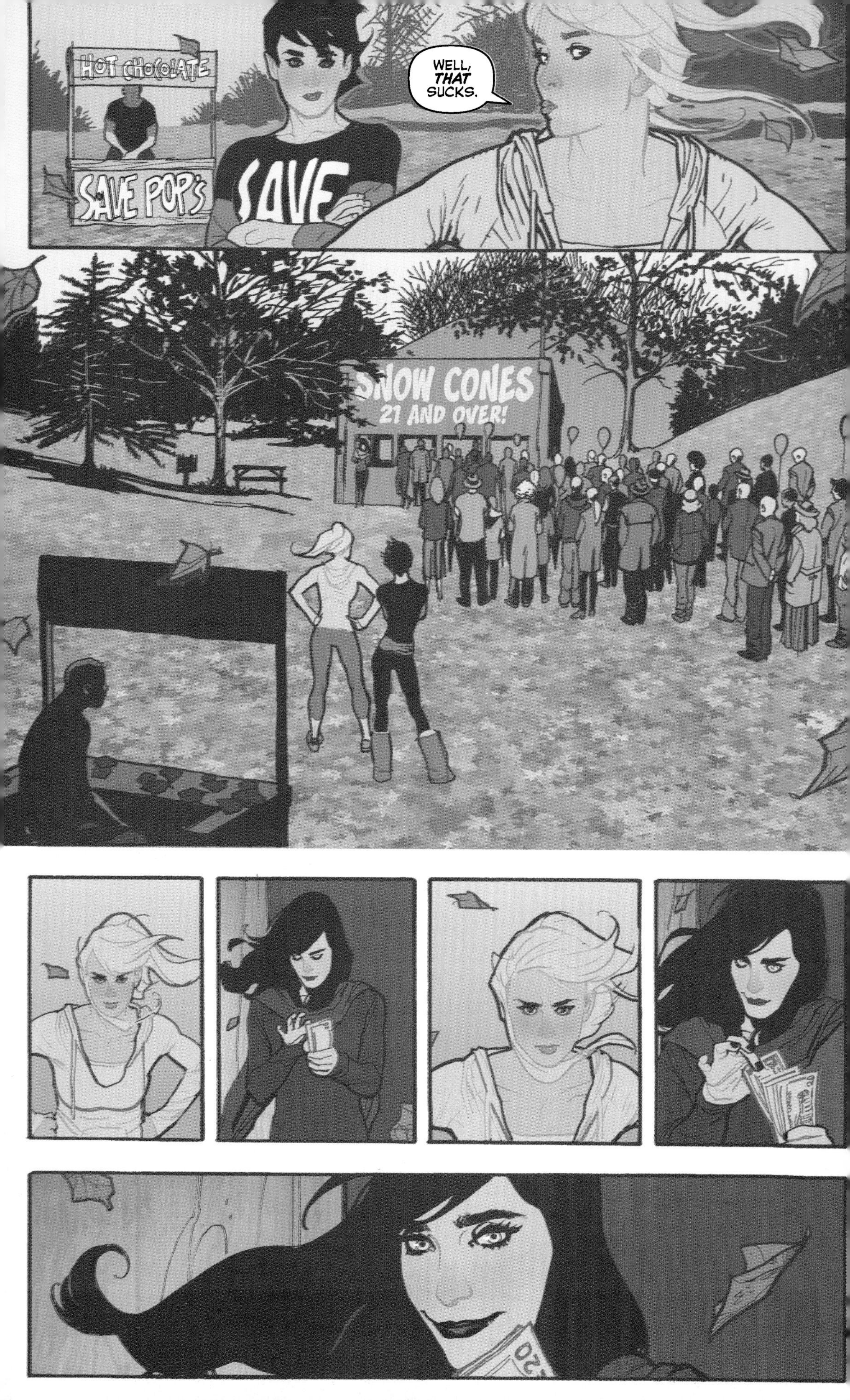
HOT CHOCOLATE
SAVE POP'S
SAVE
WELL, *THAT* SUCKS.
SNOW CONES
21 AND OVER!

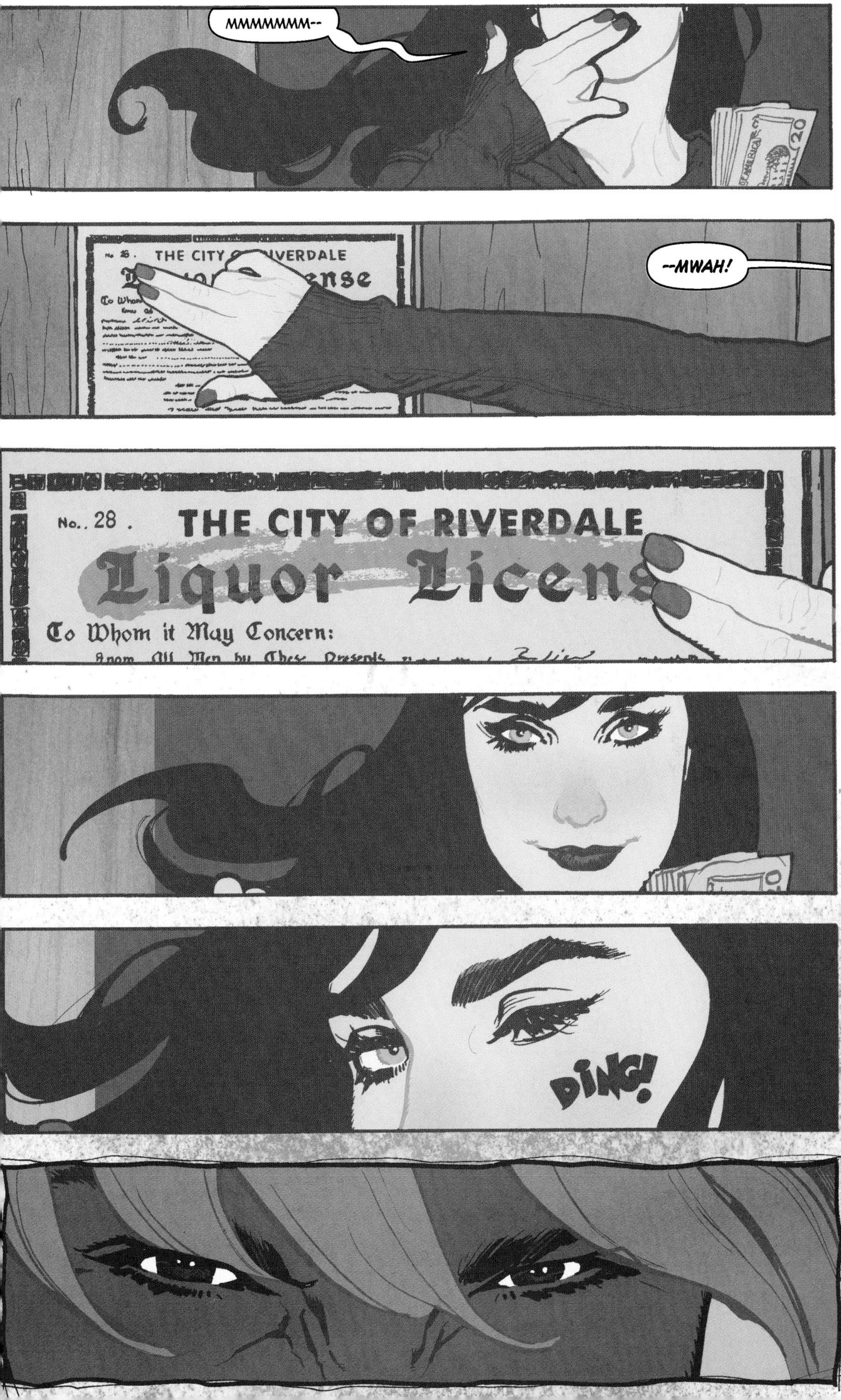
MMMMMMM--
--MWAH!
No. 28 . THE CITY OF RIVERDALE
Liquor Licens
To Whom it May Concern:
DING!

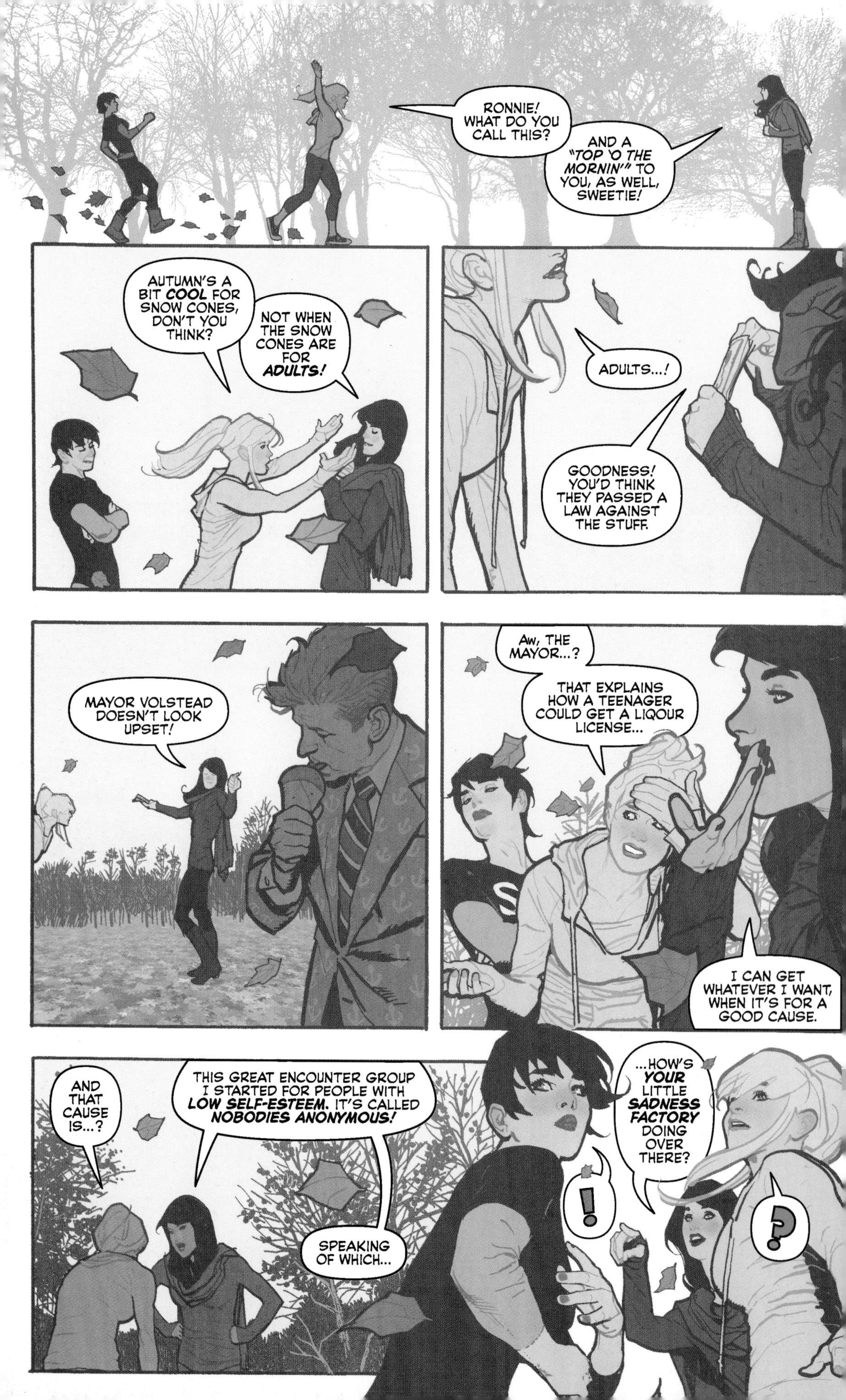
RONNIE! WHAT DO YOU CALL THIS?
AND A "TOP 'O THE MORNIN'" TO YOU, AS WELL, SWEETIE!
AUTUMN'S A BIT COOL FOR SNOW CONES, DON'T YOU THINK?
NOT WHEN THE SNOW CONES ARE FOR ADULTS!
ADULTS...!
GOODNESS! YOU'D THINK THEY PASSED A LAW AGAINST THE STUFF.
MAYOR VOLSTEAD DOESN'T LOOK UPSET!
AW, THE MAYOR...?
THAT EXPLAINS HOW A TEENAGER COULD GET A LIQOUR LICENSE...
I CAN GET WHATEVER I WANT, WHEN IT'S FOR A GOOD CAUSE.
AND THAT CAUSE IS...?
THIS GREAT ENCOUNTER GROUP I STARTED FOR PEOPLE WITH LOW SELF-ESTEEM. IT'S CALLED NOBODIES ANONYMOUS!
SPEAKING OF WHICH...
...HOW'S YOUR LITTLE SADNESS FACTORY DOING OVER THERE?
!
?

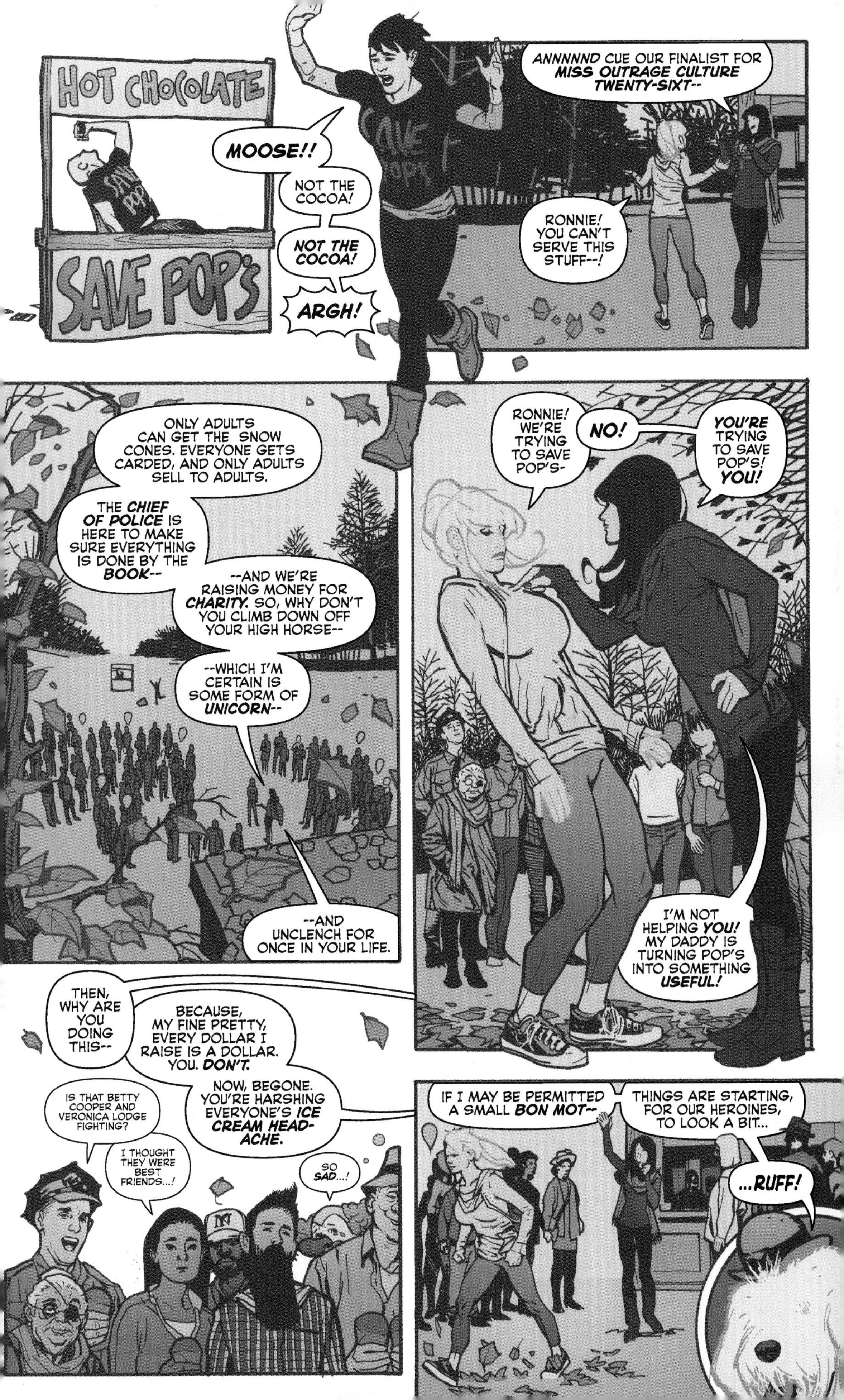
HOT CHOCOLATE
SAVE POP'S
SAVE POP'S
MOOSE!!
NOT THE COCOA!
NOT THE COCOA!
ARGH!
ANNNNND CUE OUR FINALIST FOR MISS OUTRAGE CULTURE TWENTY-SIXT--
RONNIE! YOU CAN'T SERVE THIS STUFF--!
ONLY ADULTS CAN GET THE SNOW CONES. EVERYONE GETS CARDED, AND ONLY ADULTS SELL TO ADULTS.
THE CHIEF OF POLICE IS HERE TO MAKE SURE EVERYTHING IS DONE BY THE BOOK--
--AND WE'RE RAISING MONEY FOR CHARITY. SO, WHY DON'T YOU CLIMB DOWN OFF YOUR HIGH HORSE--
--WHICH I'M CERTAIN IS SOME FORM OF UNICORN--
--AND UNCLENCH FOR ONCE IN YOUR LIFE.
RONNIE! WE'RE TRYING TO SAVE POP'S-
NO!
YOU'RE TRYING TO SAVE POP'S! YOU!
I'M NOT HELPING YOU! MY DADDY IS TURNING POP'S INTO SOMETHING USEFUL!
THEN, WHY ARE YOU DOING THIS--
BECAUSE, MY FINE PRETTY, EVERY DOLLAR I RAISE IS A DOLLAR. YOU. DON'T.
NOW, BEGONE. YOU'RE HARSHING EVERYONE'S ICE CREAM HEAD-ACHE.
IS THAT BETTY COOPER AND VERONICA LODGE FIGHTING?
I THOUGHT THEY WERE BEST FRIENDS...!
SO SAD...!
IF I MAY BE PERMITTED A SMALL BON MOT--
THINGS ARE STARTING, FOR OUR HEROINES, TO LOOK A BIT...
...RUFF!

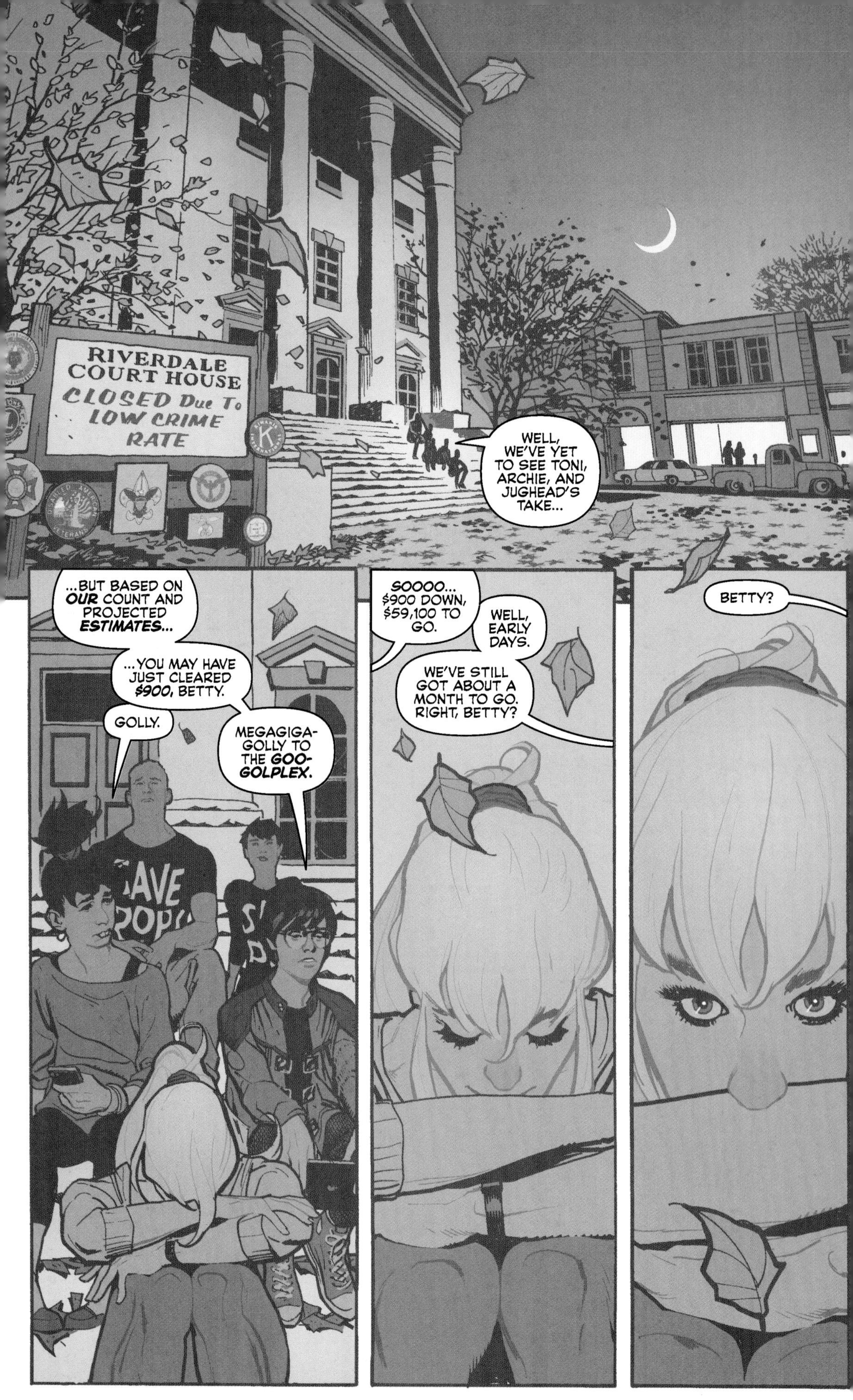
RIVERDALE COURT HOUSE
CLOSED Due To LOW CRIME RATE
WELL, WE'VE YET TO SEE TONI, ARCHIE, AND JUGHEAD'S TAKE...
...BUT BASED ON OUR COUNT AND PROJECTED ESTIMATES...
...YOU MAY HAVE JUST CLEARED $900, BETTY.
GOLLY.
MEGAGIGA-GOLLY TO THE GOO-GOLPLEX.
SOOOO... $900 DOWN, $59,100 TO GO.
WELL, EARLY DAYS.
WE'VE STILL GOT ABOUT A MONTH TO GO. RIGHT, BETTY?
BETTY?

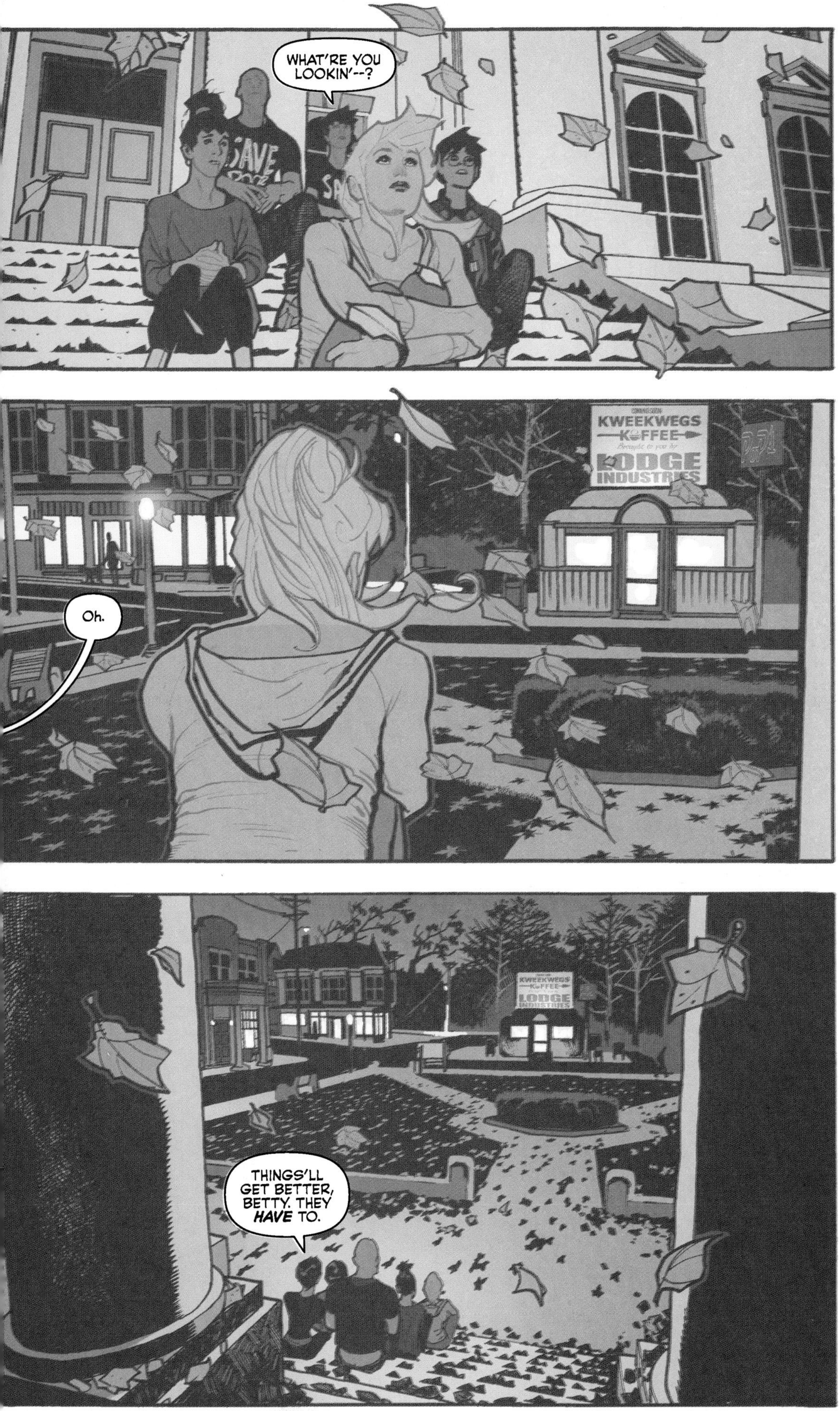

WHAT'RE YOU LOOKIN'--?
KWEEKWEGS
LODGE INDUSTRIES
Oh.
THINGS'LL GET BETTER, BETTY. THEY ***HAVE*** TO.

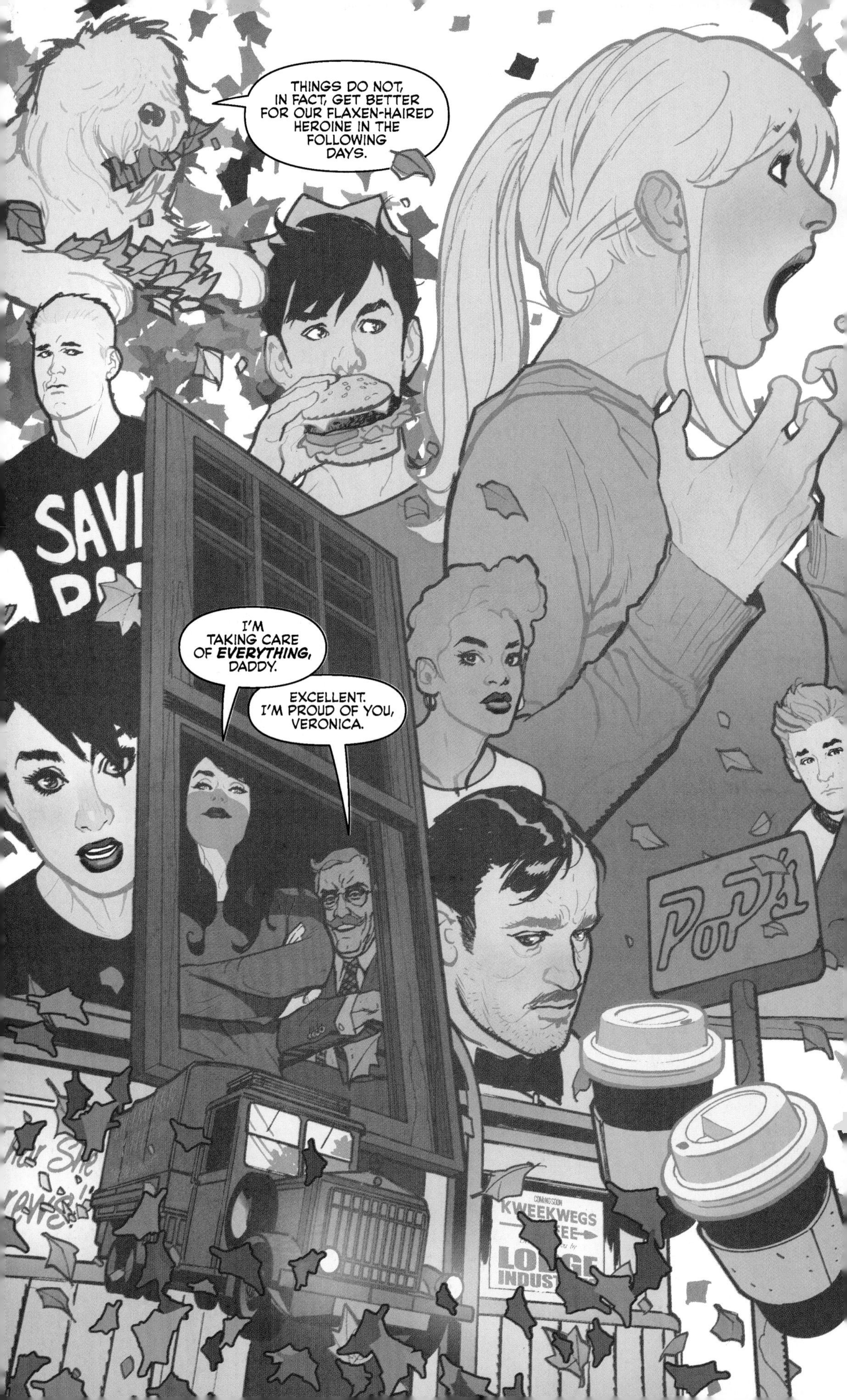
THINGS DO NOT, IN FACT, GET BETTER FOR OUR FLAXEN-HAIRED HEROINE IN THE FOLLOWING DAYS.
I'M TAKING CARE OF ***EVERYTHING***, DADDY.
EXCELLENT. I'M PROUD OF YOU, VERONICA.
COMING SOON
KWEEKWEGS

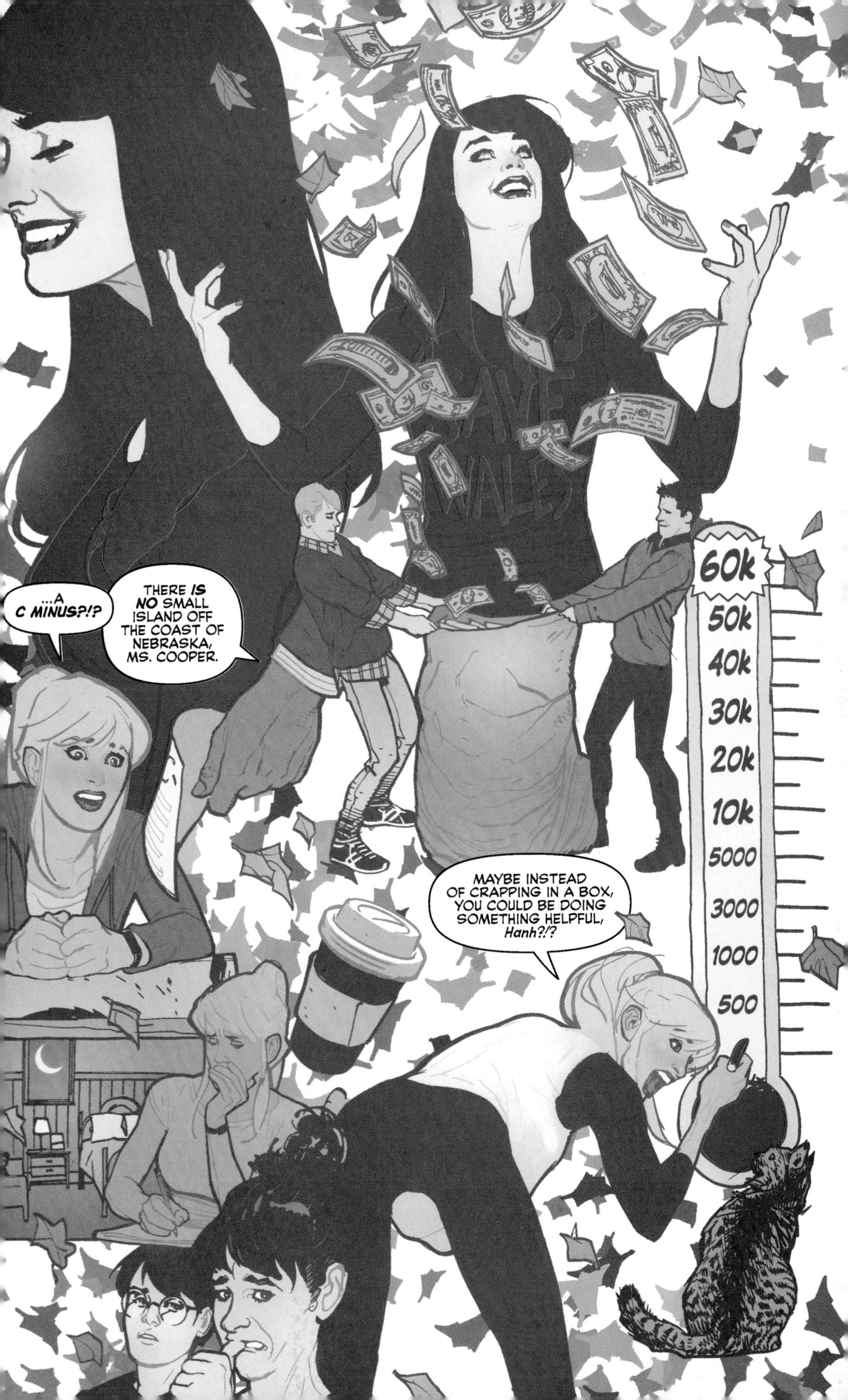

...A C MINUS?!?
THERE IS NO SMALL ISLAND OFF THE COAST OF NEBRASKA, MS. COOPER.
SAVE WALES
60k
50k
40k
30k
20k
10k
5000
3000
1000
500
MAYBE INSTEAD OF CRAPPING IN A BOX, YOU COULD BE DOING SOMETHING HELPFUL, Hanh?!?

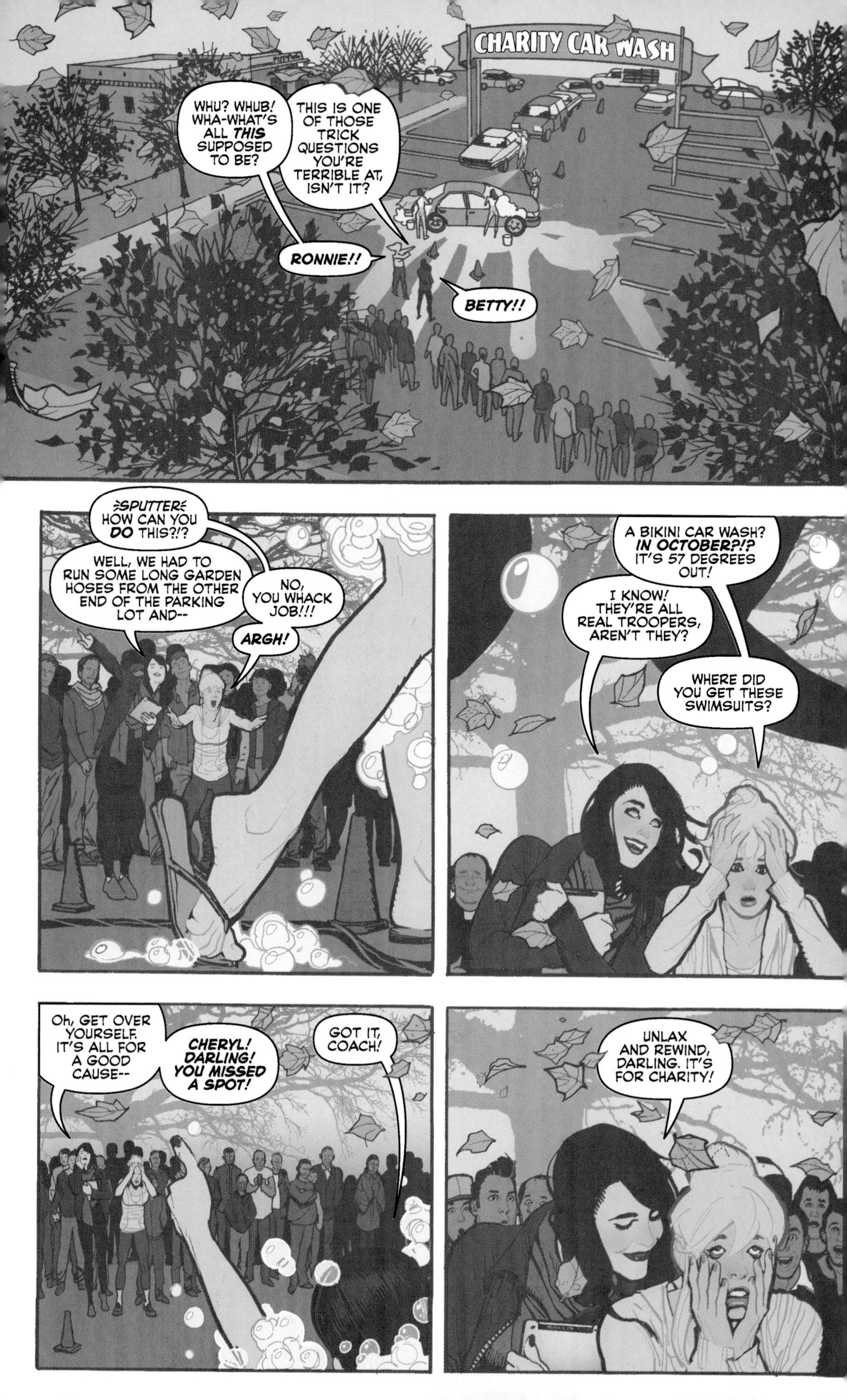
CHARITY CAR WASH
WHU? WHUB! WHA-WHAT'S ALL THIS SUPPOSED TO BE?
THIS IS ONE OF THOSE TRICK QUESTIONS YOU'RE TERRIBLE AT, ISN'T IT?
RONNIE!!
BETTY!!
SPUTTER HOW CAN YOU DO THIS?!?
WELL, WE HAD TO RUN SOME LONG GARDEN HOSES FROM THE OTHER END OF THE PARKING LOT AND--
NO, YOU WHACK JOB!!!
ARGH!
A BIKINI CAR WASH? IN OCTOBER?!? IT'S 57 DEGREES OUT!
I KNOW! THEY'RE ALL REAL TROOPERS, AREN'T THEY?
WHERE DID YOU GET THESE SWIMSUITS?
Oh, GET OVER YOURSELF. IT'S ALL FOR A GOOD CAUSE--
CHERYL! DARLING! YOU MISSED A SPOT!
GOT IT, COACH!
UNLAX AND REWIND, DARLING. IT'S FOR CHARITY!

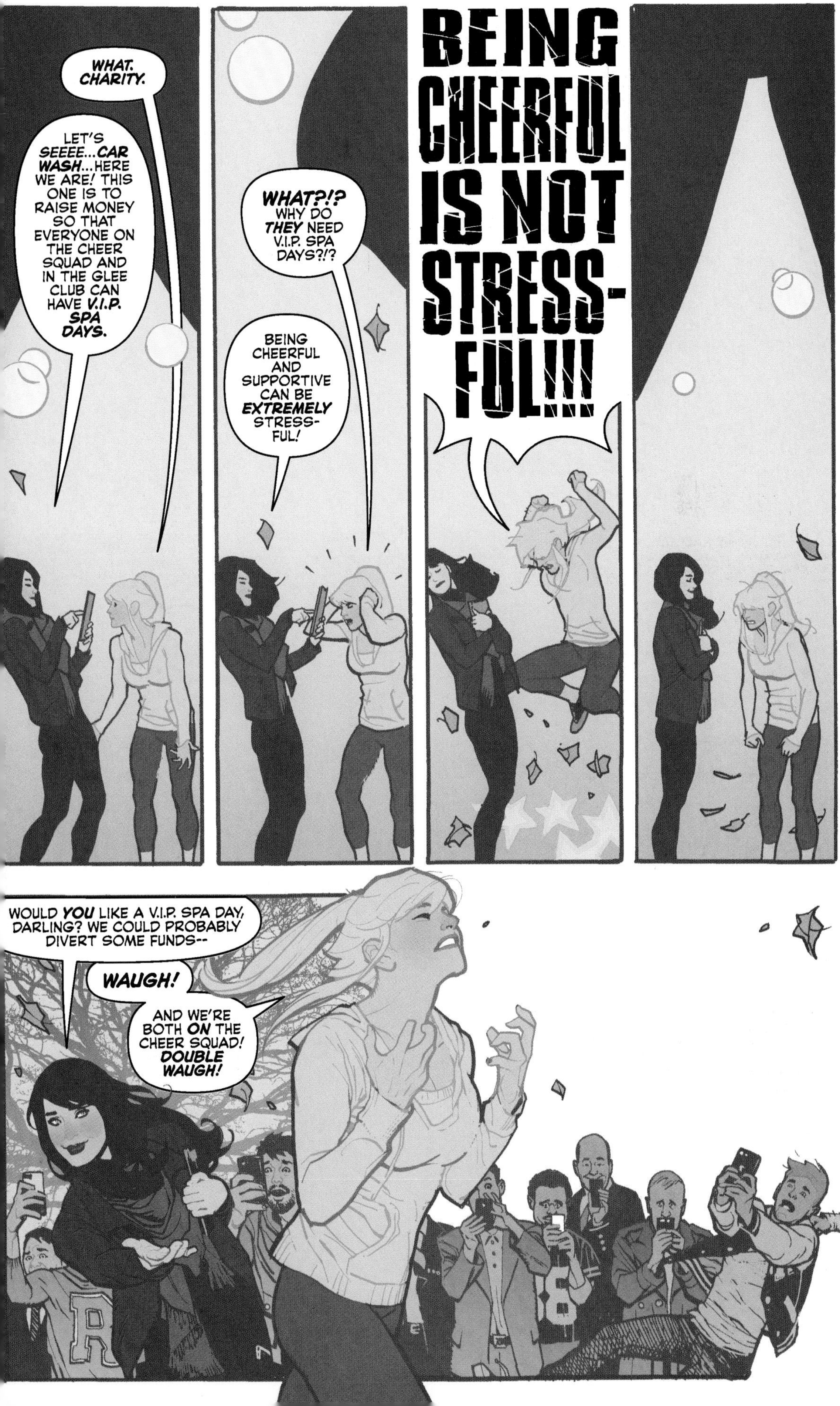

WHAT. CHARITY.
LET'S SEEEEE...CAR WASH...HERE WE ARE! THIS ONE IS TO RAISE MONEY SO THAT EVERYONE ON THE CHEER SQUAD AND IN THE GLEE CLUB CAN HAVE V.I.P. SPA DAYS.
WHAT?!? WHY DO THEY NEED V.I.P. SPA DAYS?!?
BEING CHEERFUL AND SUPPORTIVE CAN BE EXTREMELY STRESS-FUL!
BEING CHEERFUL IS NOT STRESS-FUL!!!
WOULD YOU LIKE A V.I.P. SPA DAY, DARLING? WE COULD PROBABLY DIVERT SOME FUNDS--
WAUGH!
AND WE'RE BOTH ON THE CHEER SQUAD! DOUBLE WAUGH!

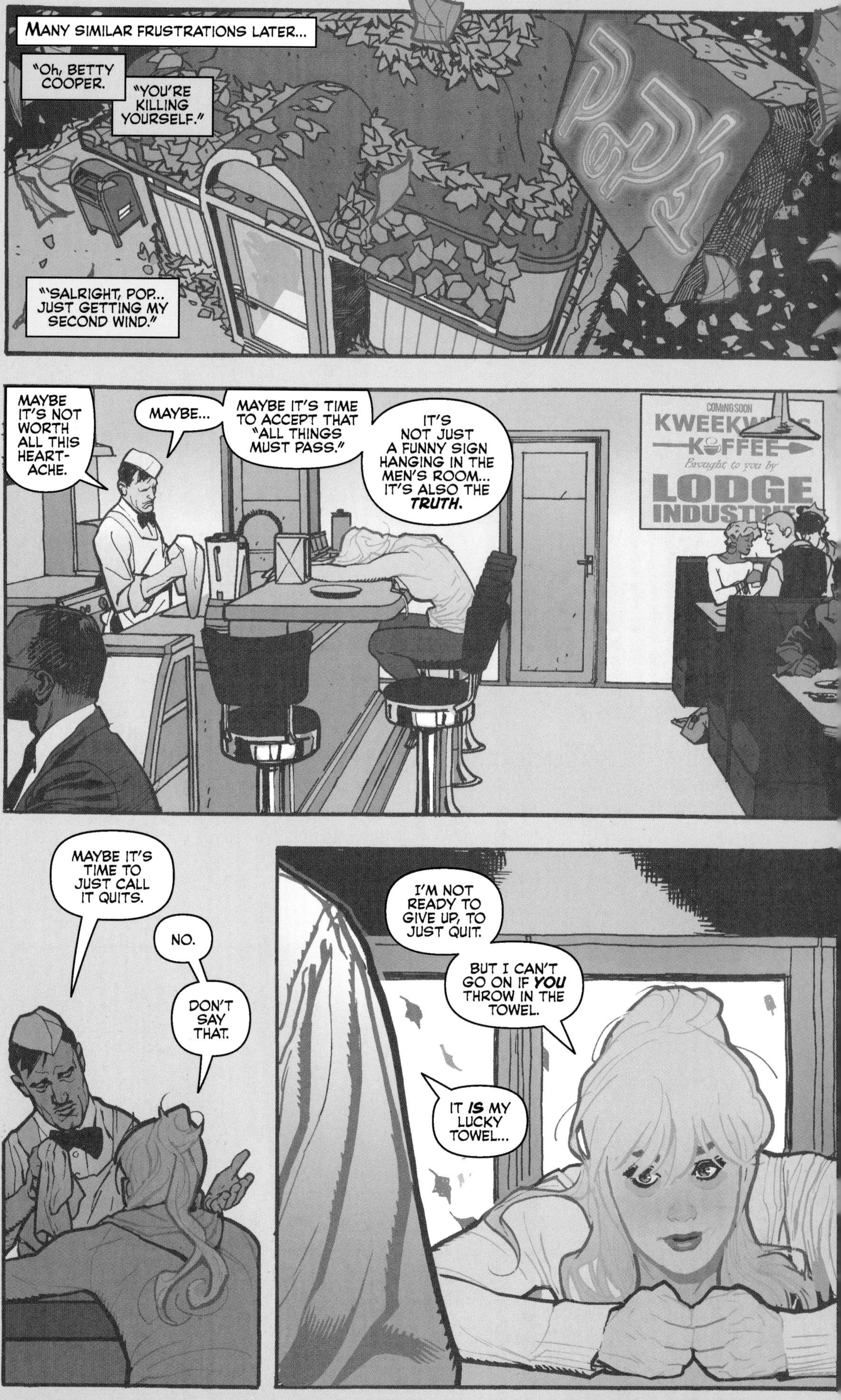

MANY SIMILAR FRUSTRATIONS LATER...
"Oh, BETTY COOPER.
"YOU'RE KILLING YOURSELF."
"'SALRIGHT, POP... JUST GETTING MY SECOND WIND."
POP'S
MAYBE IT'S NOT WORTH ALL THIS HEART-ACHE.
MAYBE...
MAYBE IT'S TIME TO ACCEPT THAT "ALL THINGS MUST PASS."
IT'S NOT JUST A FUNNY SIGN HANGING IN THE MEN'S ROOM... IT'S ALSO THE TRUTH.
COMING SOON KWEEKW KOFFEE Brought to you by LODGE INDUSTRI
MAYBE IT'S TIME TO JUST CALL IT QUITS.
NO.
DON'T SAY THAT.
I'M NOT READY TO GIVE UP, TO JUST QUIT.
BUT I CAN'T GO ON IF YOU THROW IN THE TOWEL.
IT IS MY LUCKY TOWEL...

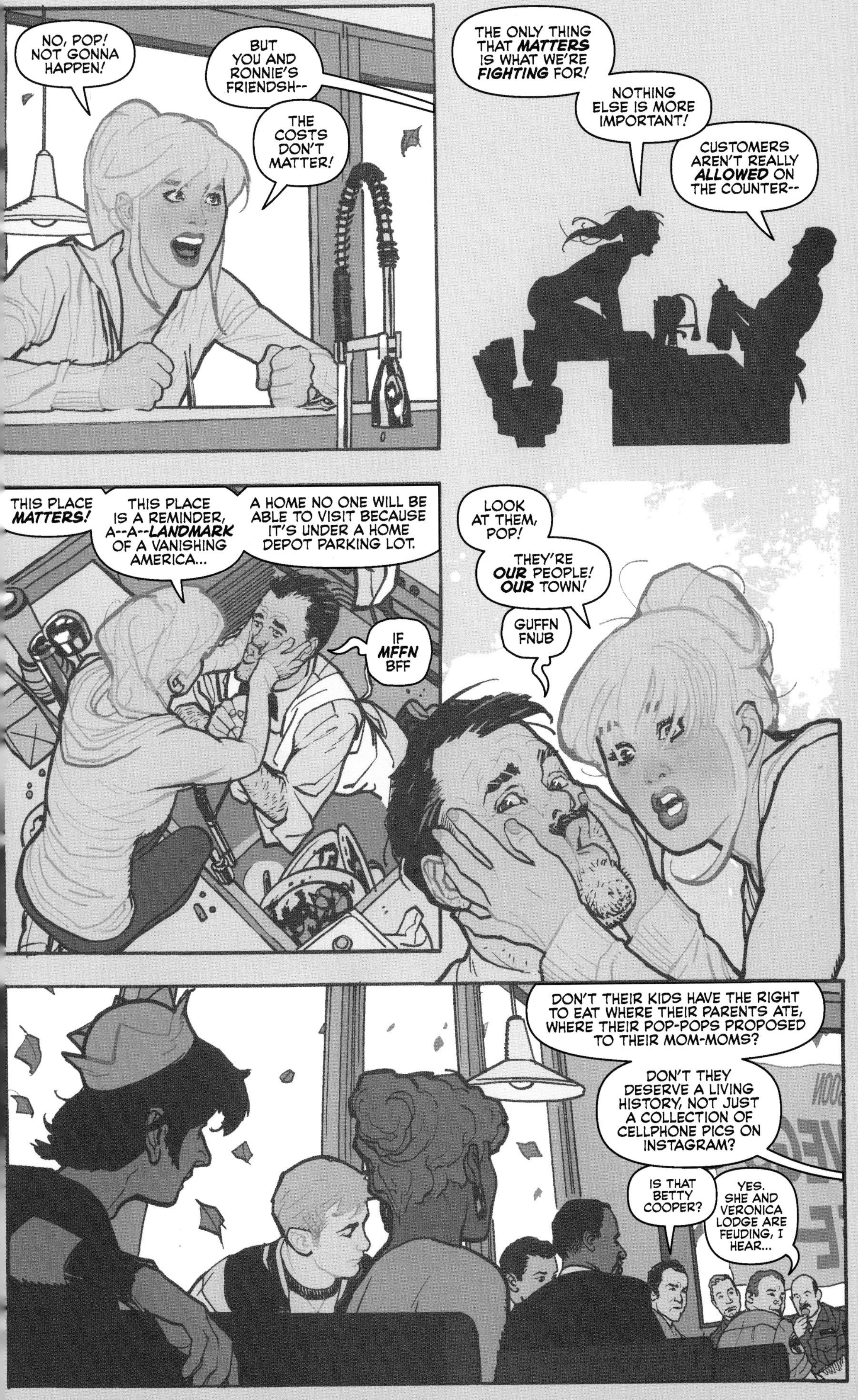
NO, POP! NOT GONNA HAPPEN!
BUT YOU AND RONNIE'S FRIENDSH--
THE COSTS DON'T MATTER!
THE ONLY THING THAT MATTERS IS WHAT WE'RE FIGHTING FOR!
NOTHING ELSE IS MORE IMPORTANT!
CUSTOMERS AREN'T REALLY ALLOWED ON THE COUNTER--
THIS PLACE MATTERS!
THIS PLACE IS A REMINDER, A--A--LANDMARK OF A VANISHING AMERICA...
A HOME NO ONE WILL BE ABLE TO VISIT BECAUSE IT'S UNDER A HOME DEPOT PARKING LOT.
IF MFFN BFF
LOOK AT THEM, POP!
THEY'RE OUR PEOPLE! OUR TOWN!
GUFFN FNUB
DON'T THEIR KIDS HAVE THE RIGHT TO EAT WHERE THEIR PARENTS ATE, WHERE THEIR POP-POPS PROPOSED TO THEIR MOM-MOMS?
DON'T THEY DESERVE A LIVING HISTORY, NOT JUST A COLLECTION OF CELLPHONE PICS ON INSTAGRAM?
IS THAT BETTY COOPER?
YES. SHE AND VERONICA LODGE ARE FEUDING, I HEAR...

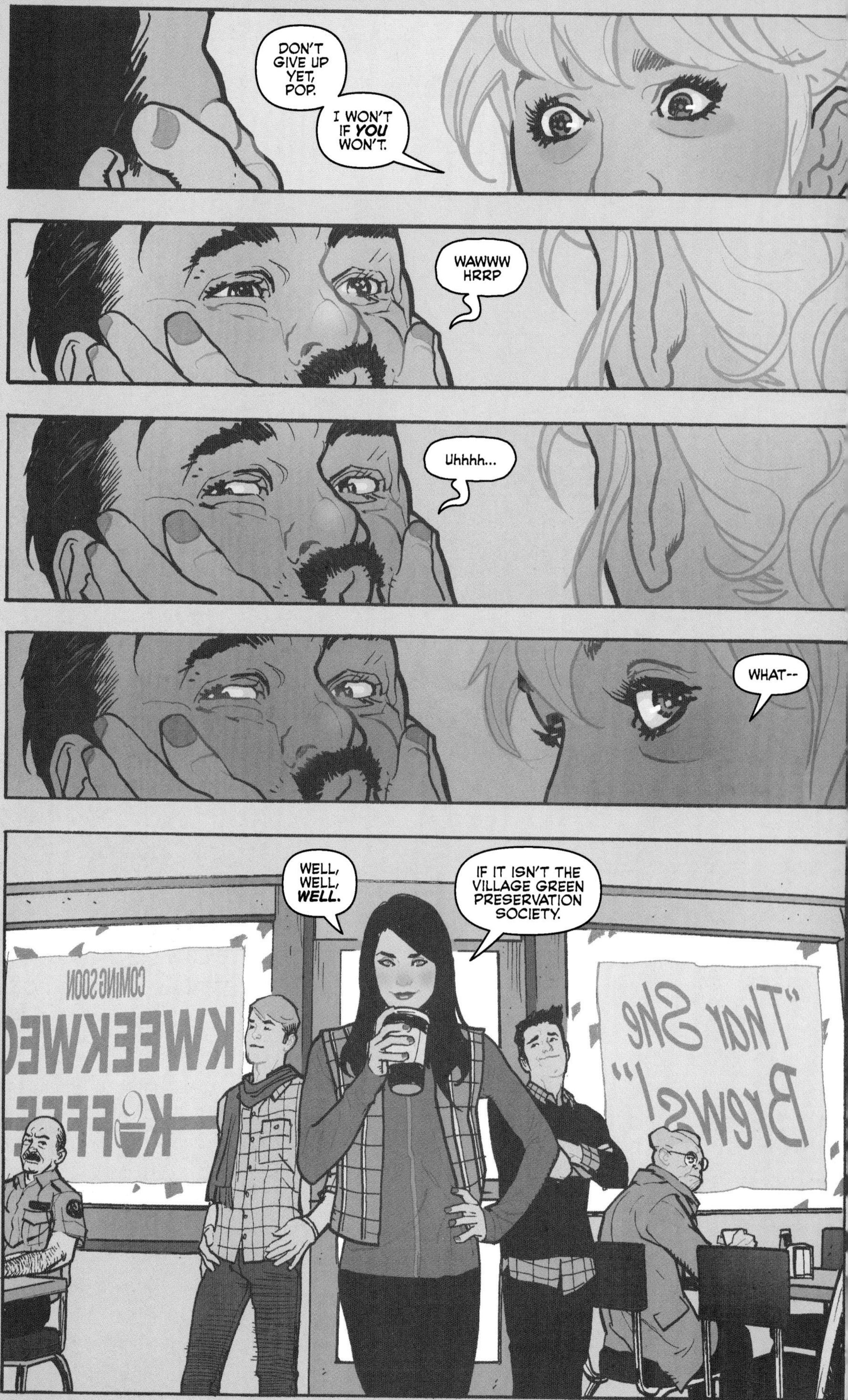
DON'T GIVE UP YET, POP.
I WON'T IF **YOU** WON'T.
WAWWW HRRP
Uhhhh...
WHAT--
WELL, WELL, **WELL.**
IF IT ISN'T THE VILLAGE GREEN PRESERVATION SOCIETY.
COMING SOON KWEEKWEG KOFFEE
"Thar She Brews!"

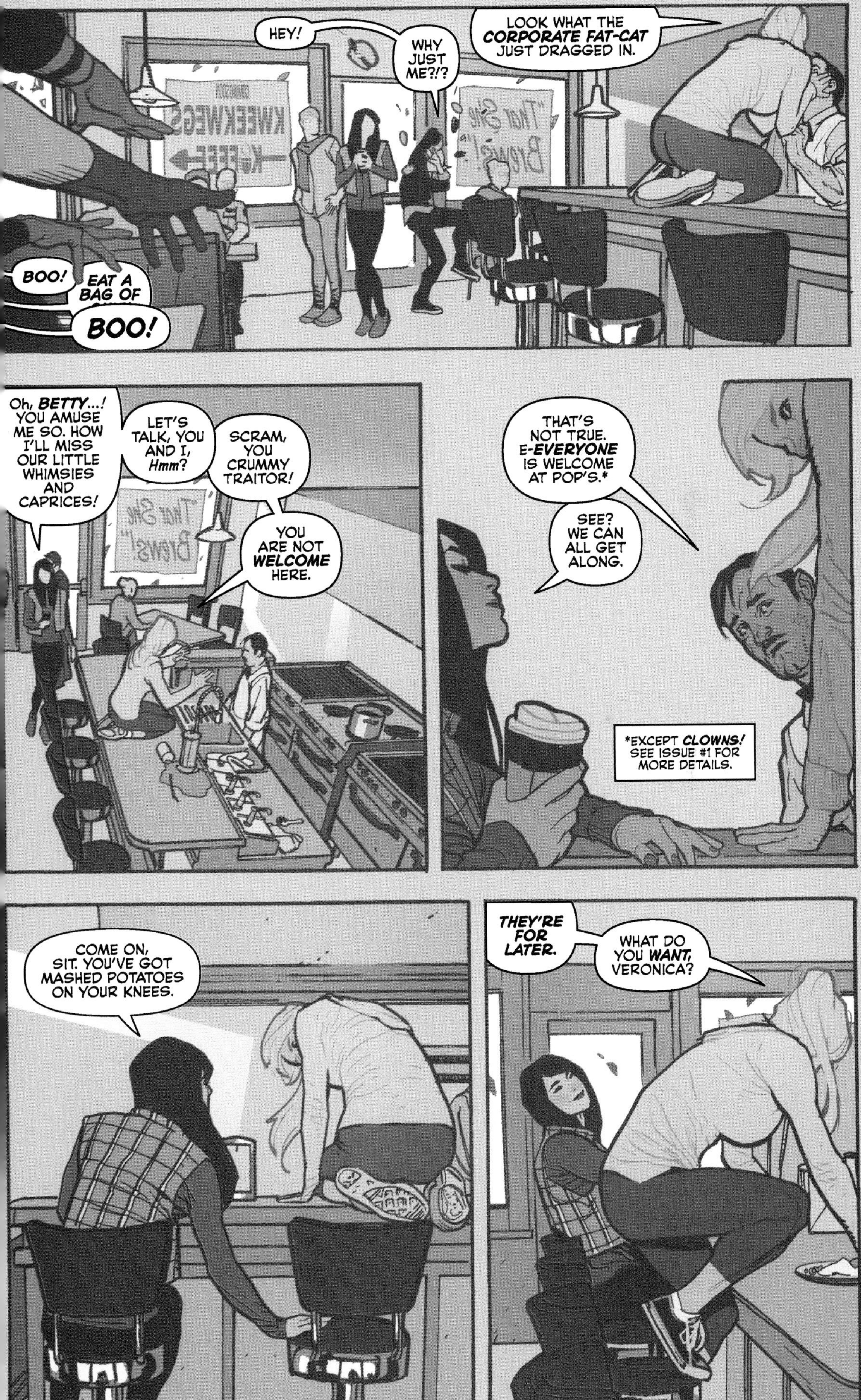
HEY!
WHY JUST ME?!?
LOOK WHAT THE *CORPORATE FAT-CAT* JUST DRAGGED IN.
BOO!
EAT A BAG OF
BOO!
Oh, *BETTY...!* YOU AMUSE ME SO. HOW I'LL MISS OUR LITTLE WHIMSIES AND CAPRICES!
LET'S TALK, YOU AND I, *Hmm*?
SCRAM, YOU CRUMMY TRAITOR!
YOU ARE NOT *WELCOME* HERE.
THAT'S NOT TRUE. E-*EVERYONE* IS WELCOME AT POP'S.*
SEE? WE CAN ALL GET ALONG.
*EXCEPT *CLOWNS!* SEE ISSUE #1 FOR MORE DETAILS.
COME ON, SIT. YOU'VE GOT MASHED POTATOES ON YOUR KNEES.
THEY'RE FOR LATER.
WHAT DO YOU *WANT,* VERONICA?

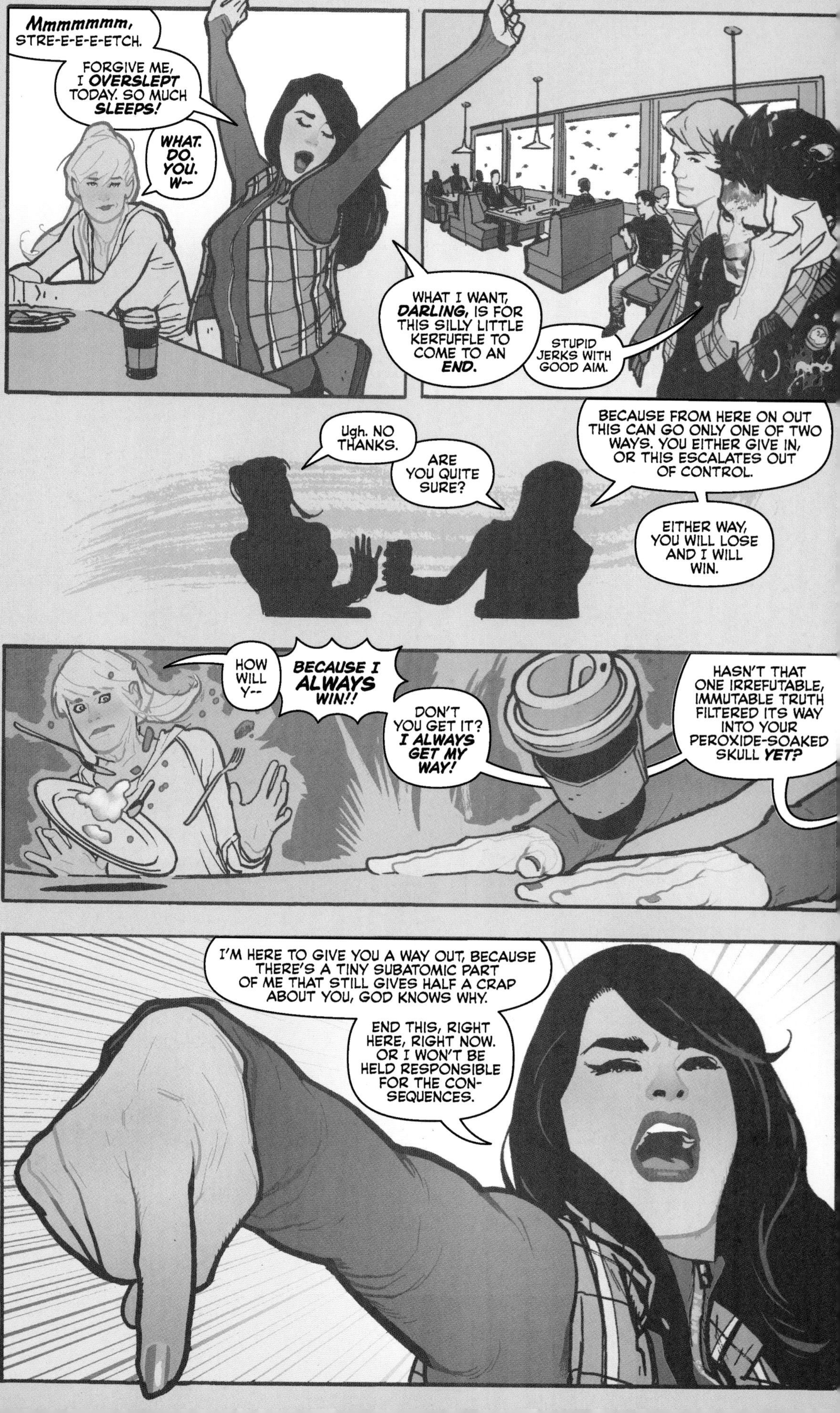
Mmmmmmm, STRE-E-E-E-ETCH.
FORGIVE ME, I OVERSLEPT TODAY. SO MUCH SLEEPS!
WHAT. DO. YOU. W--
WHAT I WANT, DARLING, IS FOR THIS SILLY LITTLE KERFUFFLE TO COME TO AN END.
STUPID JERKS WITH GOOD AIM.
Ugh. NO THANKS.
ARE YOU QUITE SURE?
BECAUSE FROM HERE ON OUT THIS CAN GO ONLY ONE OF TWO WAYS. YOU EITHER GIVE IN, OR THIS ESCALATES OUT OF CONTROL.
EITHER WAY, YOU WILL LOSE AND I WILL WIN.
HOW WILL Y--
BECAUSE I ALWAYS WIN!!
DON'T YOU GET IT? I ALWAYS GET MY WAY!
HASN'T THAT ONE IRREFUTABLE, IMMUTABLE TRUTH FILTERED ITS WAY INTO YOUR PEROXIDE-SOAKED SKULL YET?
I'M HERE TO GIVE YOU A WAY OUT, BECAUSE THERE'S A TINY SUBATOMIC PART OF ME THAT STILL GIVES HALF A CRAP ABOUT YOU, GOD KNOWS WHY.
END THIS, RIGHT HERE, RIGHT NOW. OR I WON'T BE HELD RESPONSIBLE FOR THE CON-SEQUENCES.

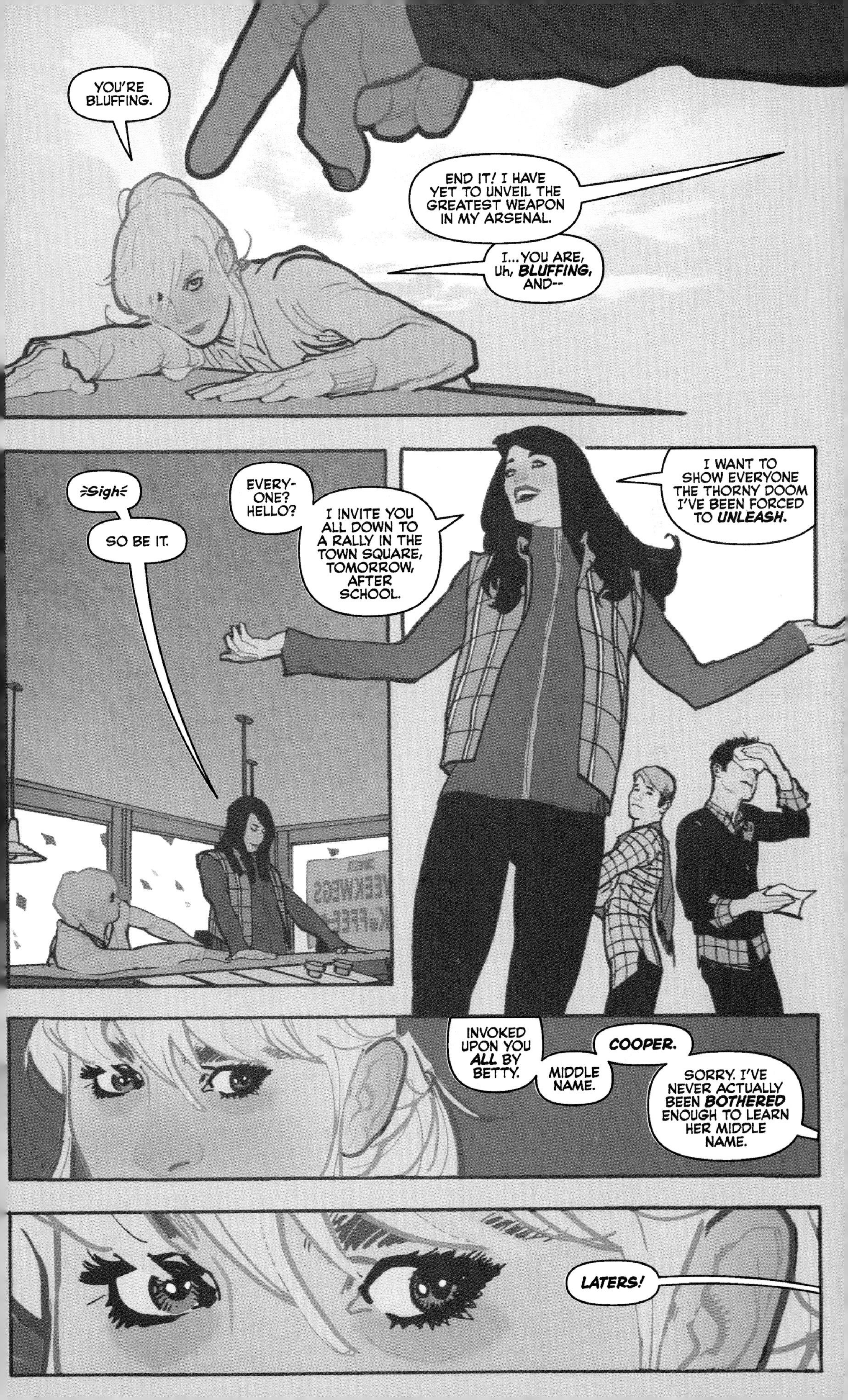

YOU'RE BLUFFING.
END IT! I HAVE YET TO UNVEIL THE GREATEST WEAPON IN MY ARSENAL.
I...YOU ARE, Uh, BLUFFING, AND--
Sigh
SO BE IT.
EVERY-ONE? HELLO?
I INVITE YOU ALL DOWN TO A RALLY IN THE TOWN SQUARE, TOMORROW, AFTER SCHOOL.
I WANT TO SHOW EVERYONE THE THORNY DOOM I'VE BEEN FORCED TO UNLEASH.
INVOKED UPON YOU ALL BY BETTY.
MIDDLE NAME.
COOPER.
SORRY. I'VE NEVER ACTUALLY BEEN BOTHERED ENOUGH TO LEARN HER MIDDLE NAME.
LATERS!

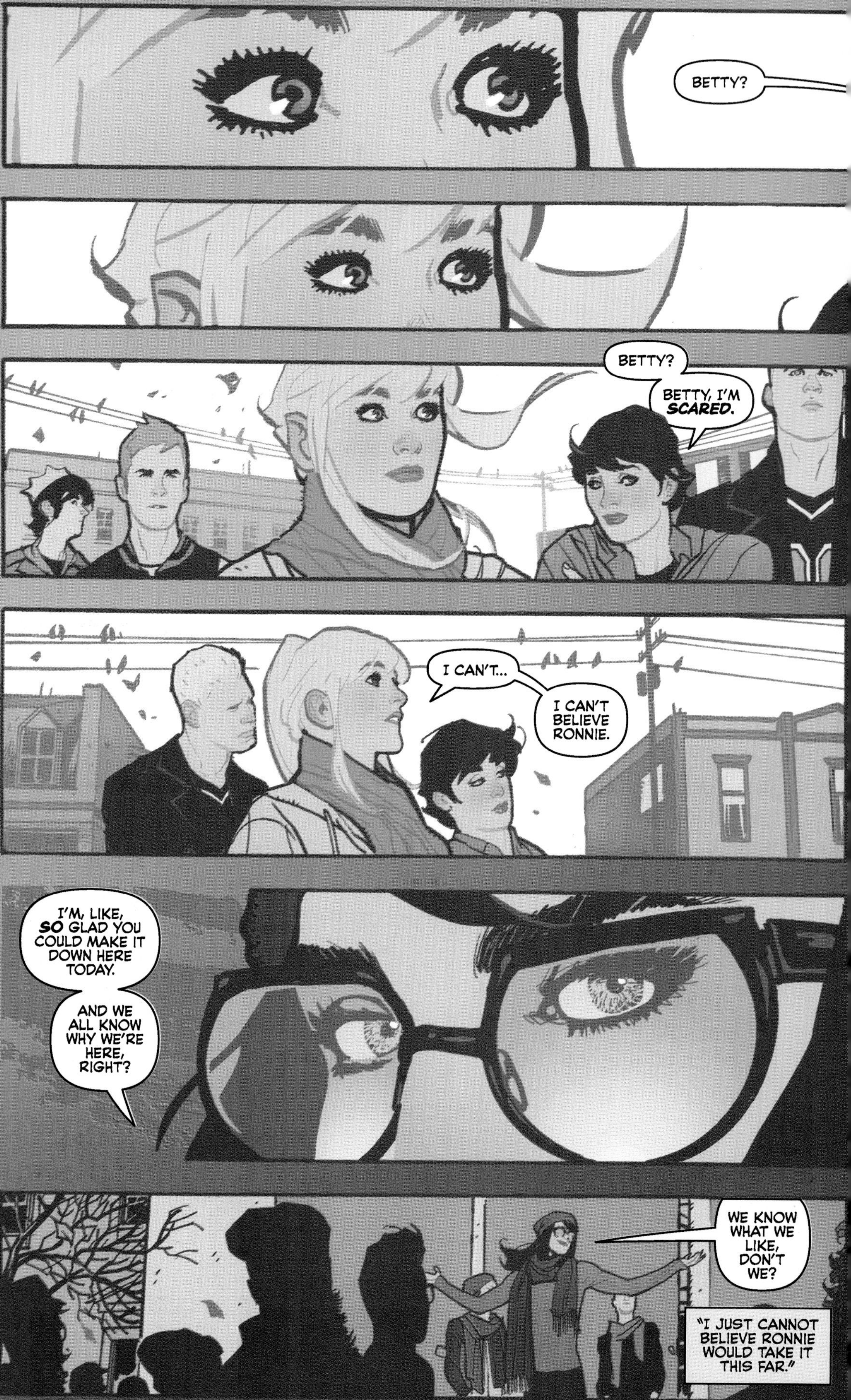

BETTY?
BETTY?
BETTY, I'M **SCARED.**
I CAN'T...
I CAN'T BELIEVE RONNIE.
I'M, LIKE, **SO** GLAD YOU COULD MAKE IT DOWN HERE TODAY.
AND WE ALL KNOW WHY WE'RE HERE, RIGHT?
WE KNOW WHAT WE LIKE, DON'T WE?
"I JUST CANNOT BELIEVE RONNIE WOULD TAKE IT THIS FAR."

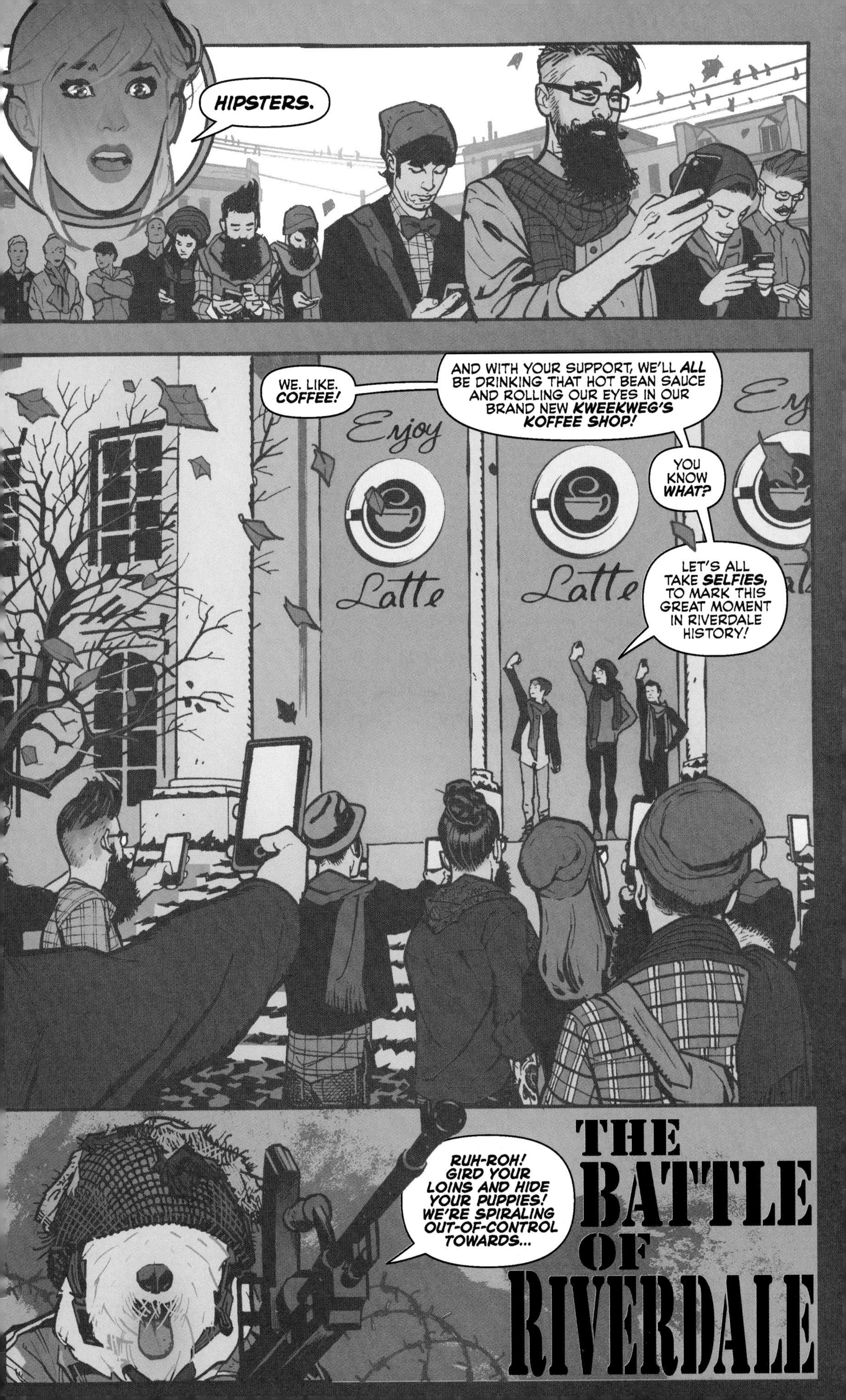
HIPSTERS.
WE. LIKE. COFFEE!
AND WITH YOUR SUPPORT, WE'LL ALL BE DRINKING THAT HOT BEAN SAUCE AND ROLLING OUR EYES IN OUR BRAND NEW KWEEKWEG'S KOFFEE SHOP!
YOU KNOW WHAT?
LET'S ALL TAKE SELFIES, TO MARK THIS GREAT MOMENT IN RIVERDALE HISTORY!
Enjoy
Latte
RUH-ROH! GIRD YOUR LOINS AND HIDE YOUR PUPPIES! WE'RE SPIRALING OUT-OF-CONTROL TOWARDS...
THE BATTLE OF RIVERDALE

ISSUE THREE

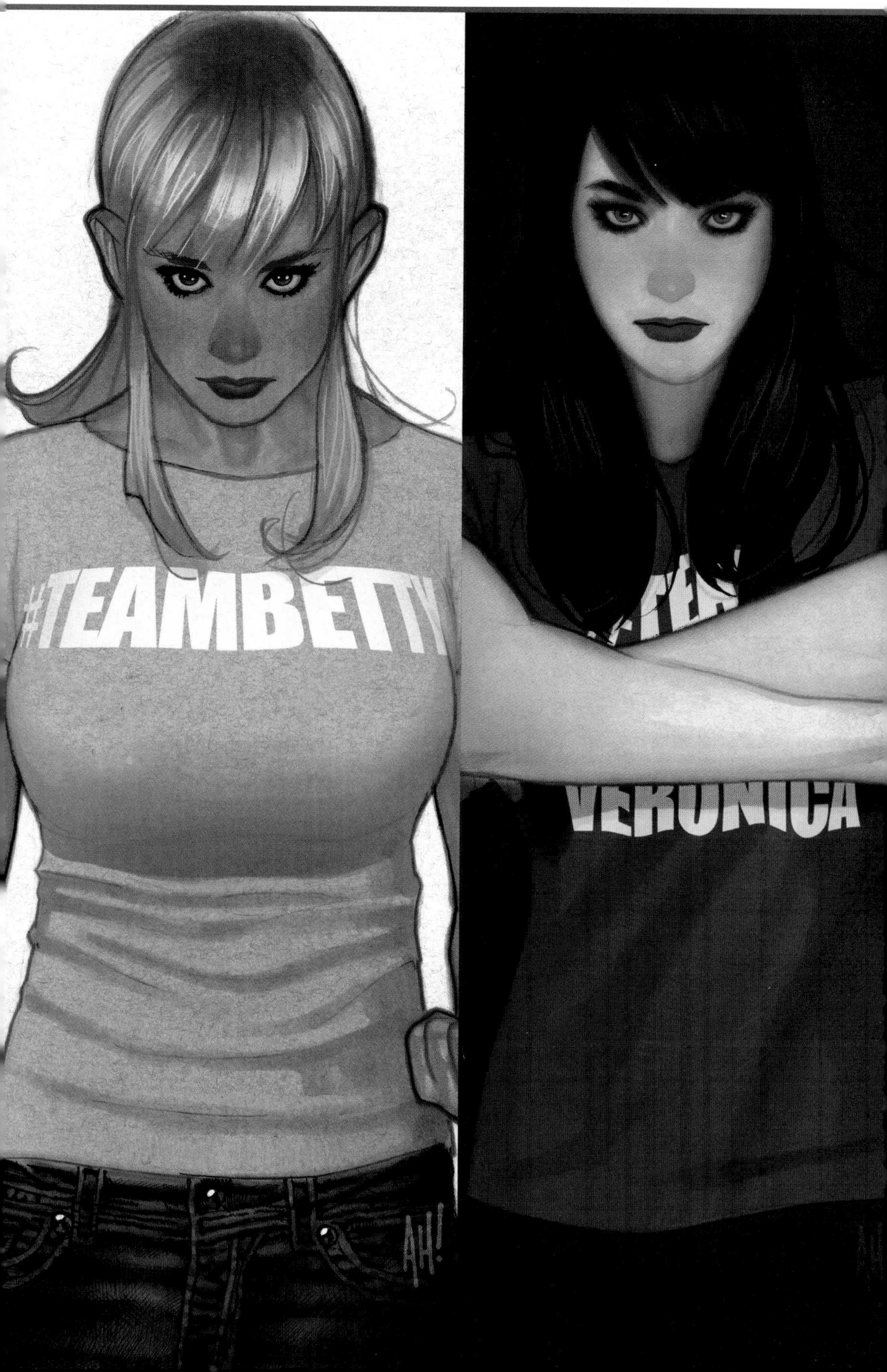
#TEAMBETTY
VERONICA
AH!

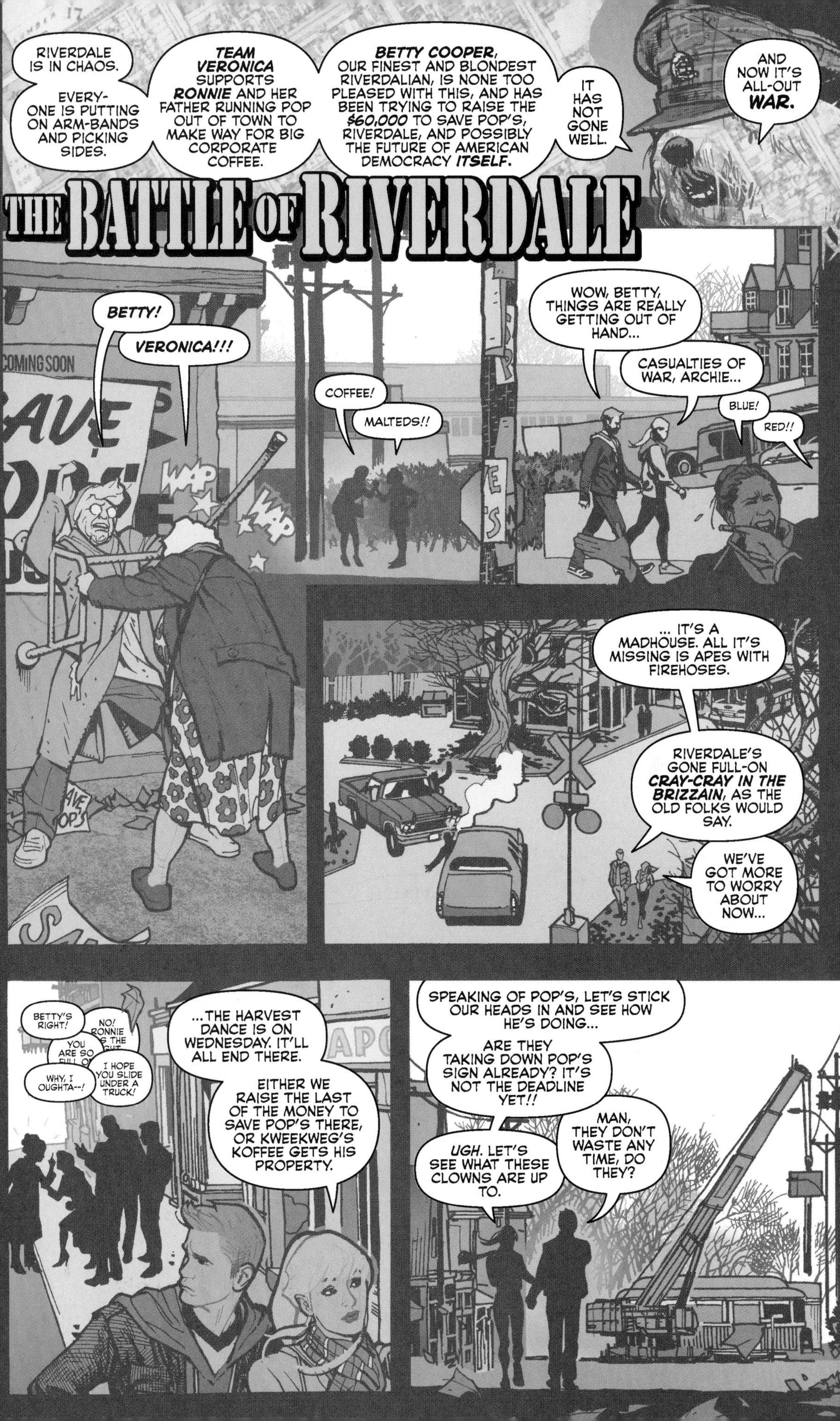

RIVERDALE IS IN CHAOS.
EVERYONE IS PUTTING ON ARM-BANDS AND PICKING SIDES.
TEAM VERONICA SUPPORTS RONNIE AND HER FATHER RUNNING POP OUT OF TOWN TO MAKE WAY FOR BIG CORPORATE COFFEE.
BETTY COOPER, OUR FINEST AND BLONDEST RIVERDALIAN, IS NONE TOO PLEASED WITH THIS, AND HAS BEEN TRYING TO RAISE THE $60,000 TO SAVE POP'S, RIVERDALE, AND POSSIBLY THE FUTURE OF AMERICAN DEMOCRACY ITSELF.
IT HAS NOT GONE WELL.
AND NOW IT'S ALL-OUT WAR.
THE BATTLE OF RIVERDALE
BETTY!
VERONICA!!!
COMING SOON
WAP
WAP
COFFEE!
MALTEDS!!
WOW, BETTY, THINGS ARE REALLY GETTING OUT OF HAND...
CASUALTIES OF WAR, ARCHIE...
BLUE!
RED!!
... IT'S A MADHOUSE. ALL IT'S MISSING IS APES WITH FIREHOSES.
RIVERDALE'S GONE FULL-ON CRAY-CRAY IN THE BRIZZAIN, AS THE OLD FOLKS WOULD SAY.
WE'VE GOT MORE TO WORRY ABOUT NOW...
BETTY'S RIGHT!
YOU ARE SO
WHY, I OUGHTA--!
I HOPE YOU SLIDE UNDER A TRUCK!
...THE HARVEST DANCE IS ON WEDNESDAY. IT'LL ALL END THERE.
EITHER WE RAISE THE LAST OF THE MONEY TO SAVE POP'S THERE, OR KWEEKWEG'S KOFFEE GETS HIS PROPERTY.
SPEAKING OF POP'S, LET'S STICK OUR HEADS IN AND SEE HOW HE'S DOING...
ARE THEY TAKING DOWN POP'S SIGN ALREADY? IT'S NOT THE DEADLINE YET!!
MAN, THEY DON'T WASTE ANY TIME, DO THEY?
UGH. LET'S SEE WHAT THESE CLOWNS ARE UP TO.

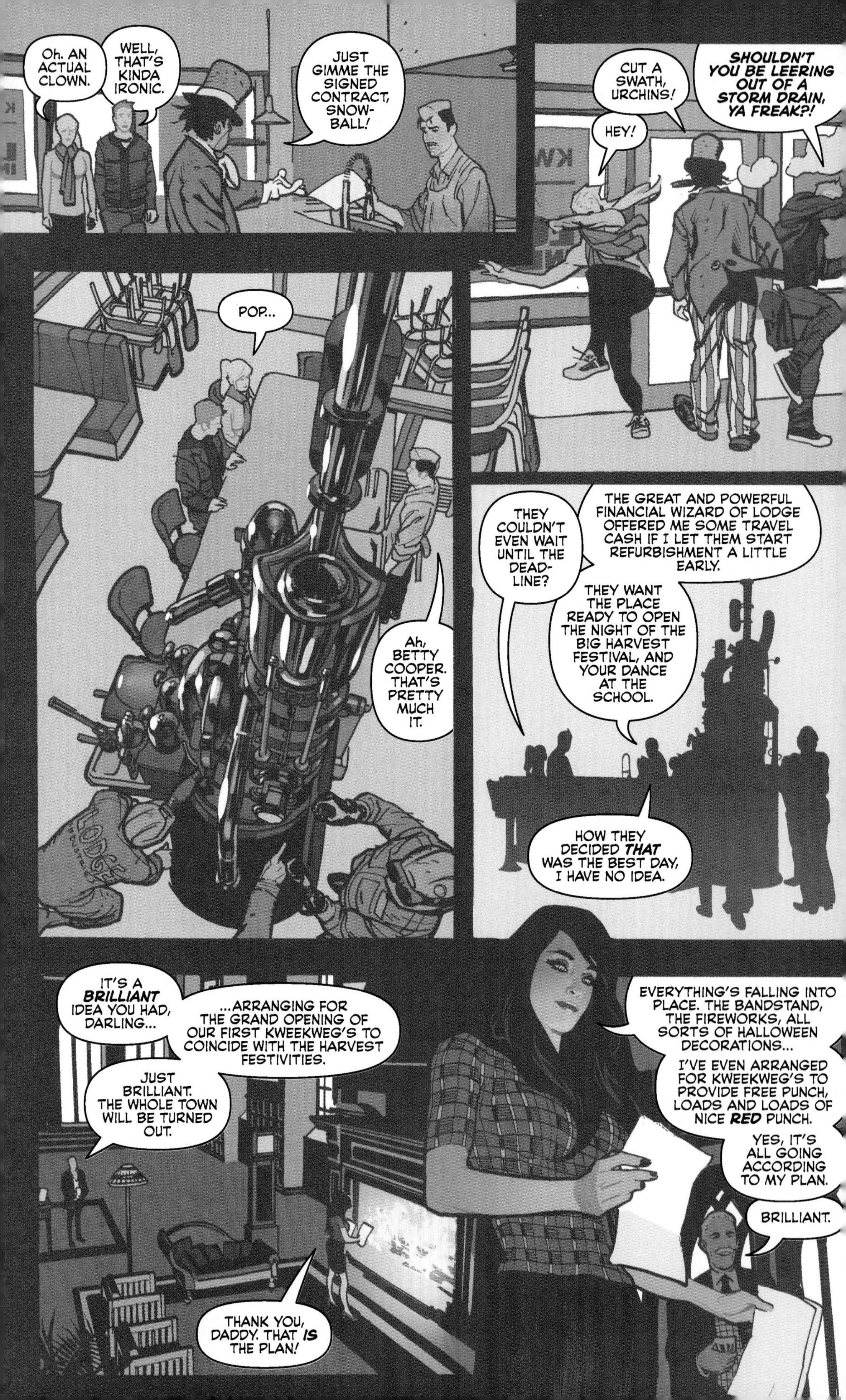

Oh. AN ACTUAL CLOWN.
WELL, THAT'S KINDA IRONIC.
JUST GIMME THE SIGNED CONTRACT, SNOW-BALL!
CUT A SWATH, URCHINS!
HEY!
SHOULDN'T YOU BE LEERING OUT OF A STORM DRAIN, YA FREAK?!
POP...
Ah, BETTY COOPER. THAT'S PRETTY MUCH IT.
THEY COULDN'T EVEN WAIT UNTIL THE DEAD-LINE?
THE GREAT AND POWERFUL FINANCIAL WIZARD OF LODGE OFFERED ME SOME TRAVEL CASH IF I LET THEM START REFURBISHMENT A LITTLE EARLY.
THEY WANT THE PLACE READY TO OPEN THE NIGHT OF THE BIG HARVEST FESTIVAL, AND YOUR DANCE AT THE SCHOOL.
HOW THEY DECIDED THAT WAS THE BEST DAY, I HAVE NO IDEA.
IT'S A BRILLIANT IDEA YOU HAD, DARLING...
...ARRANGING FOR THE GRAND OPENING OF OUR FIRST KWEEKWEG'S TO COINCIDE WITH THE HARVEST FESTIVITIES.
JUST BRILLIANT. THE WHOLE TOWN WILL BE TURNED OUT.
THANK YOU, DADDY. THAT IS THE PLAN!
EVERYTHING'S FALLING INTO PLACE. THE BANDSTAND, THE FIREWORKS, ALL SORTS OF HALLOWEEN DECORATIONS...
I'VE EVEN ARRANGED FOR KWEEKWEG'S TO PROVIDE FREE PUNCH, LOADS AND LOADS OF NICE RED PUNCH.
YES, IT'S ALL GOING ACCORDING TO MY PLAN.
BRILLIANT.

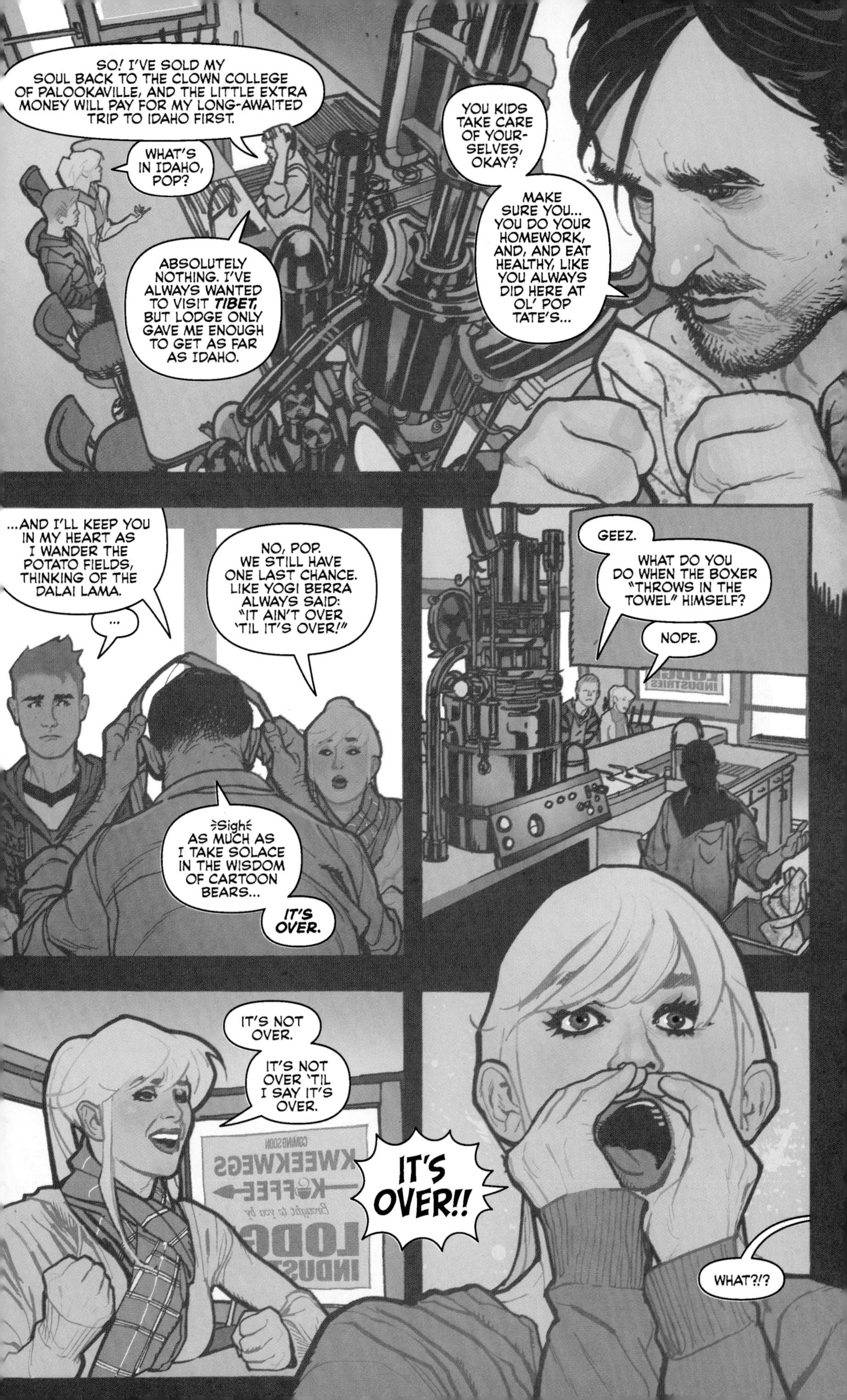

SO! I'VE SOLD MY SOUL BACK TO THE CLOWN COLLEGE OF PALOOKAVILLE, AND THE LITTLE EXTRA MONEY WILL PAY FOR MY LONG-AWAITED TRIP TO IDAHO FIRST.
WHAT'S IN IDAHO, POP?
ABSOLUTELY NOTHING. I'VE ALWAYS WANTED TO VISIT *TIBET*, BUT LODGE ONLY GAVE ME ENOUGH TO GET AS FAR AS IDAHO.
YOU KIDS TAKE CARE OF YOUR-SELVES, OKAY?
MAKE SURE YOU... YOU DO YOUR HOMEWORK, AND, AND EAT HEALTHY, LIKE YOU ALWAYS DID HERE AT OL' POP TATE'S...
...AND I'LL KEEP YOU IN MY HEART AS I WANDER THE POTATO FIELDS, THINKING OF THE DALAI LAMA.
...
NO, POP. WE STILL HAVE ONE LAST CHANCE. LIKE YOGI BERRA ALWAYS SAID: "IT AIN'T OVER 'TIL IT'S OVER!"
Sigh AS MUCH AS I TAKE SOLACE IN THE WISDOM OF CARTOON BEARS...
IT'S OVER.
GEEZ.
WHAT DO YOU DO WHEN THE BOXER "THROWS IN THE TOWEL" HIMSELF?
NOPE.
IT'S NOT OVER.
IT'S NOT OVER 'TIL I SAY IT'S OVER.
IT'S OVER!!
WHAT?!?

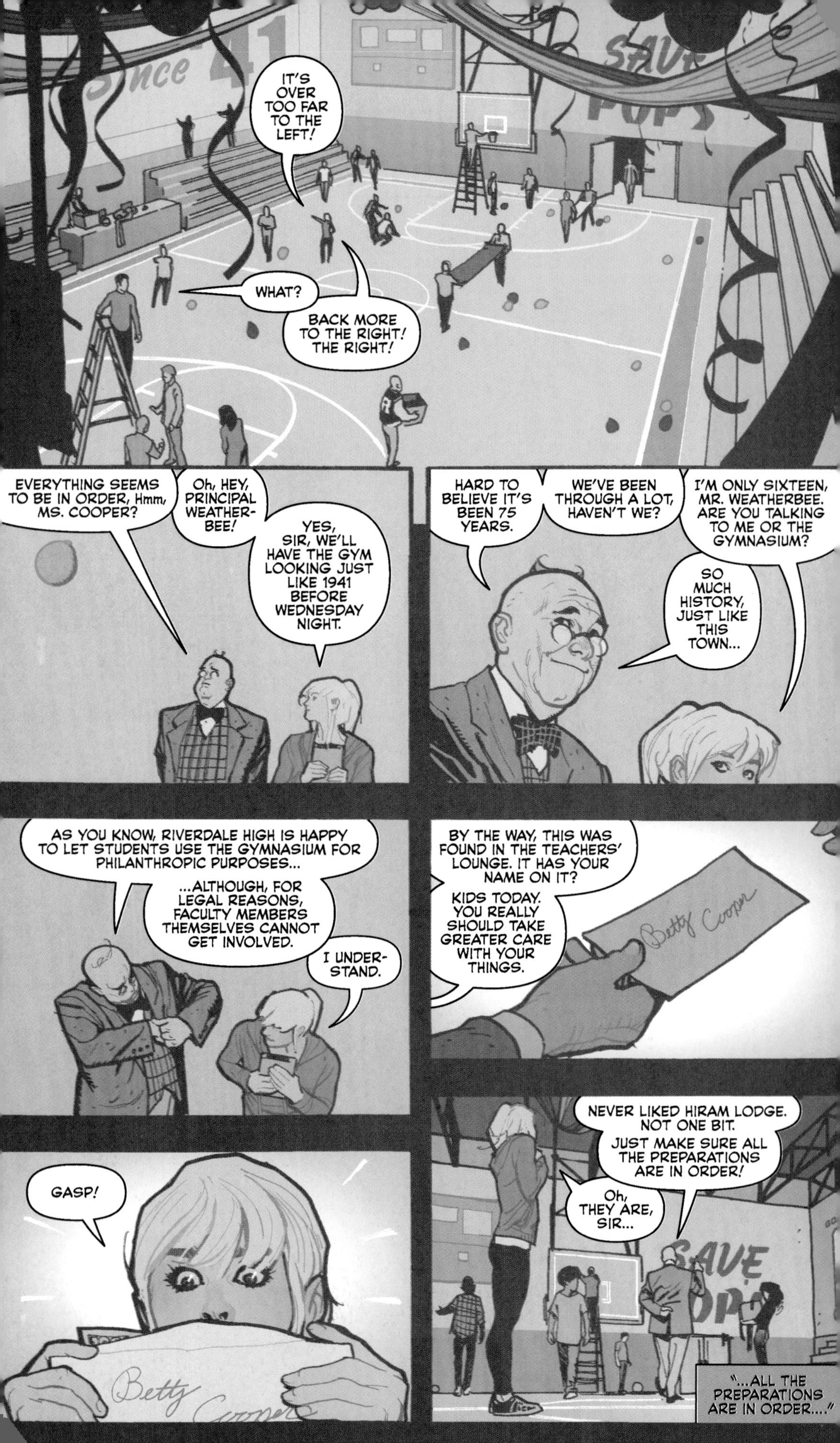
SINCE 41
SAVE POPS
IT'S OVER TOO FAR TO THE LEFT!
WHAT?
BACK MORE TO THE RIGHT! THE RIGHT!
EVERYTHING SEEMS TO BE IN ORDER, Hmm, MS. COOPER?
Oh, HEY, PRINCIPAL WEATHER-BEE!
YES, SIR, WE'LL HAVE THE GYM LOOKING JUST LIKE 1941 BEFORE WEDNESDAY NIGHT.
HARD TO BELIEVE IT'S BEEN 75 YEARS.
WE'VE BEEN THROUGH A LOT, HAVEN'T WE?
I'M ONLY SIXTEEN, MR. WEATHERBEE. ARE YOU TALKING TO ME OR THE GYMNASIUM?
SO MUCH HISTORY, JUST LIKE THIS TOWN...
AS YOU KNOW, RIVERDALE HIGH IS HAPPY TO LET STUDENTS USE THE GYMNASIUM FOR PHILANTHROPIC PURPOSES...
...ALTHOUGH, FOR LEGAL REASONS, FACULTY MEMBERS THEMSELVES CANNOT GET INVOLVED.
I UNDER-STAND.
BY THE WAY, THIS WAS FOUND IN THE TEACHERS' LOUNGE. IT HAS YOUR NAME ON IT?
KIDS TODAY. YOU REALLY SHOULD TAKE GREATER CARE WITH YOUR THINGS.
Betty Cooper
GASP!
Betty Cooper
NEVER LIKED HIRAM LODGE. NOT ONE BIT.
JUST MAKE SURE ALL THE PREPARATIONS ARE IN ORDER!
Oh, THEY ARE, SIR...
SAVE POPS
"...ALL THE PREPARATIONS ARE IN ORDER..."

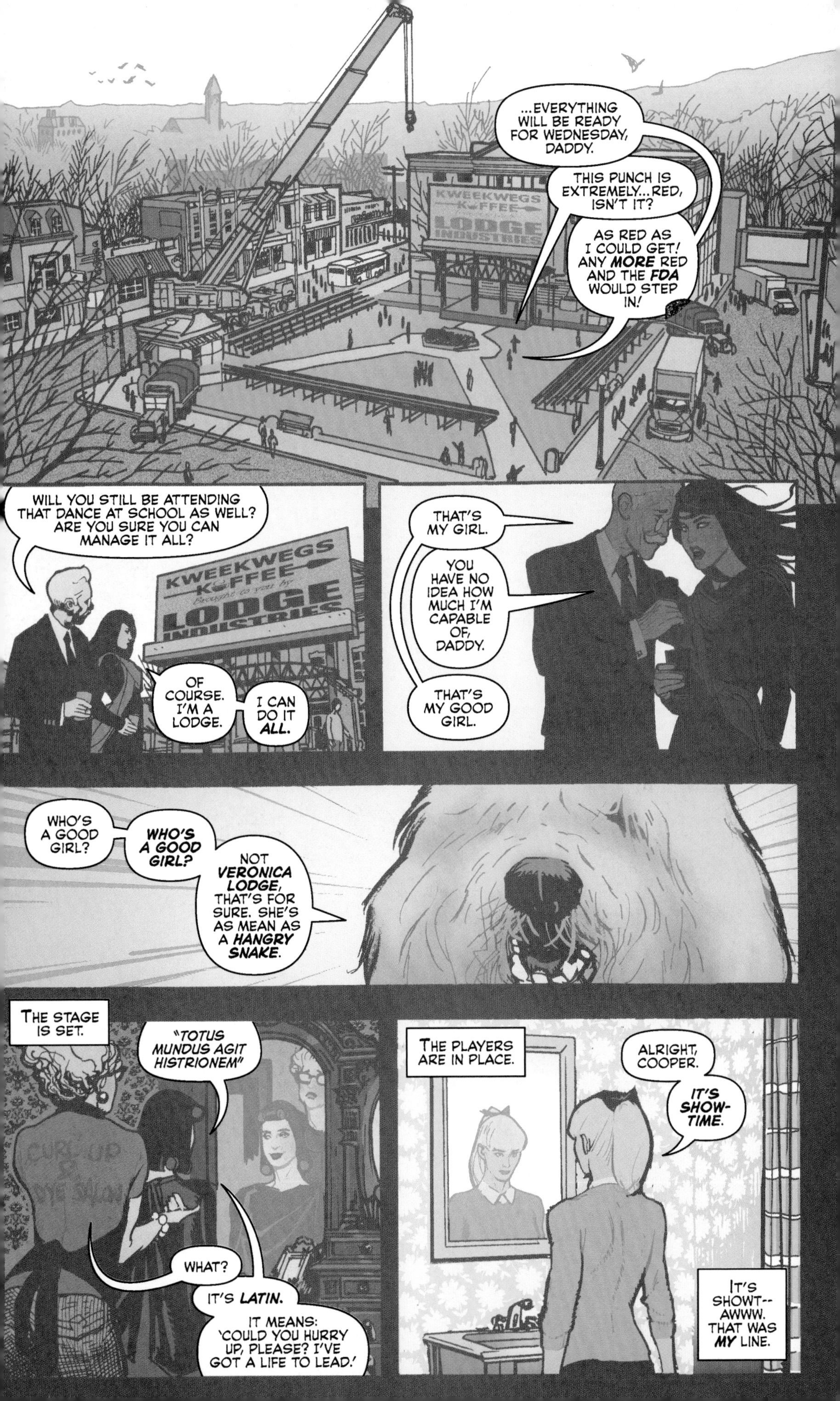

...EVERYTHING WILL BE READY FOR WEDNESDAY, DADDY.
KWEEKWEGS KOFFEE
LODGE INDUSTRIES
THIS PUNCH IS EXTREMELY...RED, ISN'T IT?
AS RED AS I COULD GET! ANY **MORE** RED AND THE **FDA** WOULD STEP IN!
WILL YOU STILL BE ATTENDING THAT DANCE AT SCHOOL AS WELL? ARE YOU SURE YOU CAN MANAGE IT ALL?
KWEEKWEGS KOFFEE Brought to you by LODGE INDUSTRIES
OF COURSE. I'M A LODGE.
I CAN DO IT **ALL.**
THAT'S MY GIRL.
YOU HAVE NO IDEA HOW MUCH I'M CAPABLE OF, DADDY.
THAT'S MY GOOD GIRL.
WHO'S A GOOD GIRL?
WHO'S A GOOD GIRL?
NOT ***VERONICA LODGE***, THAT'S FOR SURE. SHE'S AS MEAN AS A ***HANGRY SNAKE***.
THE STAGE IS SET.
"TOTUS MUNDUS AGIT HISTRIONEM"
WHAT?
IT'S ***LATIN.***
IT MEANS: 'COULD YOU HURRY UP, PLEASE? I'VE GOT A LIFE TO LEAD.'
THE PLAYERS ARE IN PLACE.
ALRIGHT, COOPER.
IT'S SHOW-TIME.
IT'S SHOWT-- AWWW. THAT WAS ***MY*** LINE.

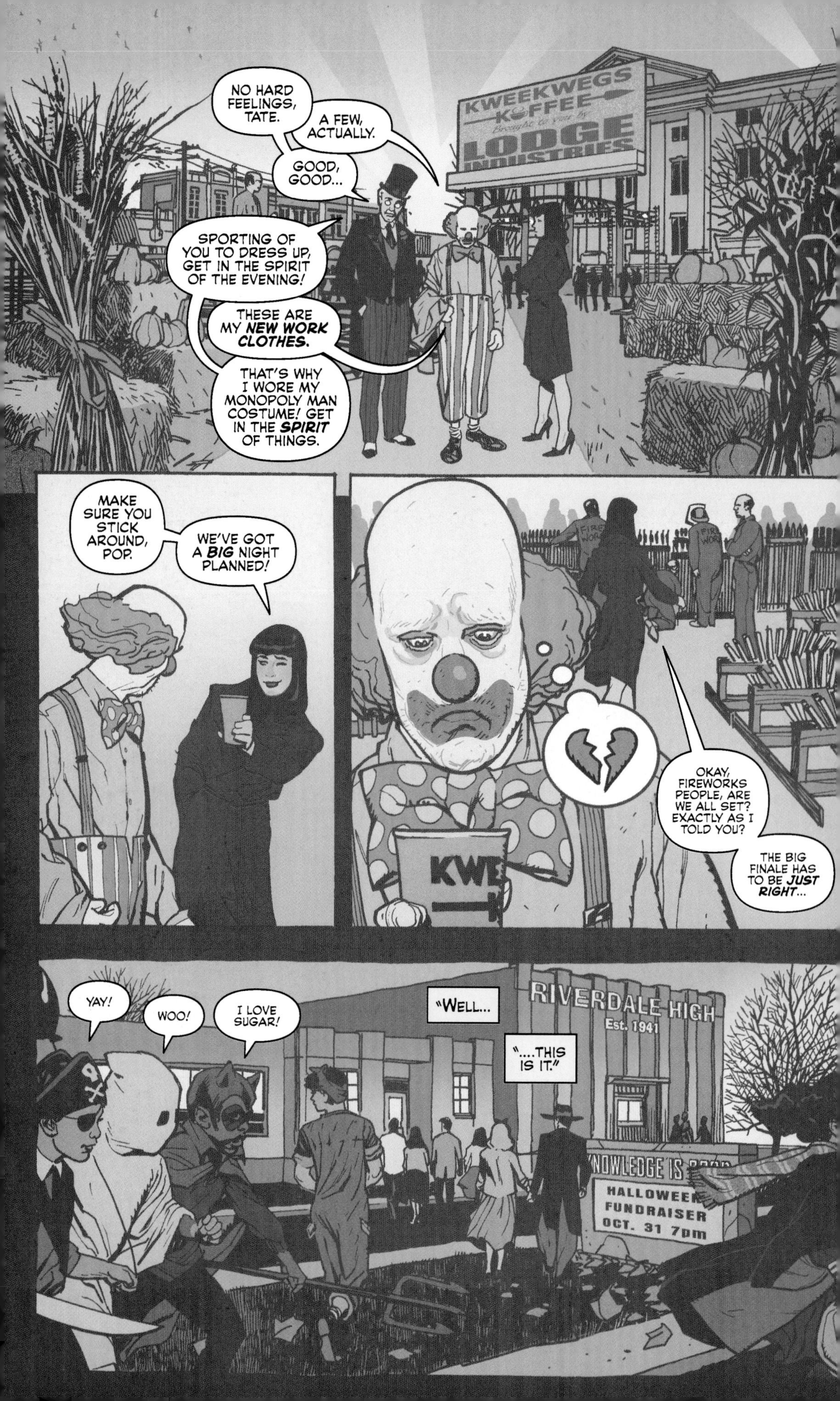
KWEEKWEGS KOFFEE Brought to you by LODGE INDUSTRIES
NO HARD FEELINGS, TATE.
A FEW, ACTUALLY.
GOOD, GOOD...
SPORTING OF YOU TO DRESS UP, GET IN THE SPIRIT OF THE EVENING!
THESE ARE MY NEW WORK CLOTHES.
THAT'S WHY I WORE MY MONOPOLY MAN COSTUME! GET IN THE SPIRIT OF THINGS.
MAKE SURE YOU STICK AROUND, POP.
WE'VE GOT A BIG NIGHT PLANNED!
KWE
OKAY, FIREWORKS PEOPLE, ARE WE ALL SET? EXACTLY AS I TOLD YOU?
THE BIG FINALE HAS TO BE JUST RIGHT...
YAY!
WOO!
I LOVE SUGAR!
"WELL...
"....THIS IS IT."
RIVERDALE HIGH Est. 1941
KNOWLEDGE IS
HALLOWEEN FUNDRAISER OCT. 31 7pm

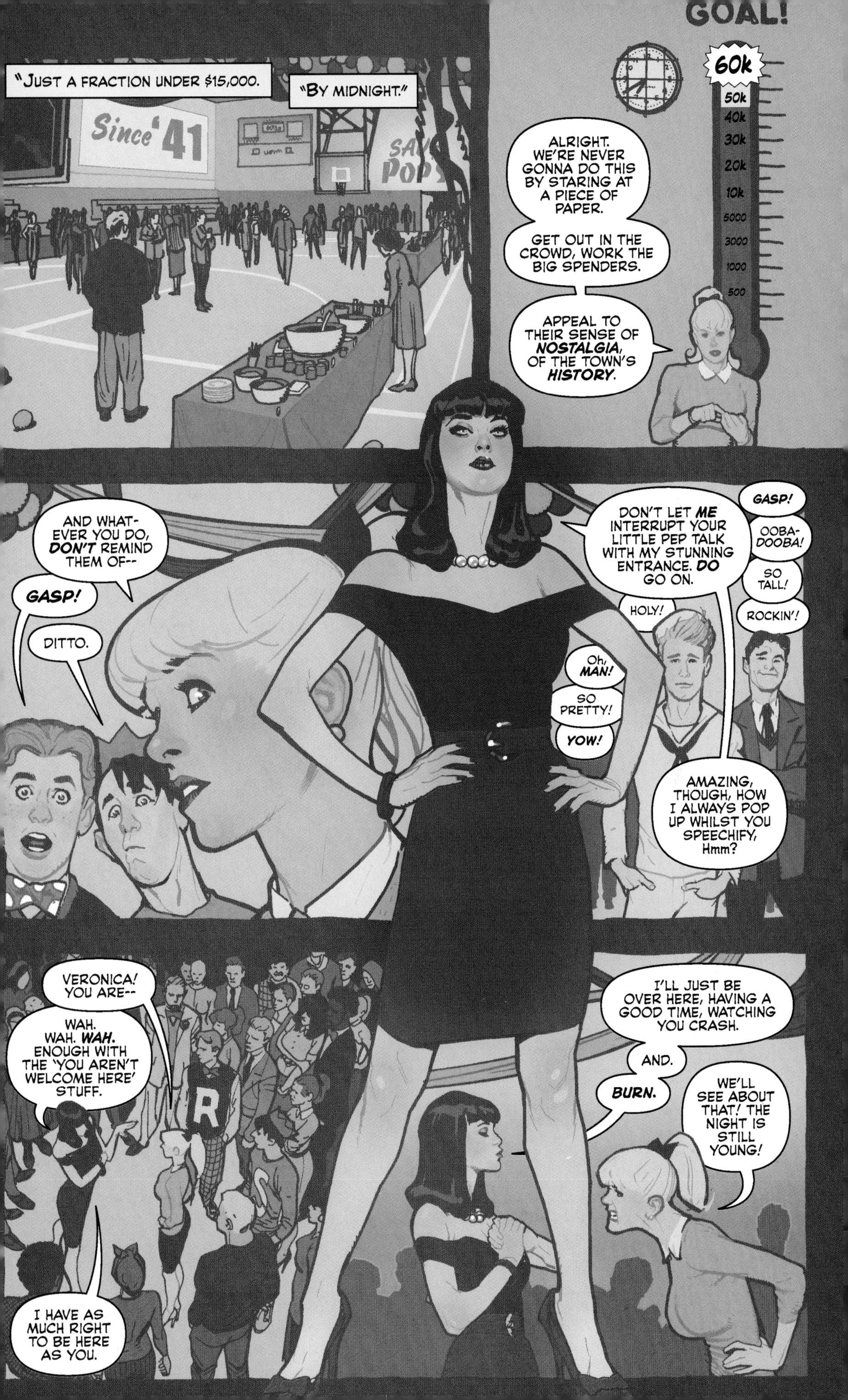

GOAL!
"JUST A FRACTION UNDER $15,000.
"BY MIDNIGHT."
Since '41
60k
50k
40k
30k
20k
10k
5000
3000
1000
500
ALRIGHT. WE'RE NEVER GONNA DO THIS BY STARING AT A PIECE OF PAPER.
GET OUT IN THE CROWD, WORK THE BIG SPENDERS.
APPEAL TO THEIR SENSE OF NOSTALGIA, OF THE TOWN'S HISTORY.
AND WHAT-EVER YOU DO, DON'T REMIND THEM OF--
GASP!
DITTO.
DON'T LET ME INTERRUPT YOUR LITTLE PEP TALK WITH MY STUNNING ENTRANCE. DO GO ON.
GASP!
OOBA-DOOBA!
SO TALL!
ROCKIN'!
HOLY!
Oh, MAN!
SO PRETTY!
YOW!
AMAZING, THOUGH, HOW I ALWAYS POP UP WHILST YOU SPEECHIFY, Hmm?
VERONICA! YOU ARE--
WAH. WAH. WAH. ENOUGH WITH THE 'YOU AREN'T WELCOME HERE' STUFF.
I HAVE AS MUCH RIGHT TO BE HERE AS YOU.
I'LL JUST BE OVER HERE, HAVING A GOOD TIME, WATCHING YOU CRASH.
AND.
BURN.
WE'LL SEE ABOUT THAT! THE NIGHT IS STILL YOUNG!

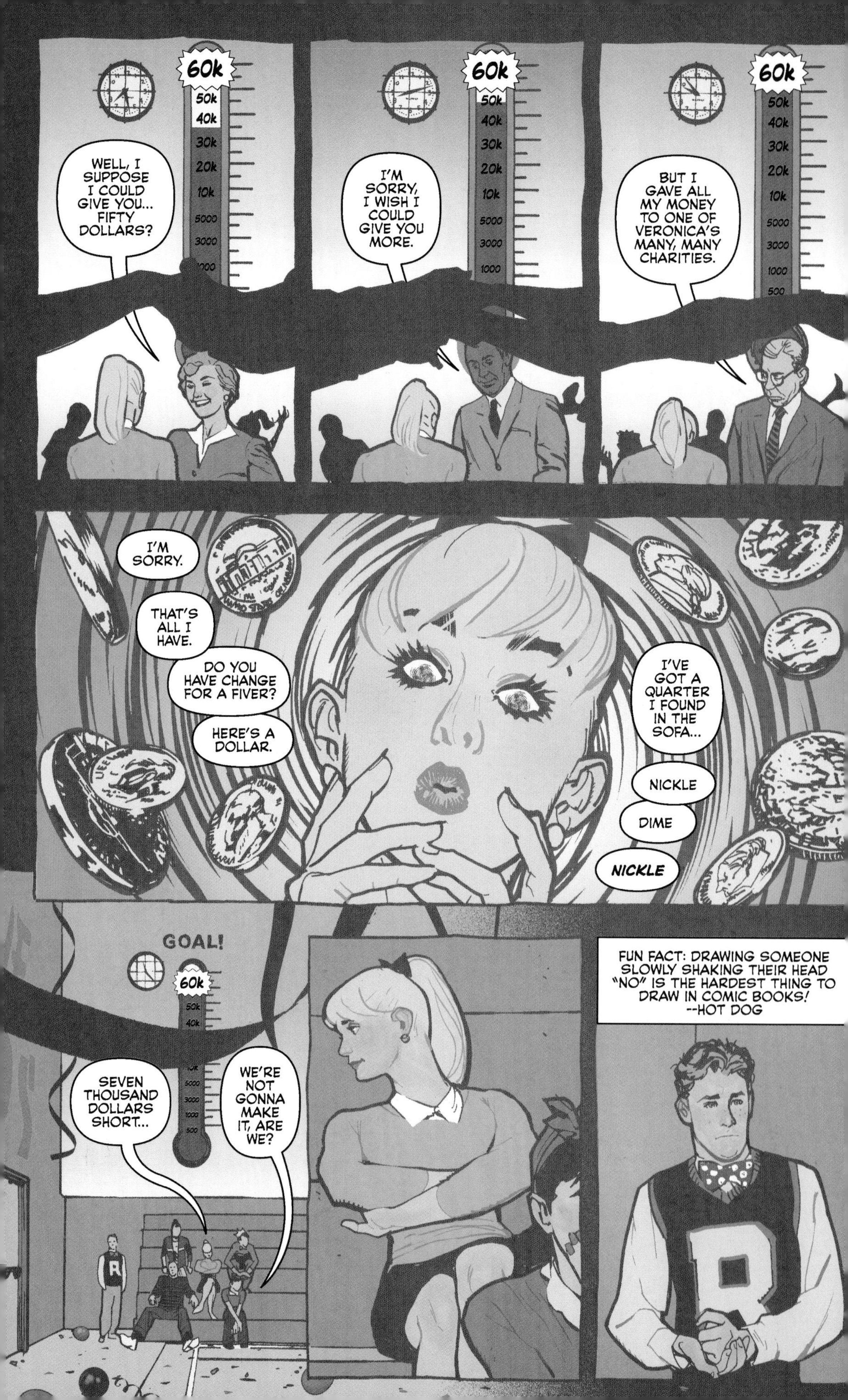
60k
50k
40k
30k
20k
10k
5000
3000
1000
WELL, I SUPPOSE I COULD GIVE YOU... FIFTY DOLLARS?
I'M SORRY, I WISH I COULD GIVE YOU MORE.
BUT I GAVE ALL MY MONEY TO ONE OF VERONICA'S MANY, MANY CHARITIES.
I'M SORRY.
THAT'S ALL I HAVE.
DO YOU HAVE CHANGE FOR A FIVER?
HERE'S A DOLLAR.
I'VE GOT A QUARTER I FOUND IN THE SOFA...
NICKLE
DIME
NICKLE
GOAL!
FUN FACT: DRAWING SOMEONE SLOWLY SHAKING THEIR HEAD "NO" IS THE HARDEST THING TO DRAW IN COMIC BOOKS! --HOT DOG
SEVEN THOUSAND DOLLARS SHORT...
WE'RE NOT GONNA MAKE IT, ARE WE?

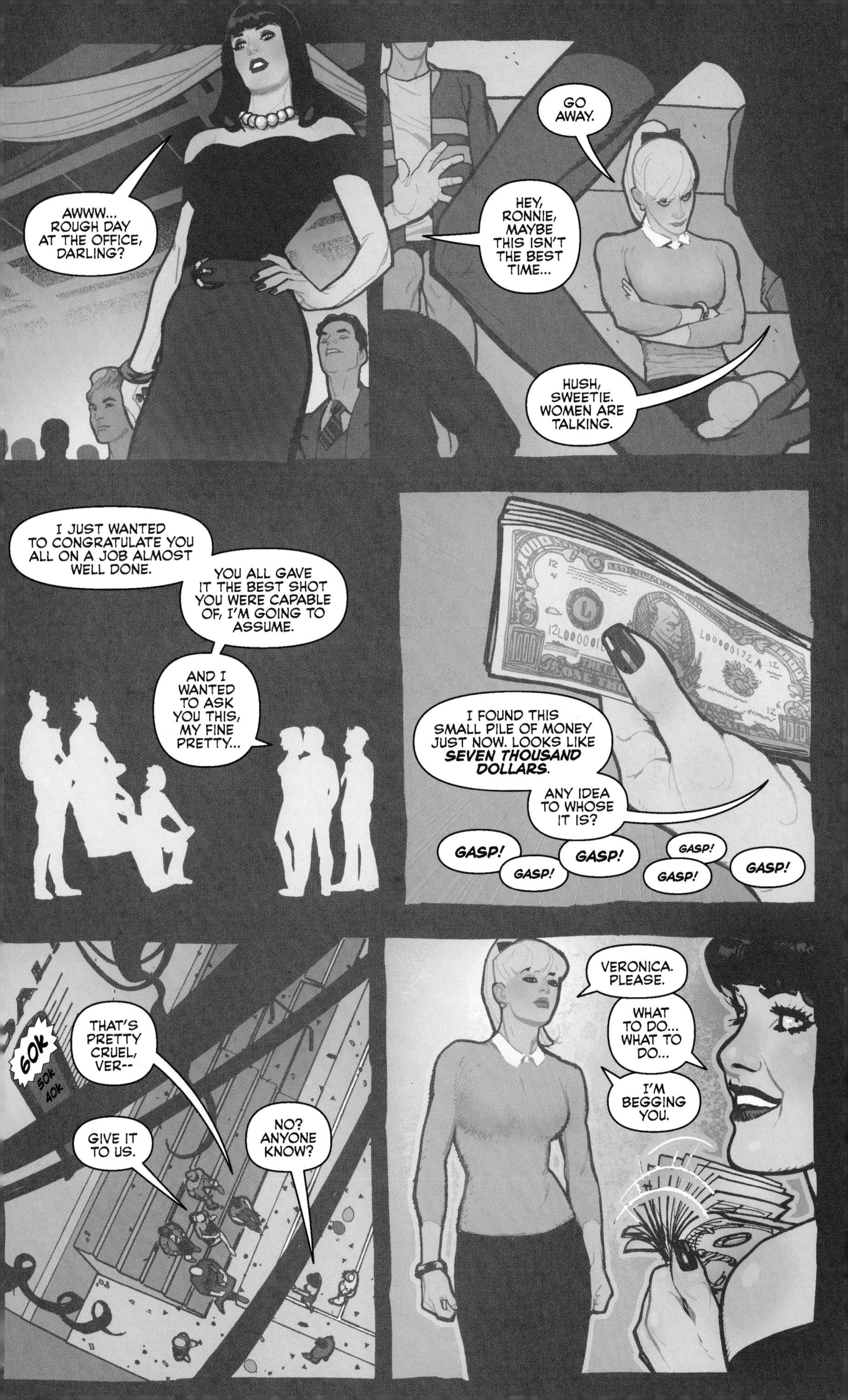

AWWW... ROUGH DAY AT THE OFFICE, DARLING?
GO AWAY.
HEY, RONNIE, MAYBE THIS ISN'T THE BEST TIME...
HUSH, SWEETIE. WOMEN ARE TALKING.
I JUST WANTED TO CONGRATULATE YOU ALL ON A JOB ALMOST WELL DONE.
YOU ALL GAVE IT THE BEST SHOT YOU WERE CAPABLE OF, I'M GOING TO ASSUME.
AND I WANTED TO ASK YOU THIS, MY FINE PRETTY...
I FOUND THIS SMALL PILE OF MONEY JUST NOW. LOOKS LIKE ***SEVEN THOUSAND DOLLARS***.
ANY IDEA TO WHOSE IT IS?
GASP!
GASP!
GASP!
GASP!
GASP!
GASP!
60K
50K
40K
THAT'S PRETTY CRUEL, VER--
GIVE IT TO US.
NO? ANYONE KNOW?
VERONICA. PLEASE.
WHAT TO DO... WHAT TO DO...
I'M BEGGING YOU.

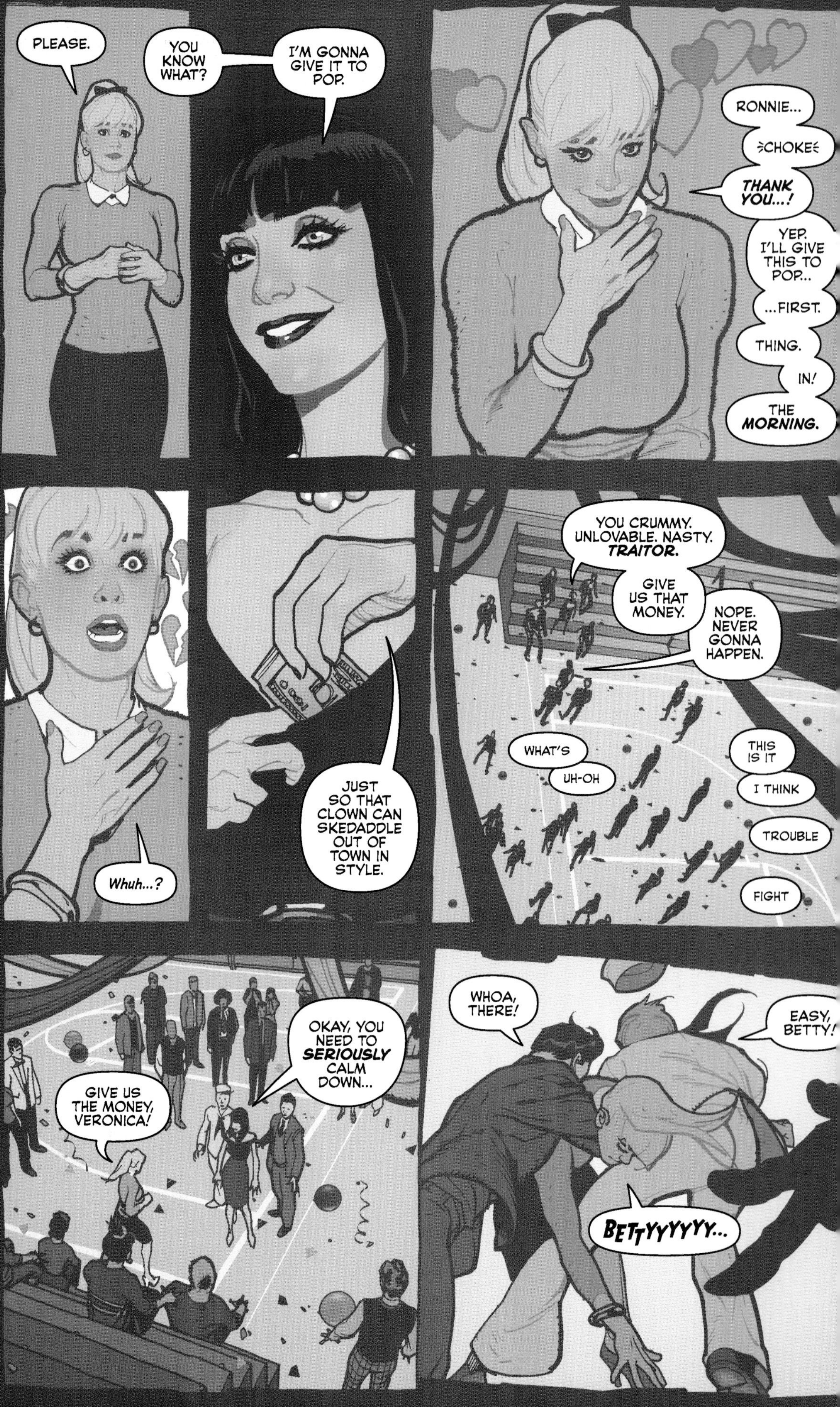
PLEASE.
YOU KNOW WHAT?
I'M GONNA GIVE IT TO POP.
RONNIE...
≽CHOKE≼
THANK YOU...!
YEP. I'LL GIVE THIS TO POP...
...FIRST.
THING.
IN!
THE *MORNING.*
Whuh...?
JUST SO THAT CLOWN CAN SKEDADDLE OUT OF TOWN IN STYLE.
YOU CRUMMY. UNLOVABLE. NASTY. *TRAITOR.*
GIVE US THAT MONEY.
NOPE. NEVER GONNA HAPPEN.
WHAT'S
UH-OH
THIS IS IT
I THINK
TROUBLE
FIGHT
GIVE US THE MONEY, VERONICA!
OKAY, YOU NEED TO *SERIOUSLY* CALM DOWN...
WHOA, THERE!
EASY, BETTY!
BETTYYYYYY...

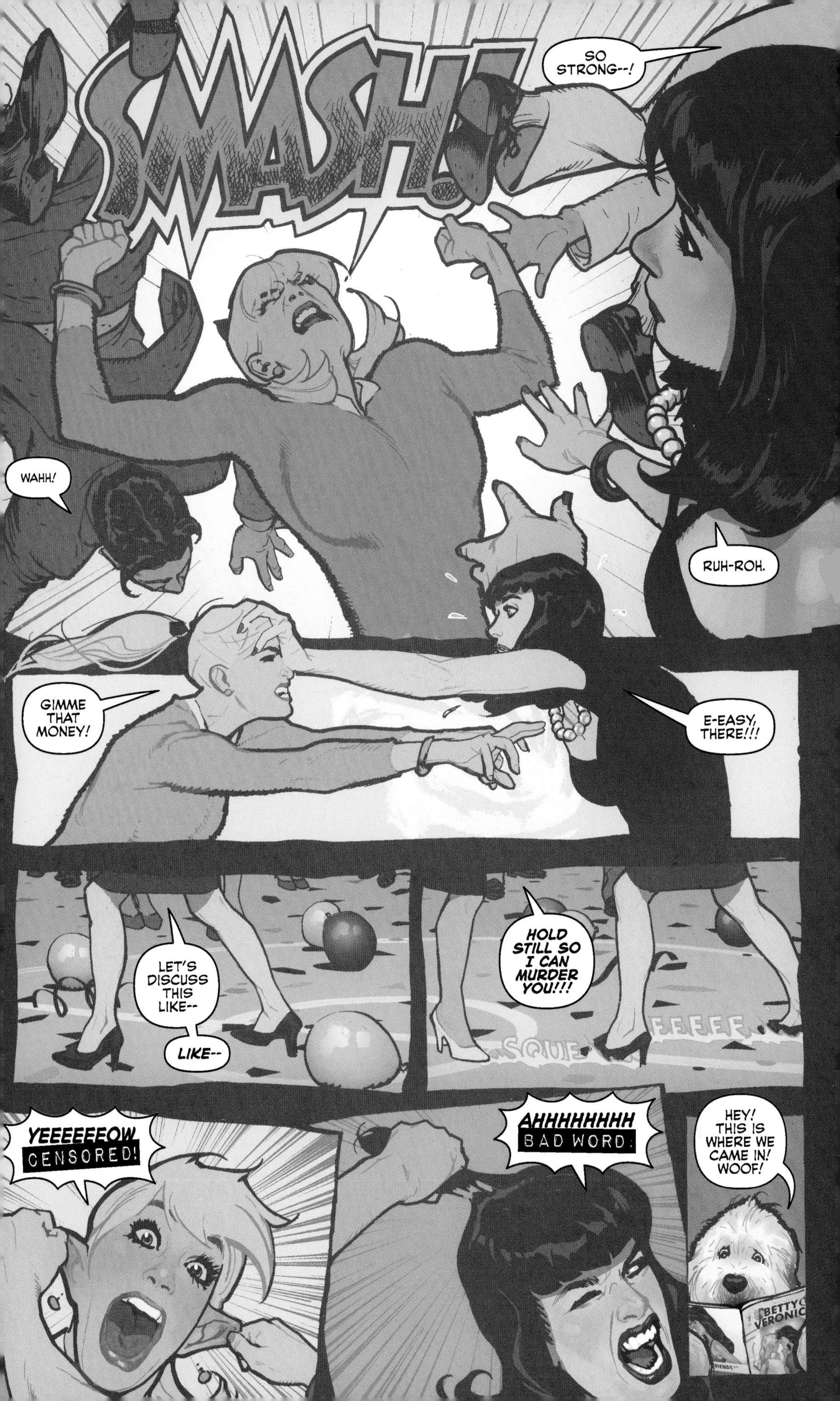
SMASH!
SO STRONG--!
WAHH!
RUH-ROH.
GIMME THAT MONEY!
E-EASY, THERE!!!
LET'S DISCUSS THIS LIKE--
LIKE--
HOLD STILL SO I CAN MURDER YOU!!!
SQUE EEEEE
YEEEEEEOW CENSORED!
AHHHHHHHH BAD WORD.
HEY! THIS IS WHERE WE CAME IN! WOOF!
BETTY VERONICA

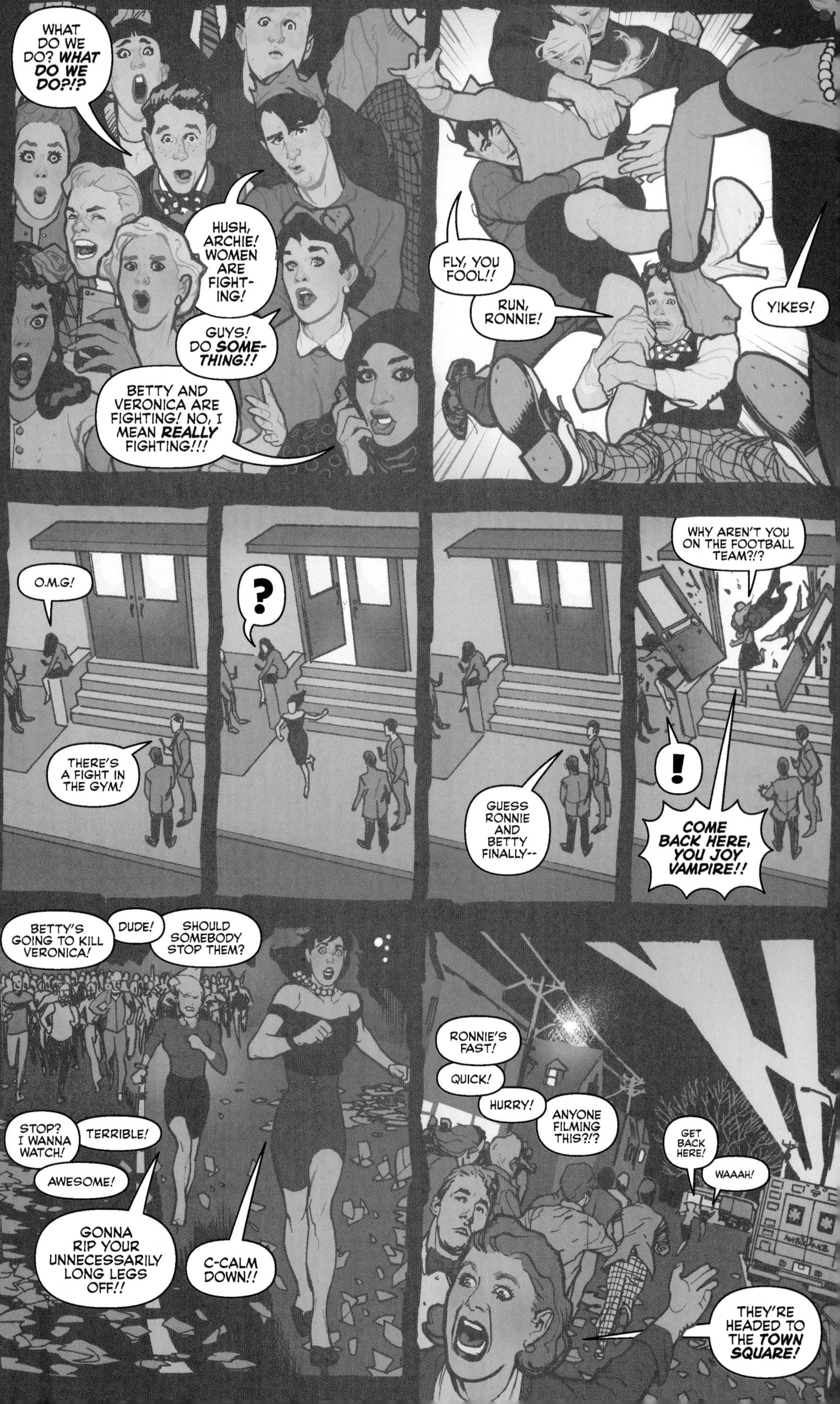
WHAT DO WE DO? WHAT DO WE DO?!?
HUSH, ARCHIE! WOMEN ARE FIGHT-ING!
GUYS! DO SOME-THING!!
BETTY AND VERONICA ARE FIGHTING! NO, I MEAN REALLY FIGHTING!!!
FLY, YOU FOOL!!
RUN, RONNIE!
YIKES!
O.M.G!
THERE'S A FIGHT IN THE GYM!
?
GUESS RONNIE AND BETTY FINALLY--
WHY AREN'T YOU ON THE FOOTBALL TEAM?!?
!
COME BACK HERE, YOU JOY VAMPIRE!!
BETTY'S GOING TO KILL VERONICA!
DUDE!
SHOULD SOMEBODY STOP THEM?
STOP? I WANNA WATCH!
TERRIBLE!
AWESOME!
GONNA RIP YOUR UNNECESSARILY LONG LEGS OFF!!
C-CALM DOWN!!
RONNIE'S FAST!
QUICK!
HURRY!
ANYONE FILMING THIS?!?
GET BACK HERE!
WAAAH!
THEY'RE HEADED TO THE TOWN SQUARE!

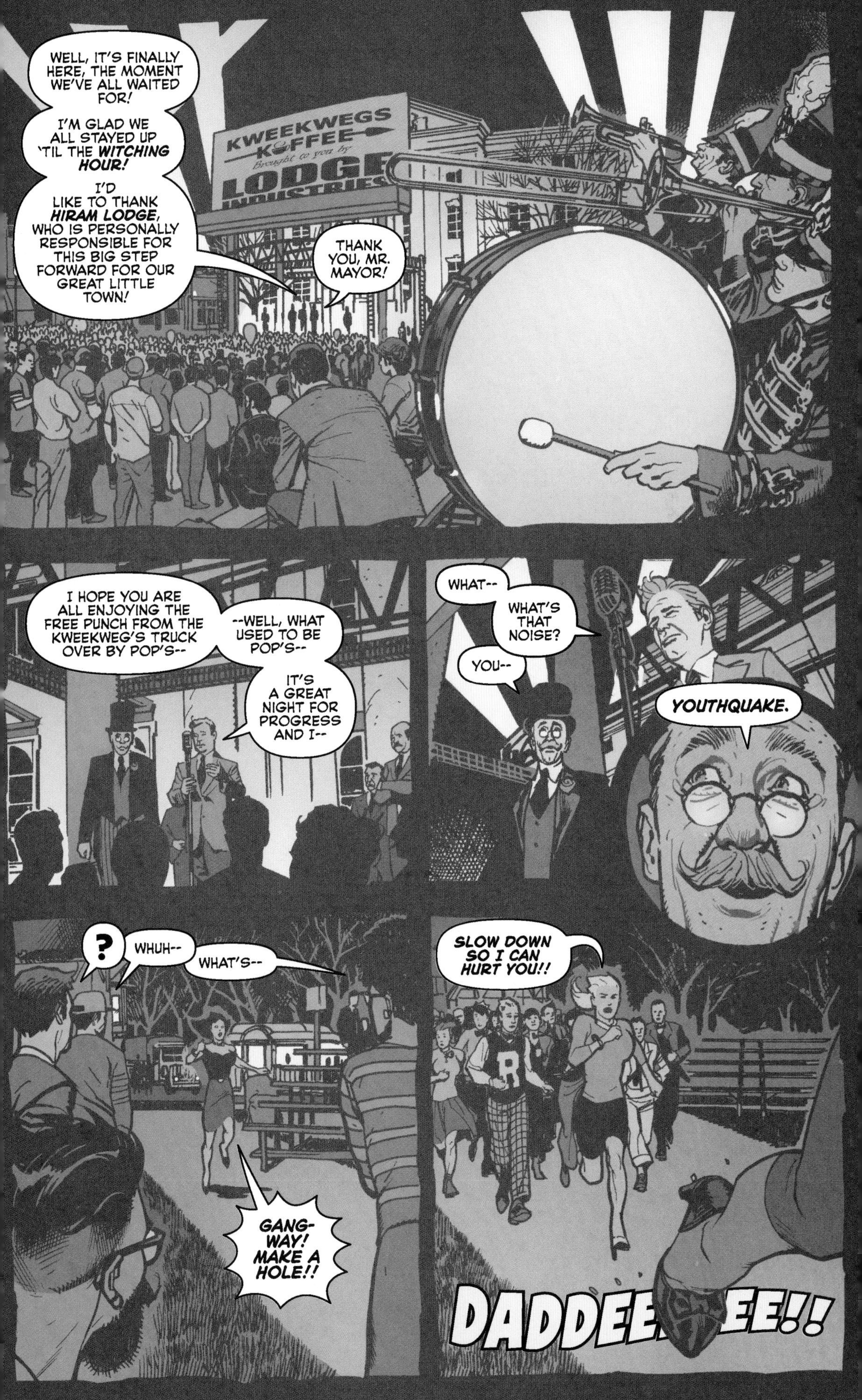
WELL, IT'S FINALLY HERE, THE MOMENT WE'VE ALL WAITED FOR!
I'M GLAD WE ALL STAYED UP 'TIL THE WITCHING HOUR!
I'D LIKE TO THANK HIRAM LODGE, WHO IS PERSONALLY RESPONSIBLE FOR THIS BIG STEP FORWARD FOR OUR GREAT LITTLE TOWN!
KWEEKWEGS KOFFEE
Brought to you by
LODGE INDUSTRIES
THANK YOU, MR. MAYOR!
I HOPE YOU ARE ALL ENJOYING THE FREE PUNCH FROM THE KWEEKWEG'S TRUCK OVER BY POP'S--
--WELL, WHAT USED TO BE POP'S--
IT'S A GREAT NIGHT FOR PROGRESS AND I--
WHAT--
WHAT'S THAT NOISE?
YOU--
YOUTHQUAKE.
?
WHUH--
WHAT'S--
GANG-WAY! MAKE A HOLE!!
SLOW DOWN SO I CAN HURT YOU!!
DADDEE EE!!

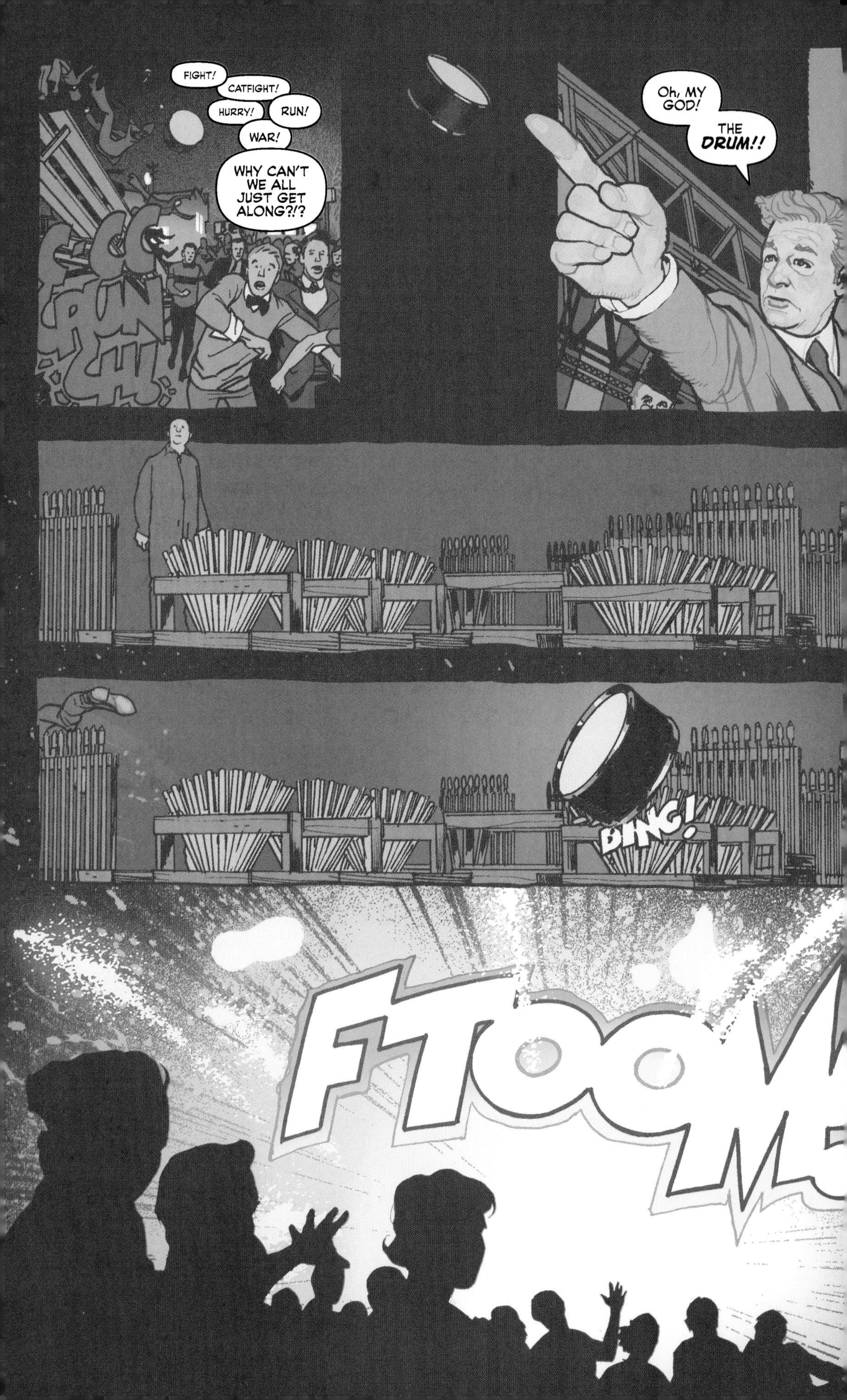
FIGHT!
CATFIGHT!
HURRY!
RUN!
WAR!
WHY CAN'T WE ALL JUST GET ALONG?!?
Oh, MY GOD!
THE DRUM!!
DING!
FTOO

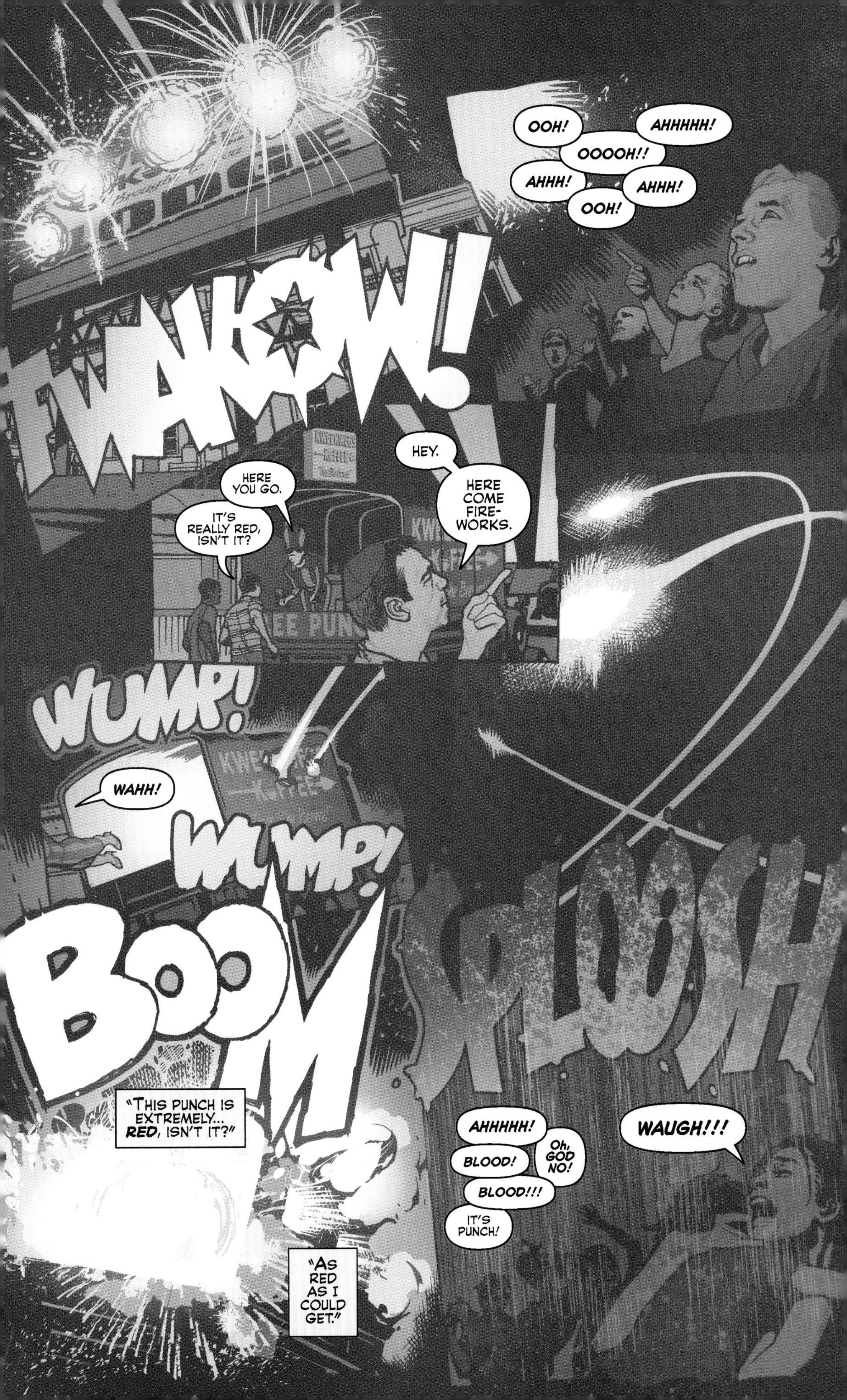
FWAKOW!
OOH!
AHHHHH!
OOOOH!!
AHHH!
AHHH!
OOH!
HERE YOU GO.
IT'S REALLY RED, ISN'T IT?
HEY.
HERE COME FIRE-WORKS.
WUMP!
WAHH!
WUMP!
BOOM
SPLOOSH
"THIS PUNCH IS EXTREMELY... **RED**, ISN'T IT?"
"AS RED AS I COULD GET."
AHHHHH!
BLOOD!
Oh, GOD NO!
BLOOD!!!
IT'S PUNCH!
WAUGH!!!

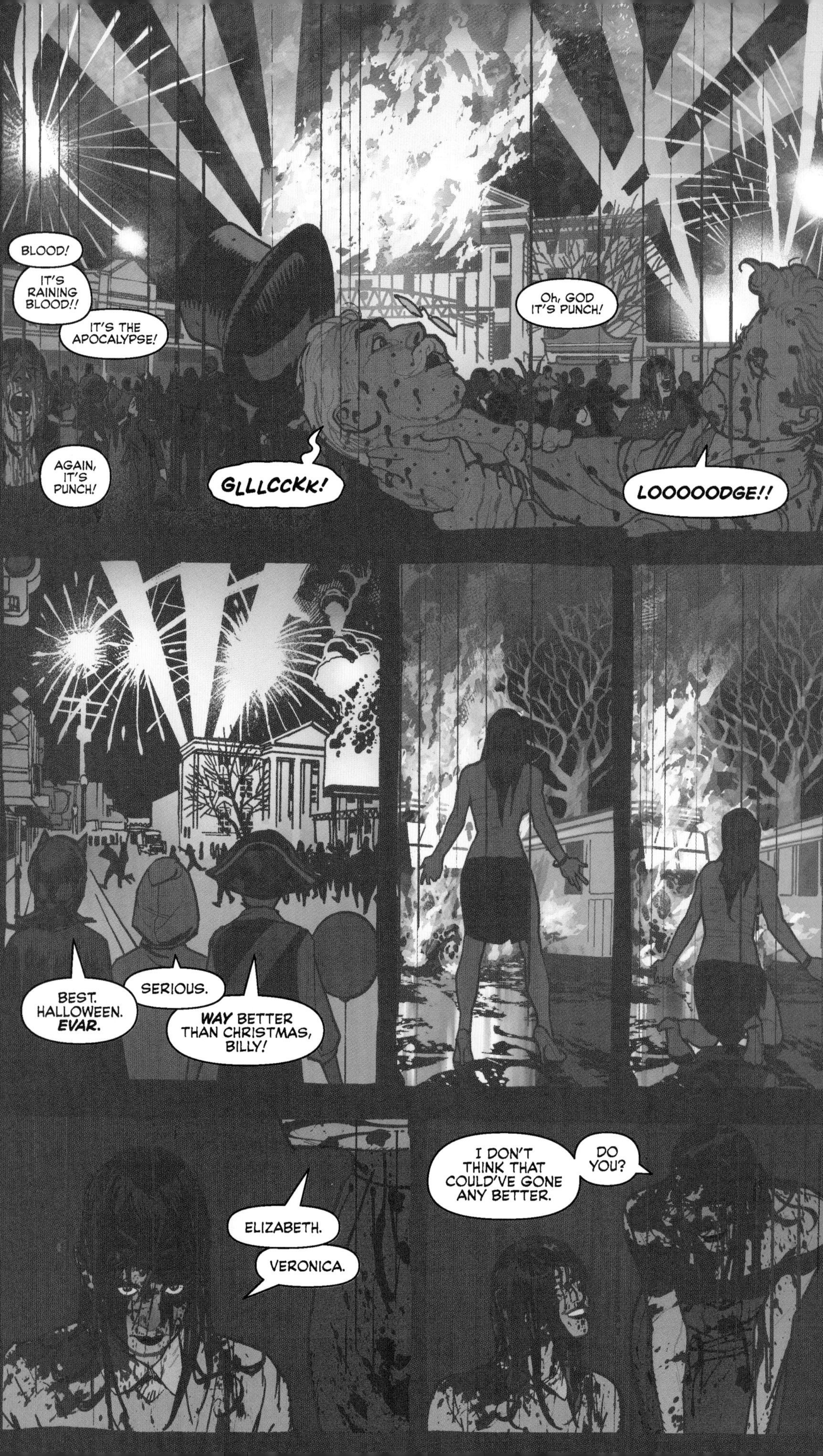
BLOOD!
IT'S RAINING BLOOD!!
IT'S THE APOCALYPSE!
AGAIN, IT'S PUNCH!
GLLLCCKK!
Oh, GOD IT'S PUNCH!
LOOOOODGE!!
BEST. HALLOWEEN. EVAR.
SERIOUS.
WAY BETTER THAN CHRISTMAS, BILLY!
ELIZABETH.
VERONICA.
I DON'T THINK THAT COULD'VE GONE ANY BETTER.
DO YOU?

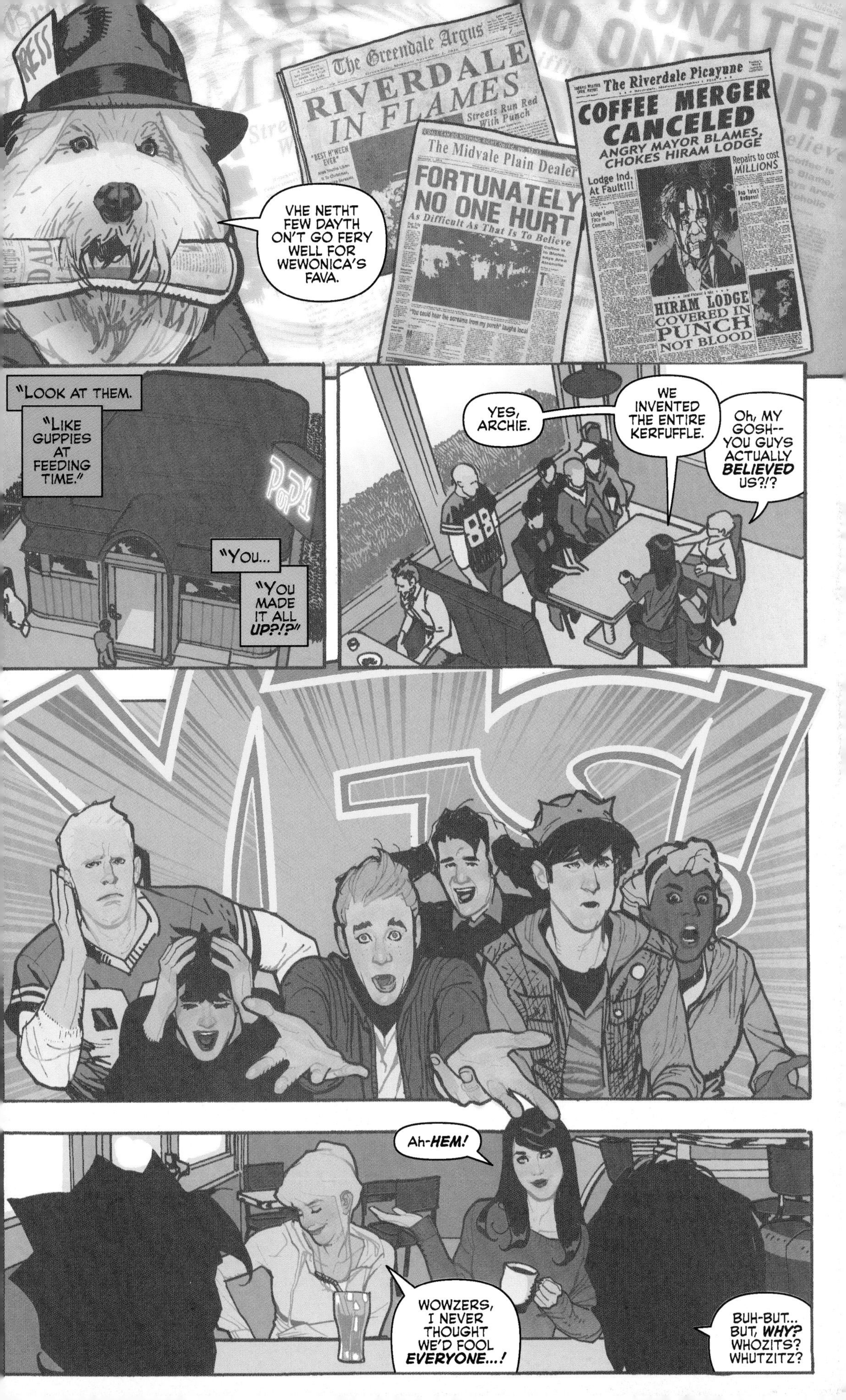
The Greendale Argus
RIVERDALE IN FLAMES
Streets Run Red With Punch
"BEST H'WEEN EVER"
The Midvale Plain Dealer
FORTUNATELY NO ONE HURT
As Difficult As That Is To Believe
"You could hear the screams from my porch" laughs local
The Riverdale Picayune
COFFEE MERGER CANCELED
ANGRY MAYOR BLAMES, CHOKES HIRAM LODGE
Repairs to cost MILLIONS
Lodge Ind. At Fault!!!
Lodge Loses Face in Community
HIRAM LODGE COVERED IN PUNCH NOT BLOOD
VHE NETHT FEW DAYTH ON'T GO FERY WELL FOR WEWONICA'S FAVA.
"LOOK AT THEM.
"LIKE GUPPIES AT FEEDING TIME."
POP'S
"YOU...
"YOU MADE IT ALL *UP?!?*"
YES, ARCHIE.
WE INVENTED THE ENTIRE KERFUFFLE.
Oh, MY GOSH-- YOU GUYS ACTUALLY *BELIEVED* US?!?
Ah-*HEM!*
WOWZERS, I NEVER THOUGHT WE'D FOOL *EVERYONE...!*
BUH-BUT... BUT, *WHY?* WHOZITS? WHUTZITZ?

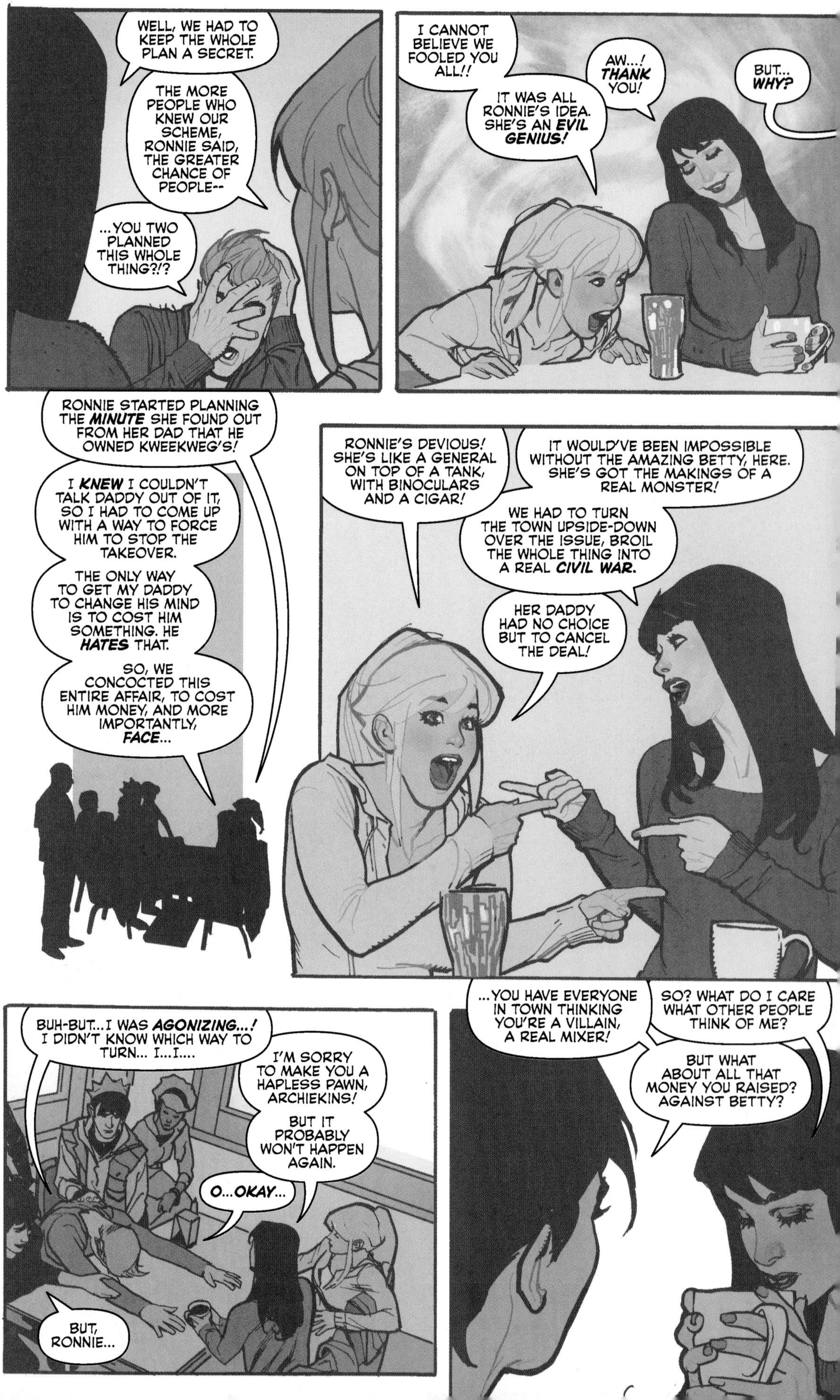
WELL, WE HAD TO KEEP THE WHOLE PLAN A SECRET.
THE MORE PEOPLE WHO KNEW OUR SCHEME, RONNIE SAID, THE GREATER CHANCE OF PEOPLE--
...YOU TWO PLANNED THIS WHOLE THING?!?
I CANNOT BELIEVE WE FOOLED YOU ALL!!
IT WAS ALL RONNIE'S IDEA. SHE'S AN EVIL GENIUS!
AW...! THANK YOU!
BUT... WHY?
RONNIE STARTED PLANNING THE MINUTE SHE FOUND OUT FROM HER DAD THAT HE OWNED KWEEKWEG'S!
I KNEW I COULDN'T TALK DADDY OUT OF IT, SO I HAD TO COME UP WITH A WAY TO FORCE HIM TO STOP THE TAKEOVER.
THE ONLY WAY TO GET MY DADDY TO CHANGE HIS MIND IS TO COST HIM SOMETHING. HE HATES THAT.
SO, WE CONCOCTED THIS ENTIRE AFFAIR, TO COST HIM MONEY, AND MORE IMPORTANTLY, FACE...
RONNIE'S DEVIOUS! SHE'S LIKE A GENERAL ON TOP OF A TANK, WITH BINOCULARS AND A CIGAR!
IT WOULD'VE BEEN IMPOSSIBLE WITHOUT THE AMAZING BETTY, HERE. SHE'S GOT THE MAKINGS OF A REAL MONSTER!
WE HAD TO TURN THE TOWN UPSIDE-DOWN OVER THE ISSUE, BROIL THE WHOLE THING INTO A REAL CIVIL WAR.
HER DADDY HAD NO CHOICE BUT TO CANCEL THE DEAL!
BUH-BUT...I WAS AGONIZING...! I DIDN'T KNOW WHICH WAY TO TURN... I...I....
I'M SORRY TO MAKE YOU A HAPLESS PAWN, ARCHIEKINS!
BUT IT PROBABLY WON'T HAPPEN AGAIN.
O...OKAY...
BUT, RONNIE...
...YOU HAVE EVERYONE IN TOWN THINKING YOU'RE A VILLAIN, A REAL MIXER!
SO? WHAT DO I CARE WHAT OTHER PEOPLE THINK OF ME?
BUT WHAT ABOUT ALL THAT MONEY YOU RAISED? AGAINST BETTY?

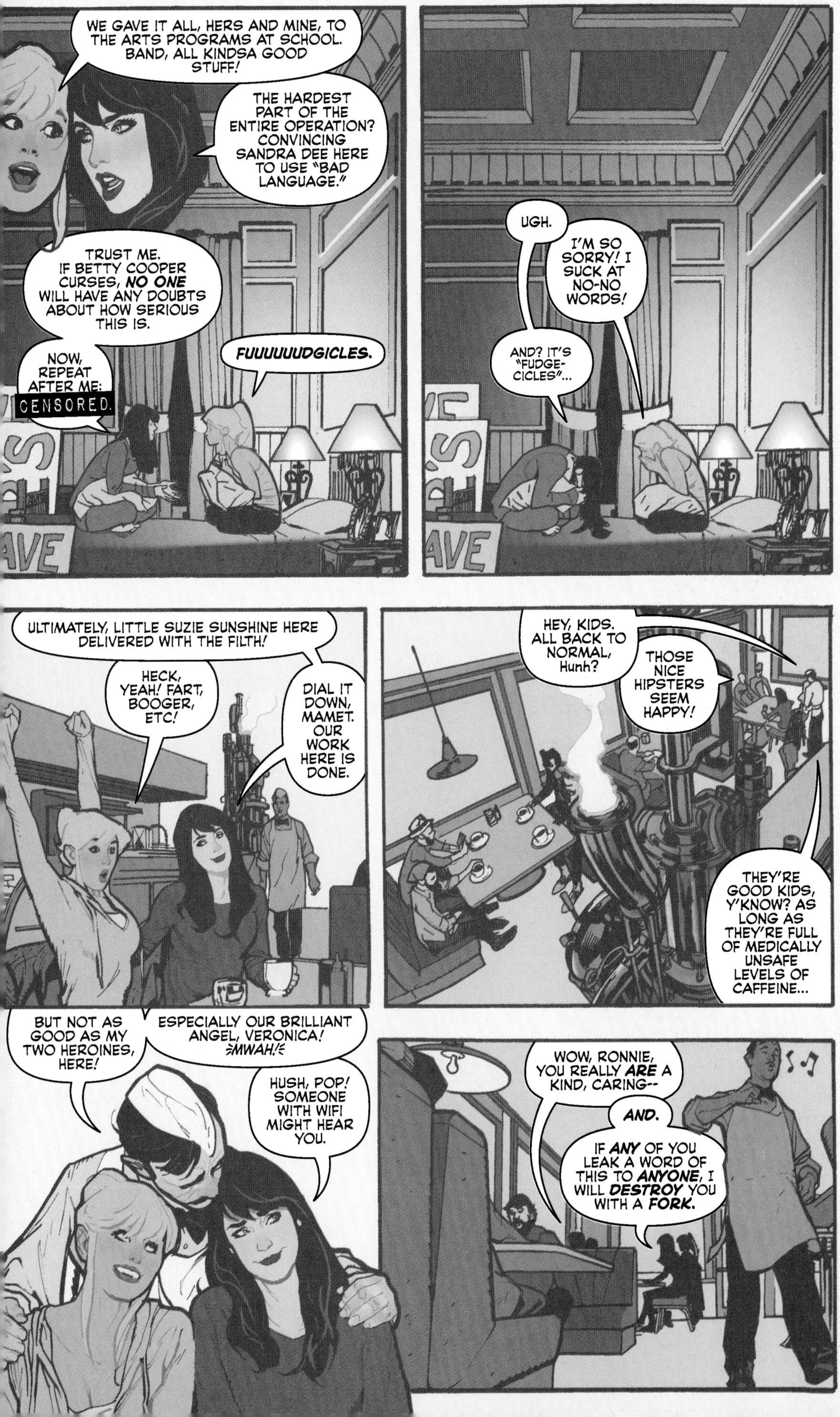
WE GAVE IT ALL, HERS AND MINE, TO THE ARTS PROGRAMS AT SCHOOL. BAND, ALL KINDSA GOOD STUFF!
THE HARDEST PART OF THE ENTIRE OPERATION? CONVINCING SANDRA DEE HERE TO USE "BAD LANGUAGE."
TRUST ME. IF BETTY COOPER CURSES, **NO ONE** WILL HAVE ANY DOUBTS ABOUT HOW SERIOUS THIS IS.
NOW, REPEAT AFTER ME: CENSORED.
FUUUUUUDGICLES.
UGH.
I'M SO SORRY! I SUCK AT NO-NO WORDS!
AND? IT'S "FUDGE-CICLES"...
ULTIMATELY, LITTLE SUZIE SUNSHINE HERE DELIVERED WITH THE FILTH!
HECK, YEAH! FART, BOOGER, ETC!
DIAL IT DOWN, MAMET. OUR WORK HERE IS DONE.
HEY, KIDS. ALL BACK TO NORMAL, Hunh?
THOSE NICE HIPSTERS SEEM HAPPY!
THEY'RE GOOD KIDS, Y'KNOW? AS LONG AS THEY'RE FULL OF MEDICALLY UNSAFE LEVELS OF CAFFEINE...
BUT NOT AS GOOD AS MY TWO HEROINES, HERE!
ESPECIALLY OUR BRILLIANT ANGEL, VERONICA! *MWAH!*
HUSH, POP! SOMEONE WITH WIFI MIGHT HEAR YOU.
WOW, RONNIE, YOU REALLY **ARE** A KIND, CARING--
AND.
IF **ANY** OF YOU LEAK A WORD OF THIS TO **ANYONE**, I WILL **DESTROY** YOU WITH A **FORK.**

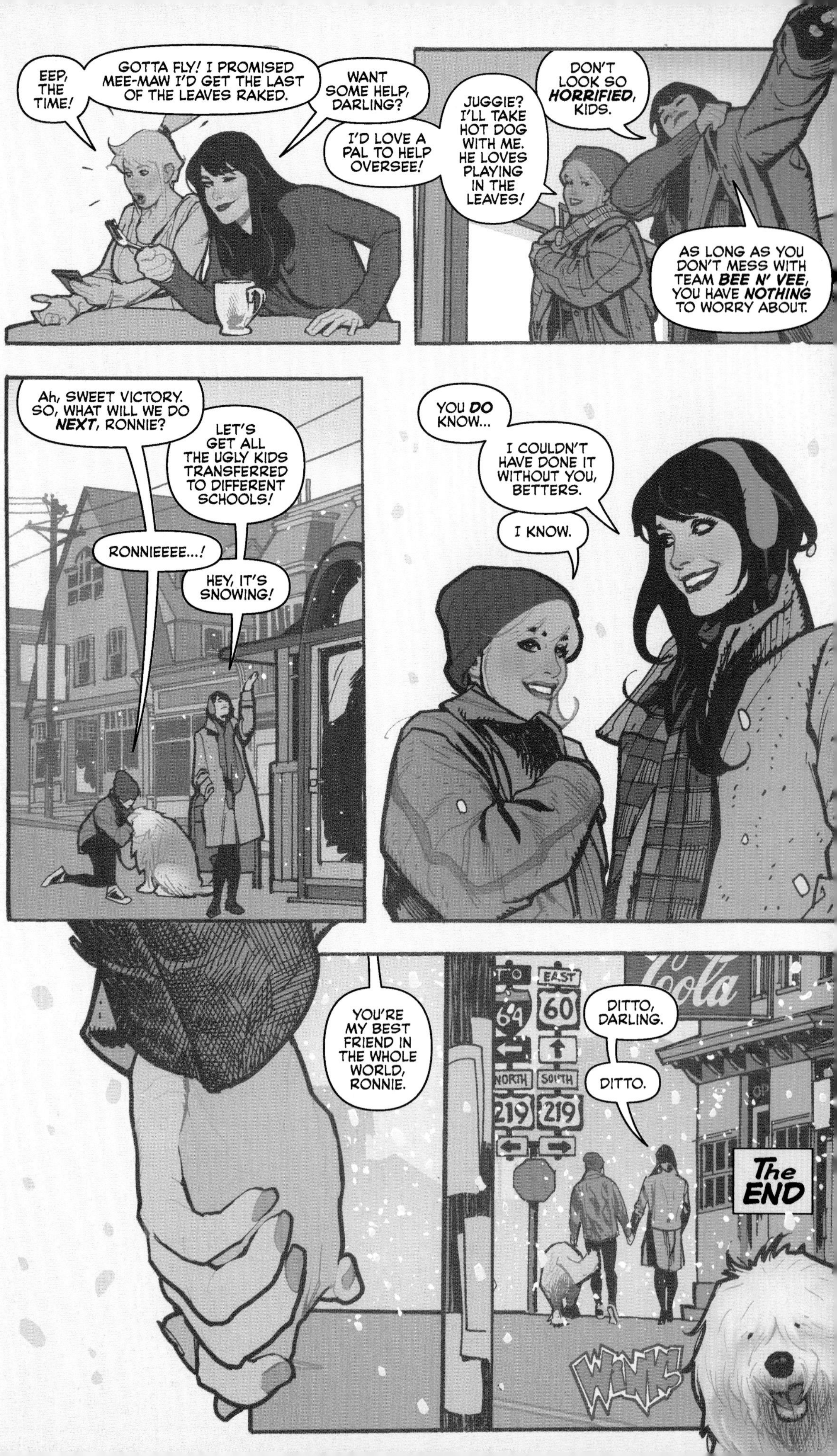

EEP, THE TIME!
GOTTA FLY! I PROMISED MEE-MAW I'D GET THE LAST OF THE LEAVES RAKED.
WANT SOME HELP, DARLING?
I'D LOVE A PAL TO HELP OVERSEE!
JUGGIE? I'LL TAKE HOT DOG WITH ME. HE LOVES PLAYING IN THE LEAVES!
DON'T LOOK SO HORRIFIED, KIDS.
AS LONG AS YOU DON'T MESS WITH TEAM BEE N' VEE, YOU HAVE NOTHING TO WORRY ABOUT.
Ah, SWEET VICTORY. SO, WHAT WILL WE DO NEXT, RONNIE?
LET'S GET ALL THE UGLY KIDS TRANSFERRED TO DIFFERENT SCHOOLS!
RONNIEEEE...!
HEY, IT'S SNOWING!
YOU DO KNOW...
I COULDN'T HAVE DONE IT WITHOUT YOU, BETTERS.
I KNOW.
YOU'RE MY BEST FRIEND IN THE WHOLE WORLD, RONNIE.
TO
64
EAST
60
NORTH
219
SOUTH
219
Cola
DITTO, DARLING.
DITTO.
The END
WINK!

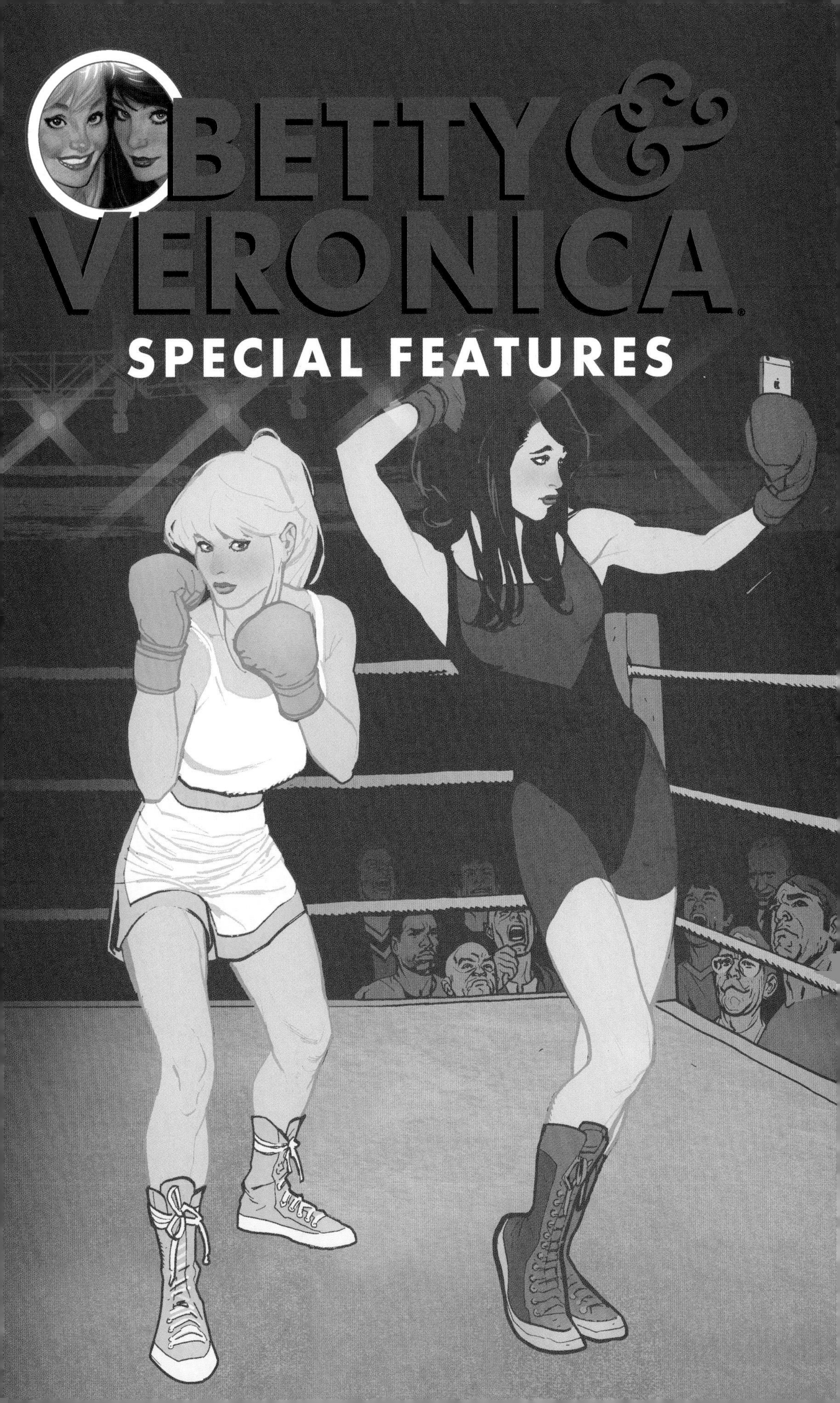
BETTY & VERONICA
SPECIAL FEATURES

BETTY & VERONICA
COVER GALLERY

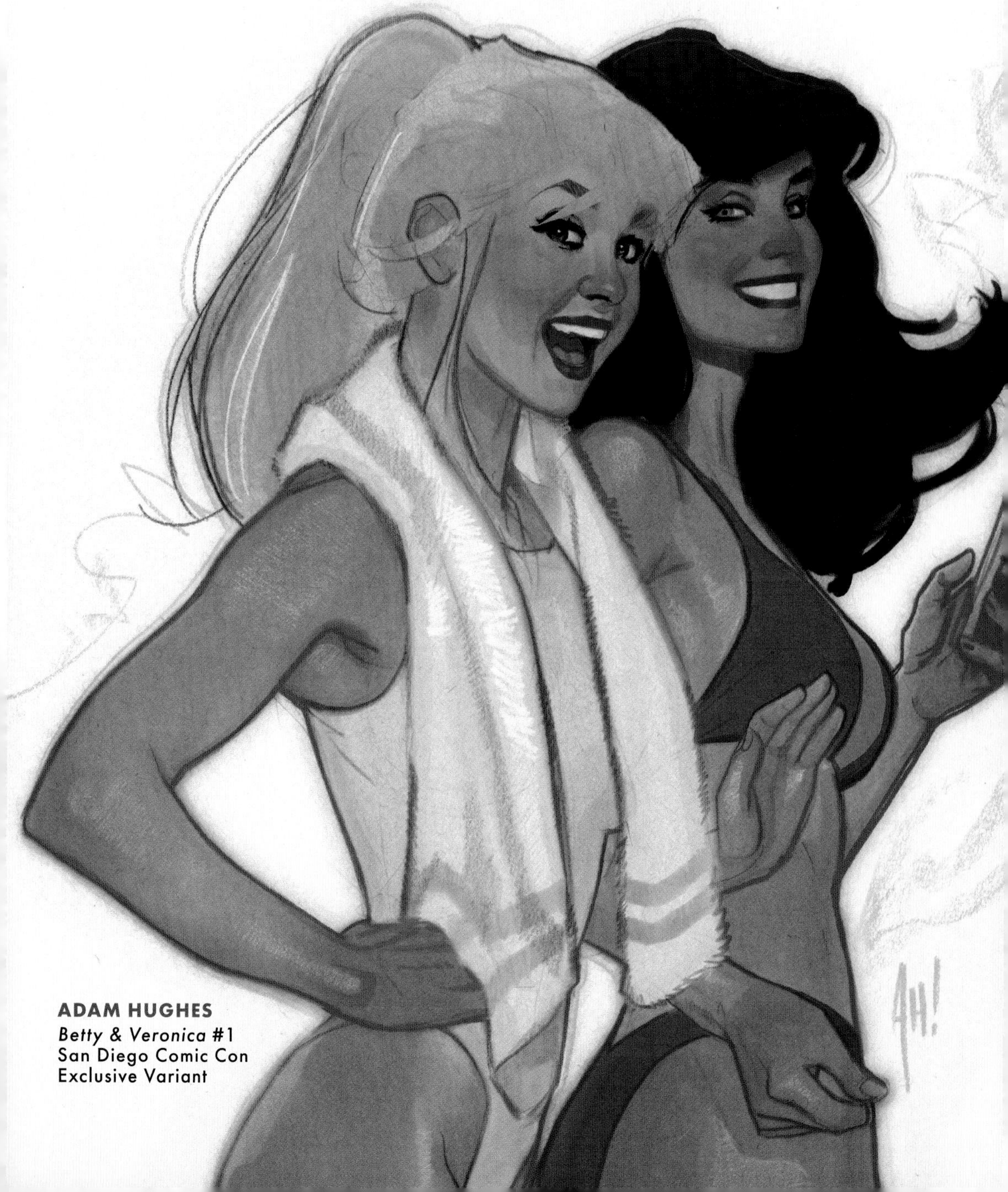

ADAM HUGHES
Betty & Veronica #1
San Diego Comic Con
Exclusive Variant

ISSUE ONE

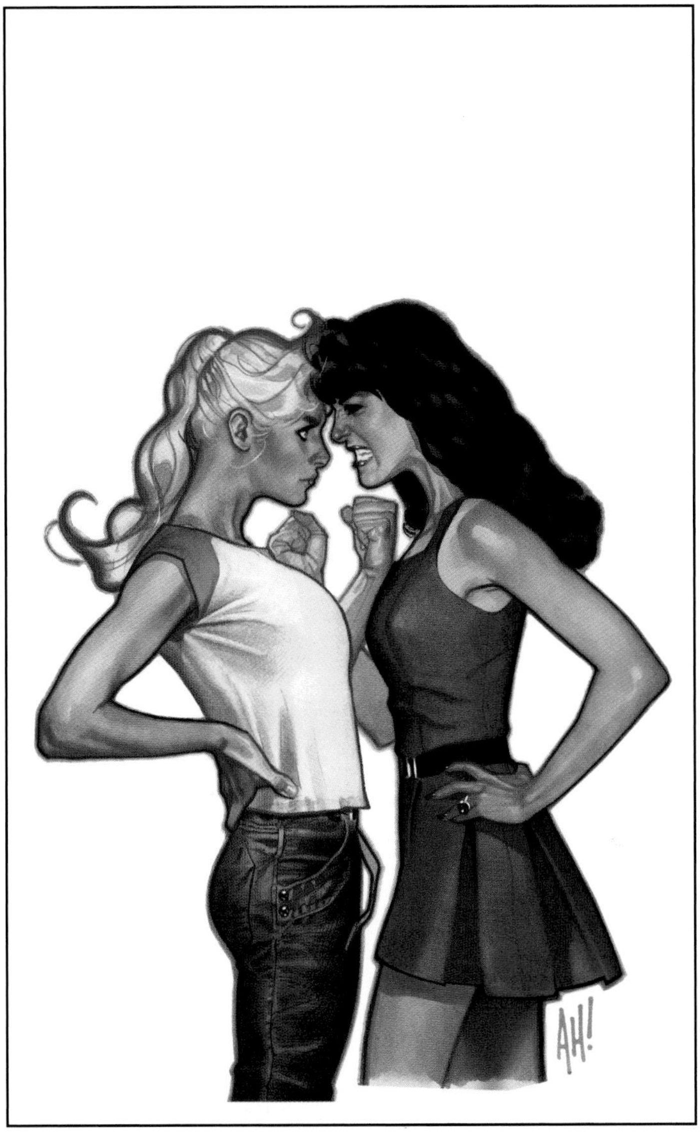
AH!

ADAM HUGHES

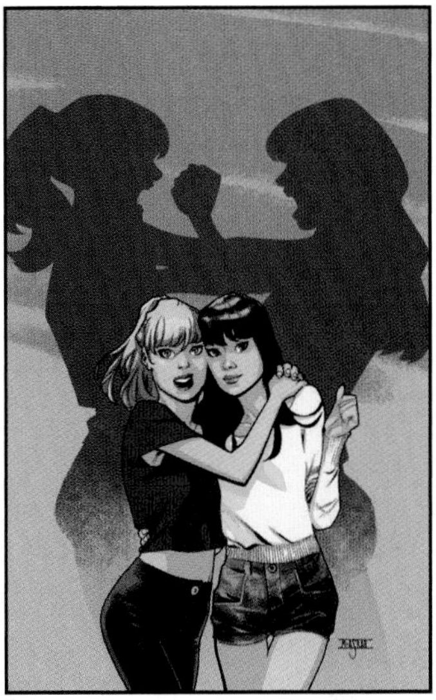

MAHMUD ASRAR

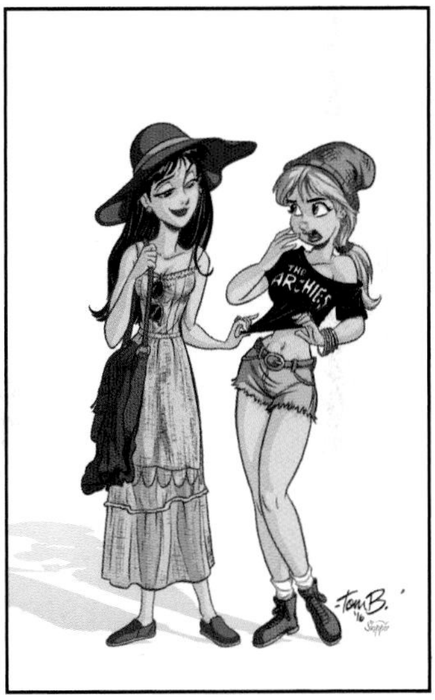
THE ARCHIES

TOM BANCROFT

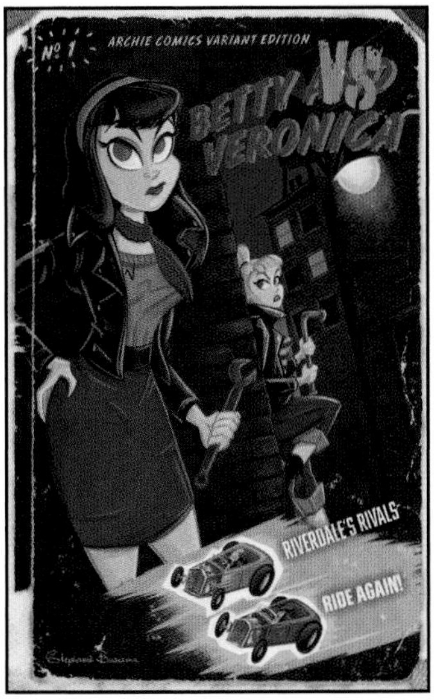
Nº 1
ARCHIE COMICS VARIANT EDITION
BETTY VS VERONICA
RIVERDALE'S RIVALS
RIDE AGAIN!

STEPHANIE BUSCEMA

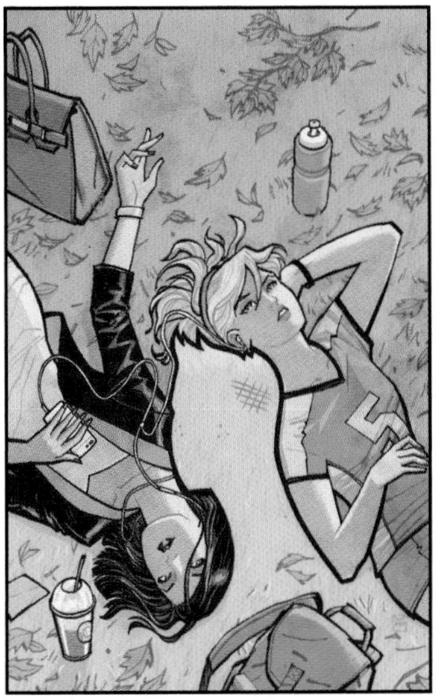

CLIFF CHIANG

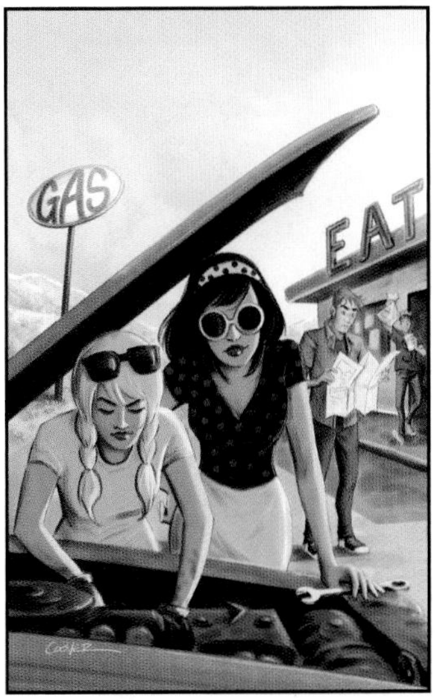
GAS
EAT

COLLEEN COOVER

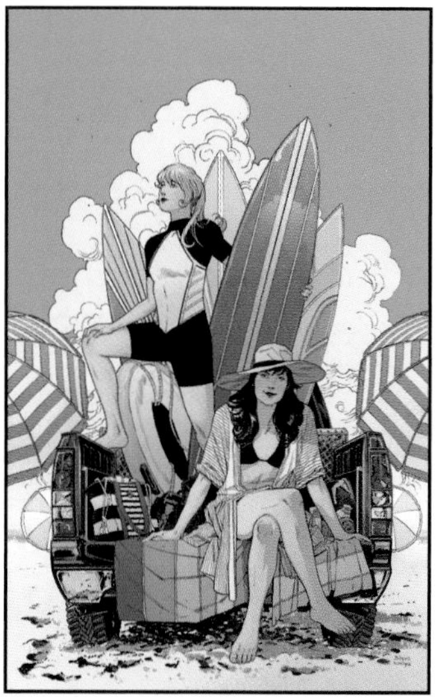

BILQUIS EVELY

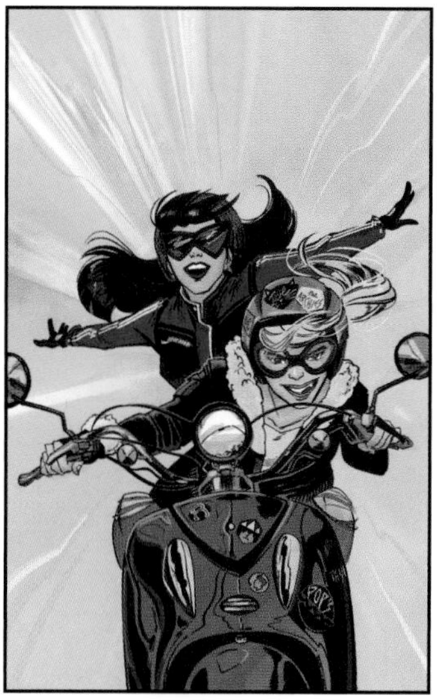

VERONICA FISH

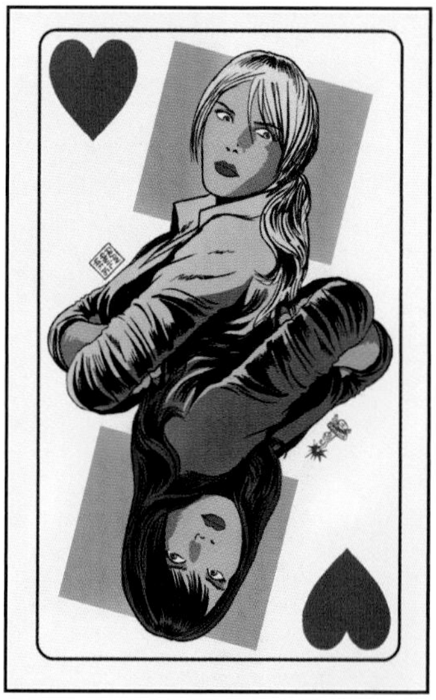

FRANCESCO FRANCAVILLA

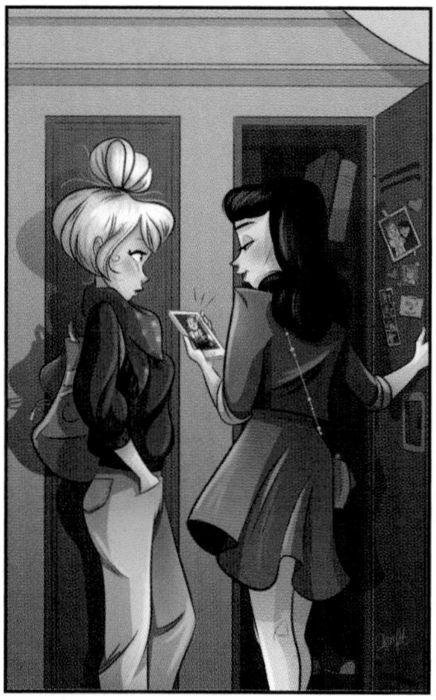

GENEVIEVE F.T.

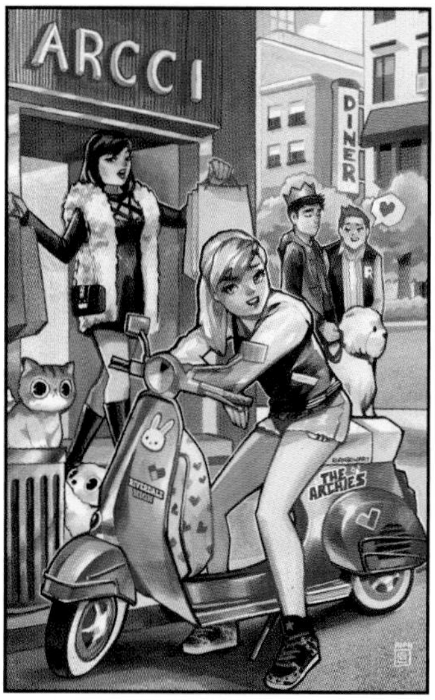
ARCCI
DINER
THE ARCHIES

RIAN GONZALES

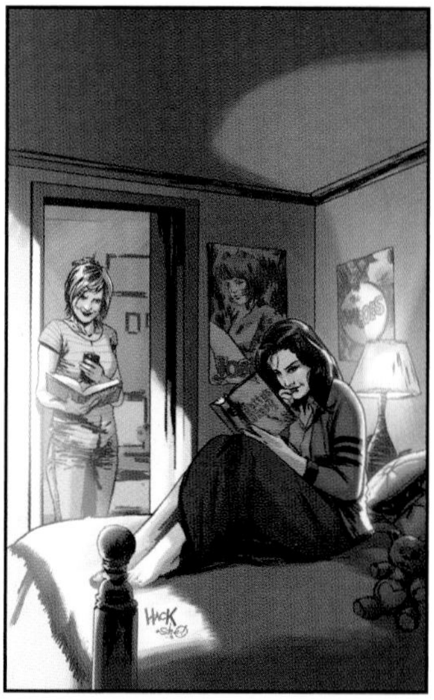

ROBERT HACK

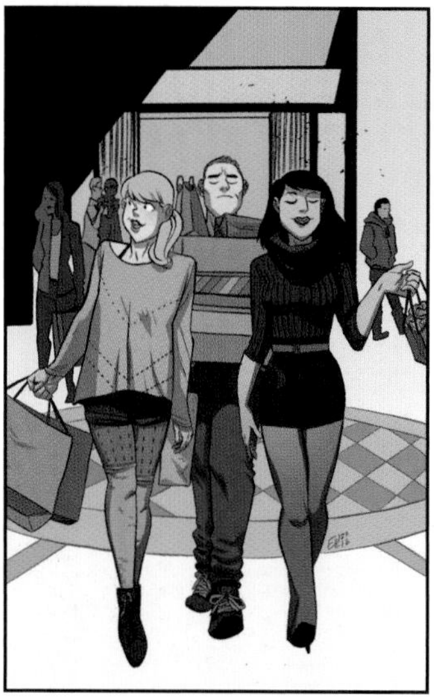

ERICA HENDERSON

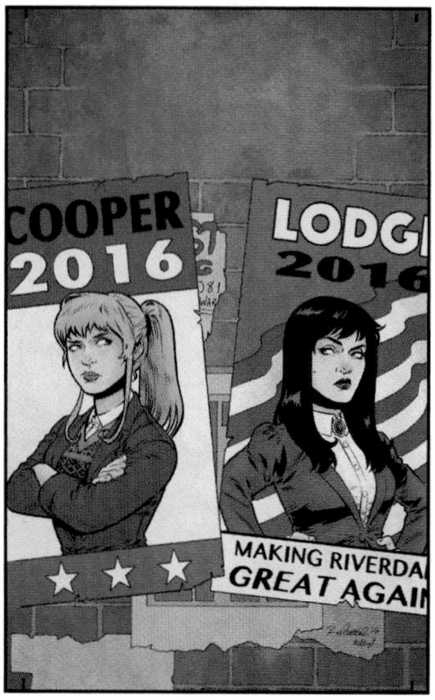
COOPER
2016
LODG
2016
MAKING RIVERDA
GREAT AGAI

REBEKAH ISAACS

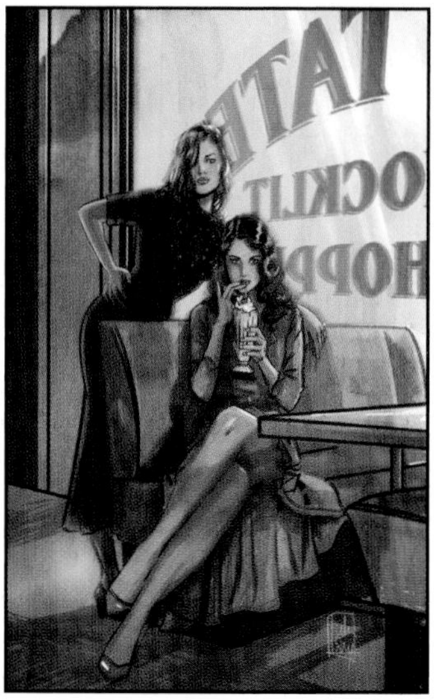

TULA LOTAY

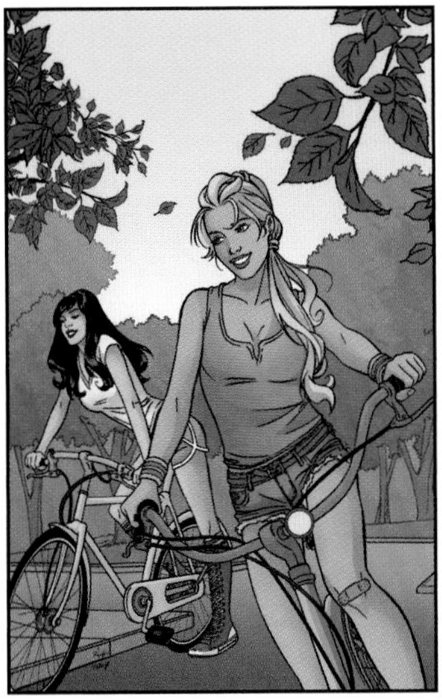

ALITHA MARTINEZ

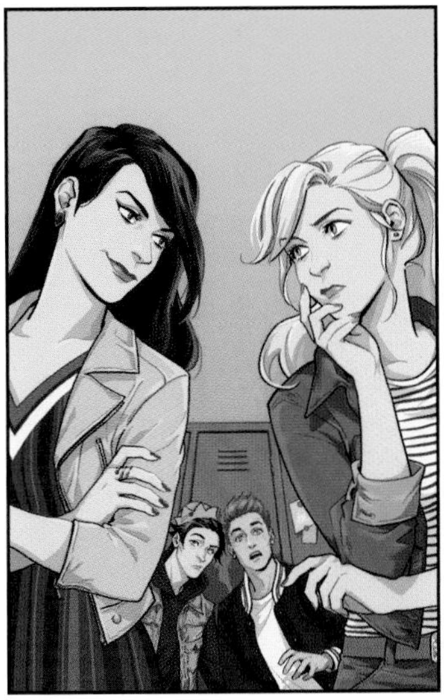

AUDREY MOK

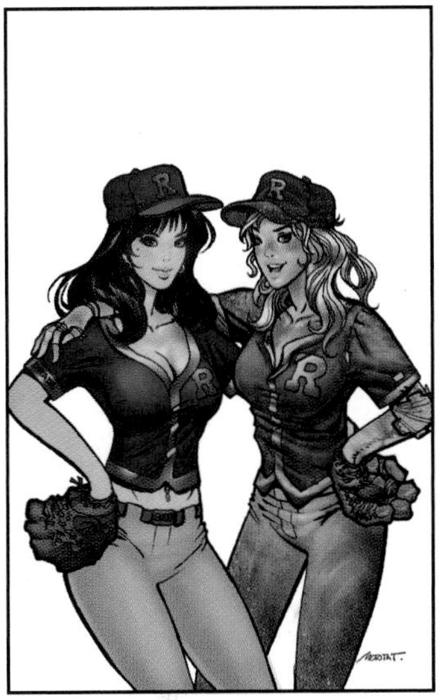

MORITAT

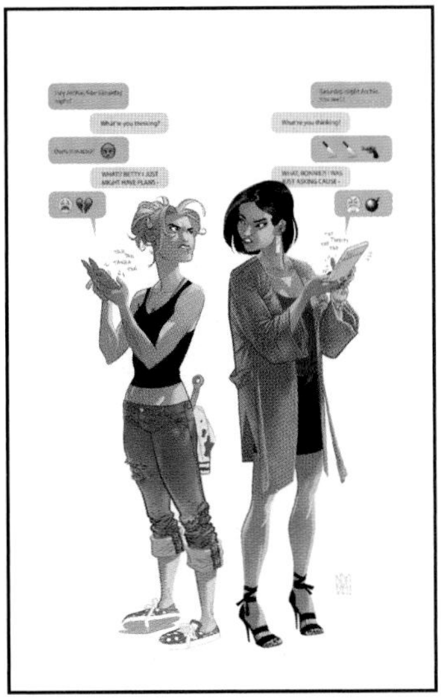

RAMON PEREZ

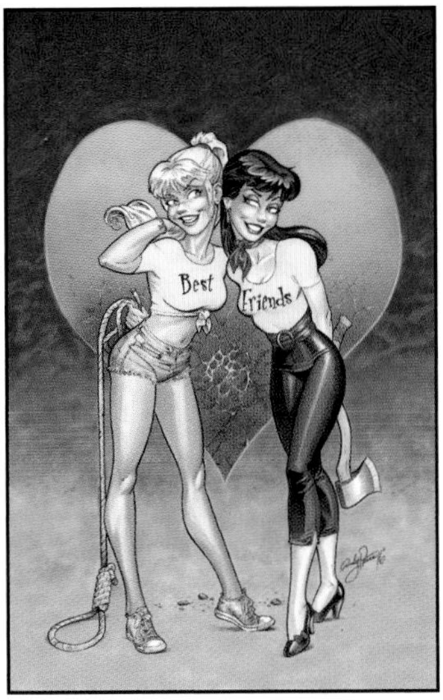
Best
Friends

ANDY PRICE

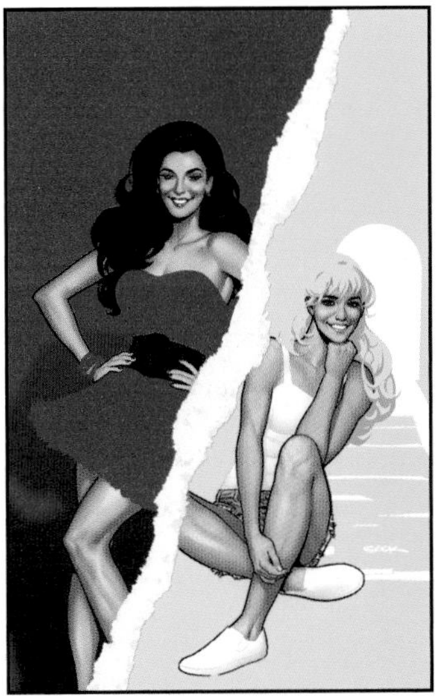

RYAN SOOK

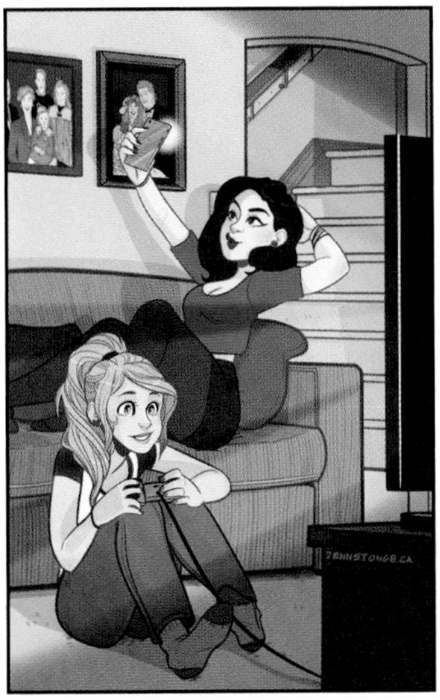

JENN ST. ONGE

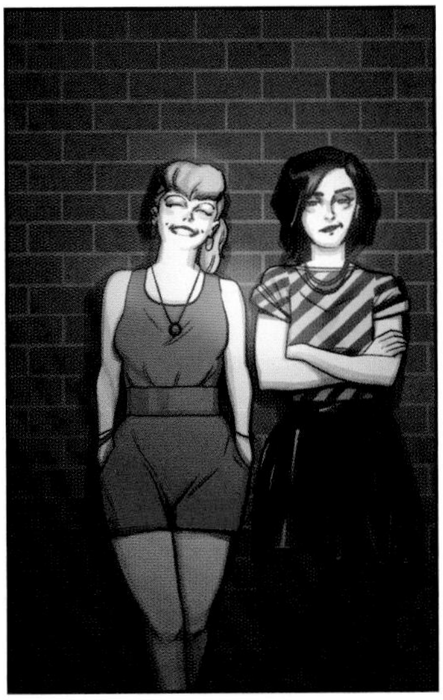

CHIP ZDARSKY

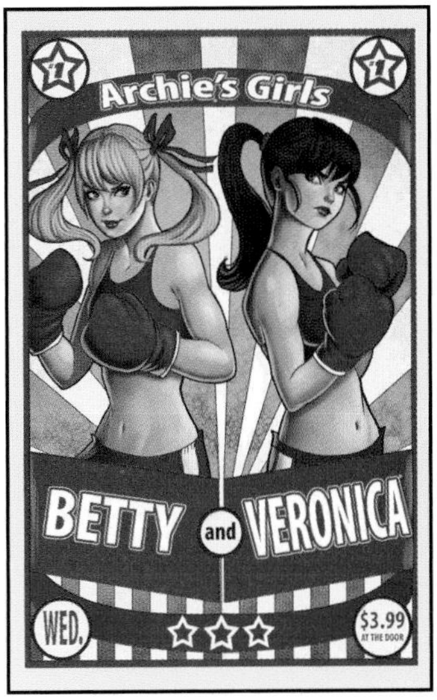
Archie's Girls
BETTY and VERONICA
WED.
$3.99 AT THE DOOR

CHRISSIE ZULLO

ISSUE TWO

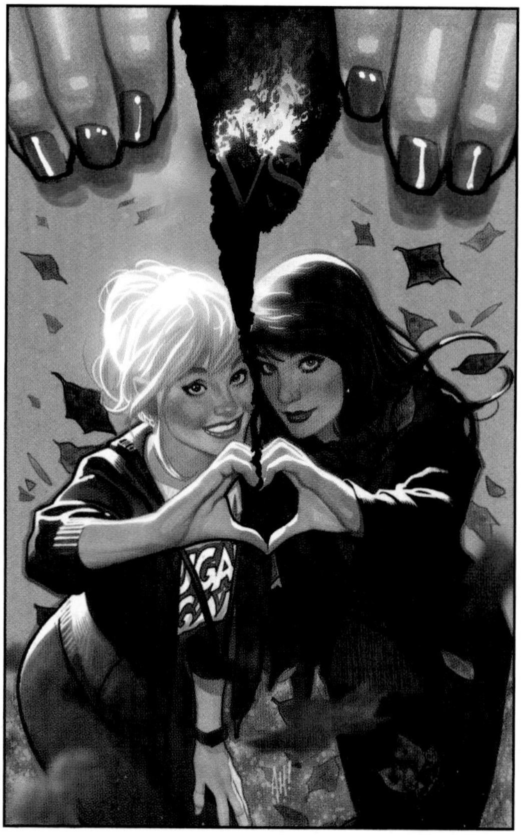
VS

ADAM HUGHES

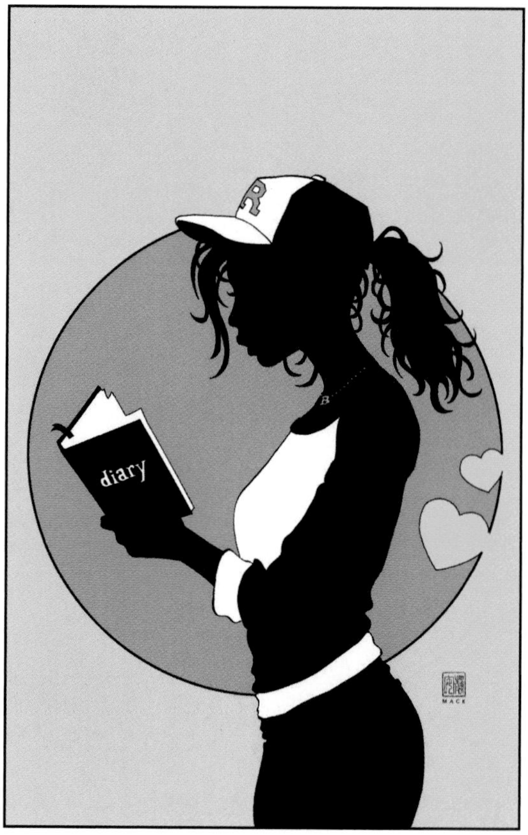
diary
MACK

DAVID MACK

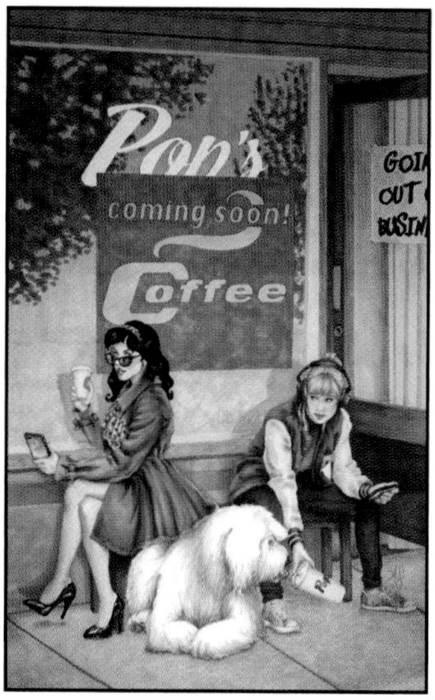
Pop's
coming soon!
Coffee

ALLISON SOHN

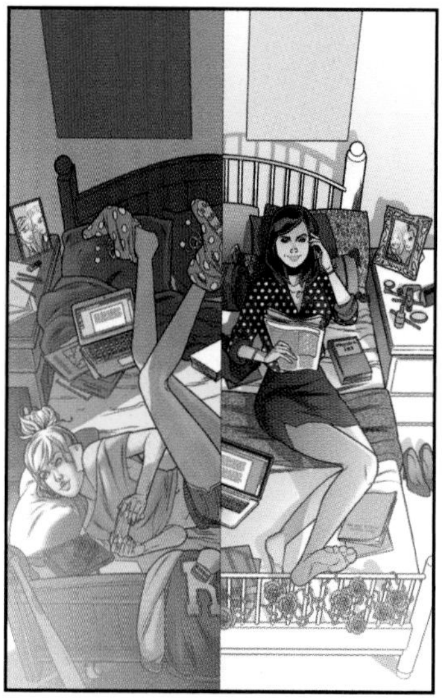

RACHAEL STOTT

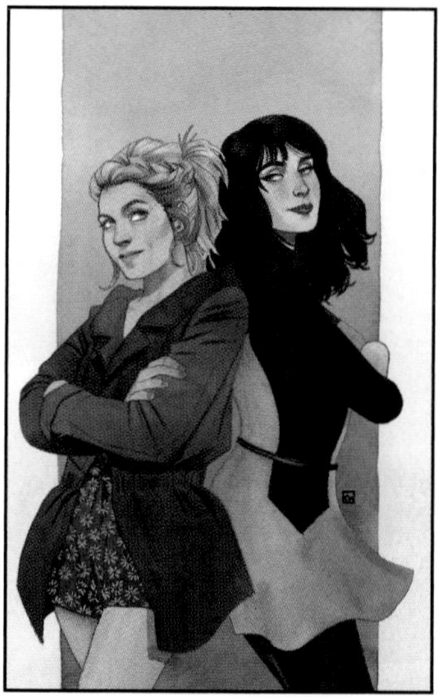

KEVIN WADA

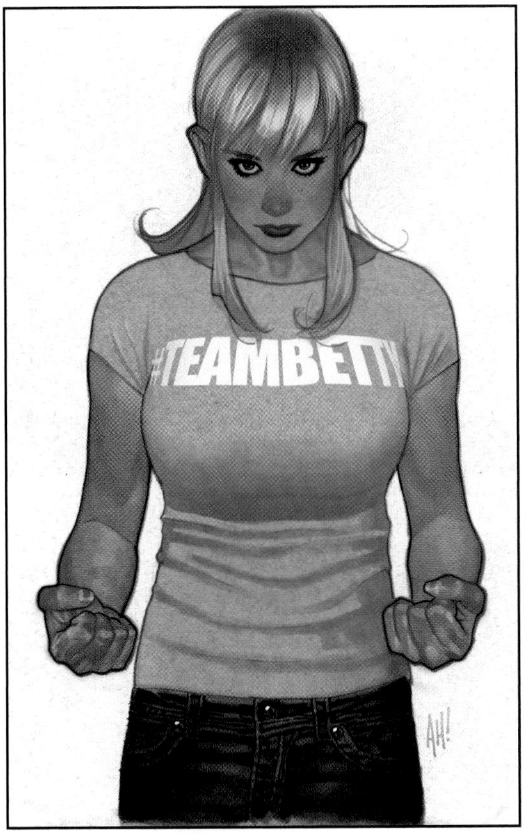
#TEAMBETTY

ADAM HUGHES

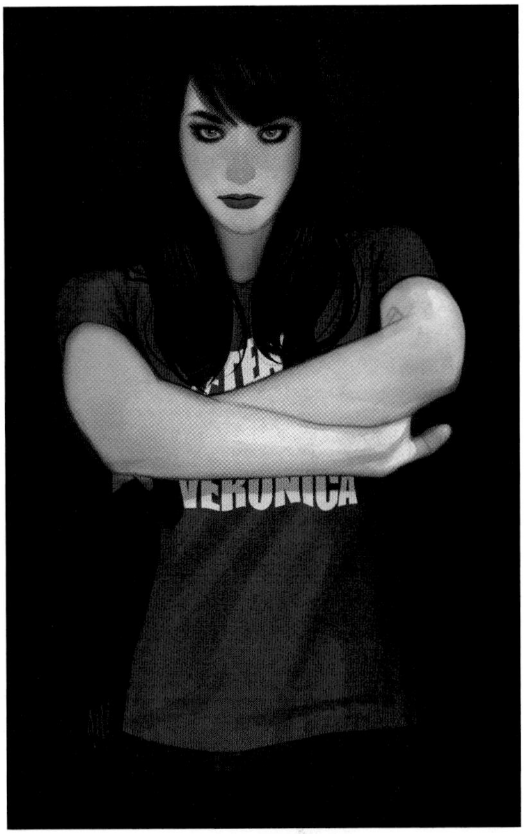
VERONICA

ADAM HUGHES

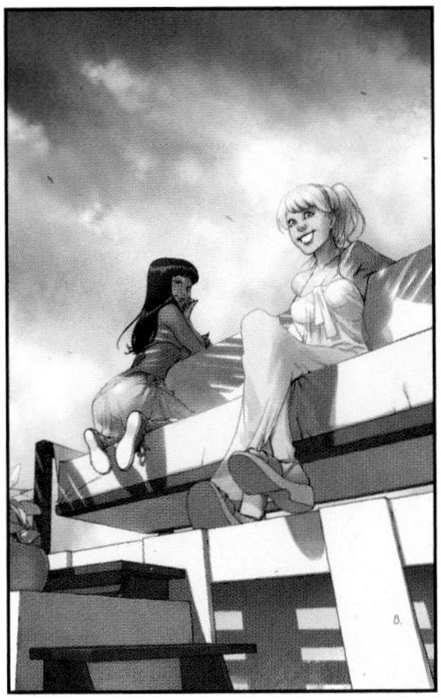

BENGAL

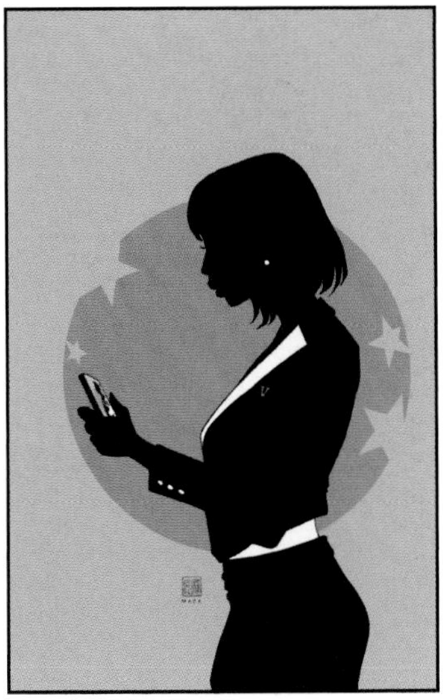

DAVID MACK

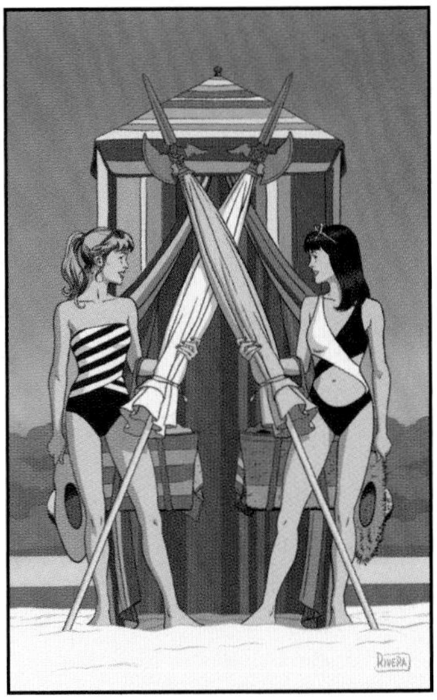
RIVERA

PAOLO RIVERA

THE COVERS THAT STARTED IT ALL...

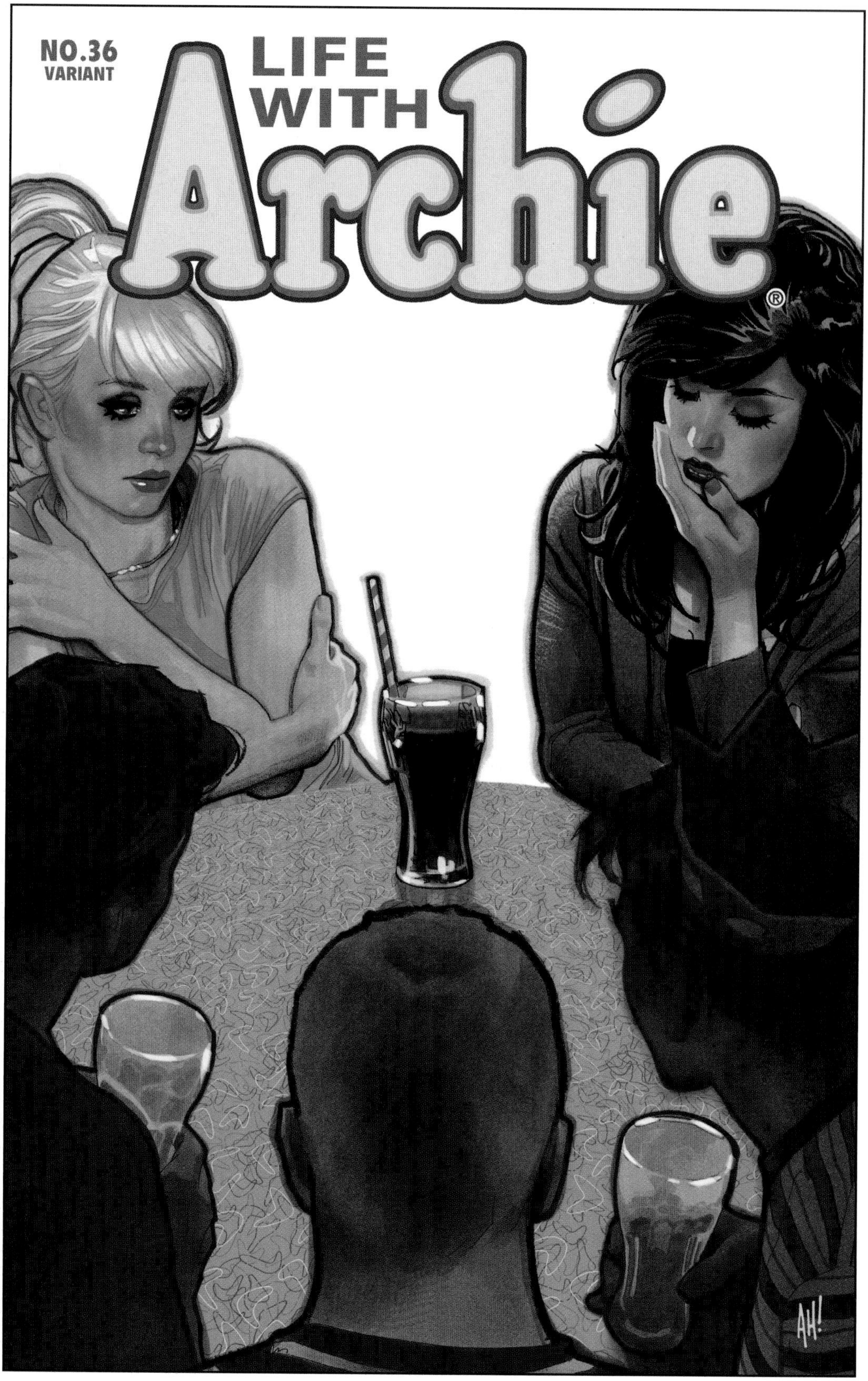
NO.36
VARIANT
LIFE
WITH
Archie
AH!

ADAM HUGHES Variant cover for *Life with Archie* #36, September 2014
(Historic Death of Archie issue)

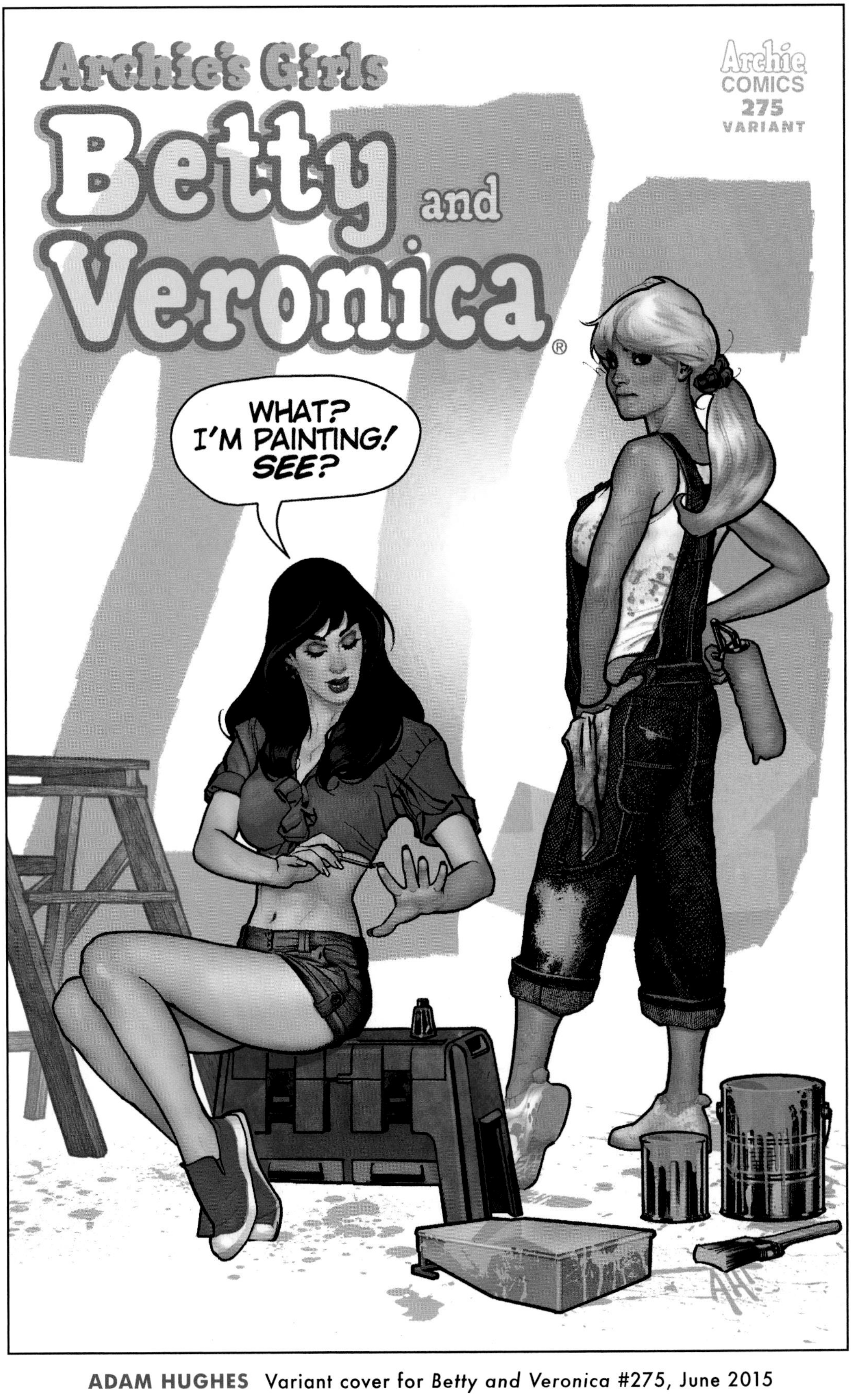
Archie's Girls
Betty and Veronica
Archie COMICS
275
VARIANT
WHAT? I'M PAINTING! SEE?

ADAM HUGHES Variant cover for *Betty and Veronica* #275, June 2015

UNRELEASED COVER

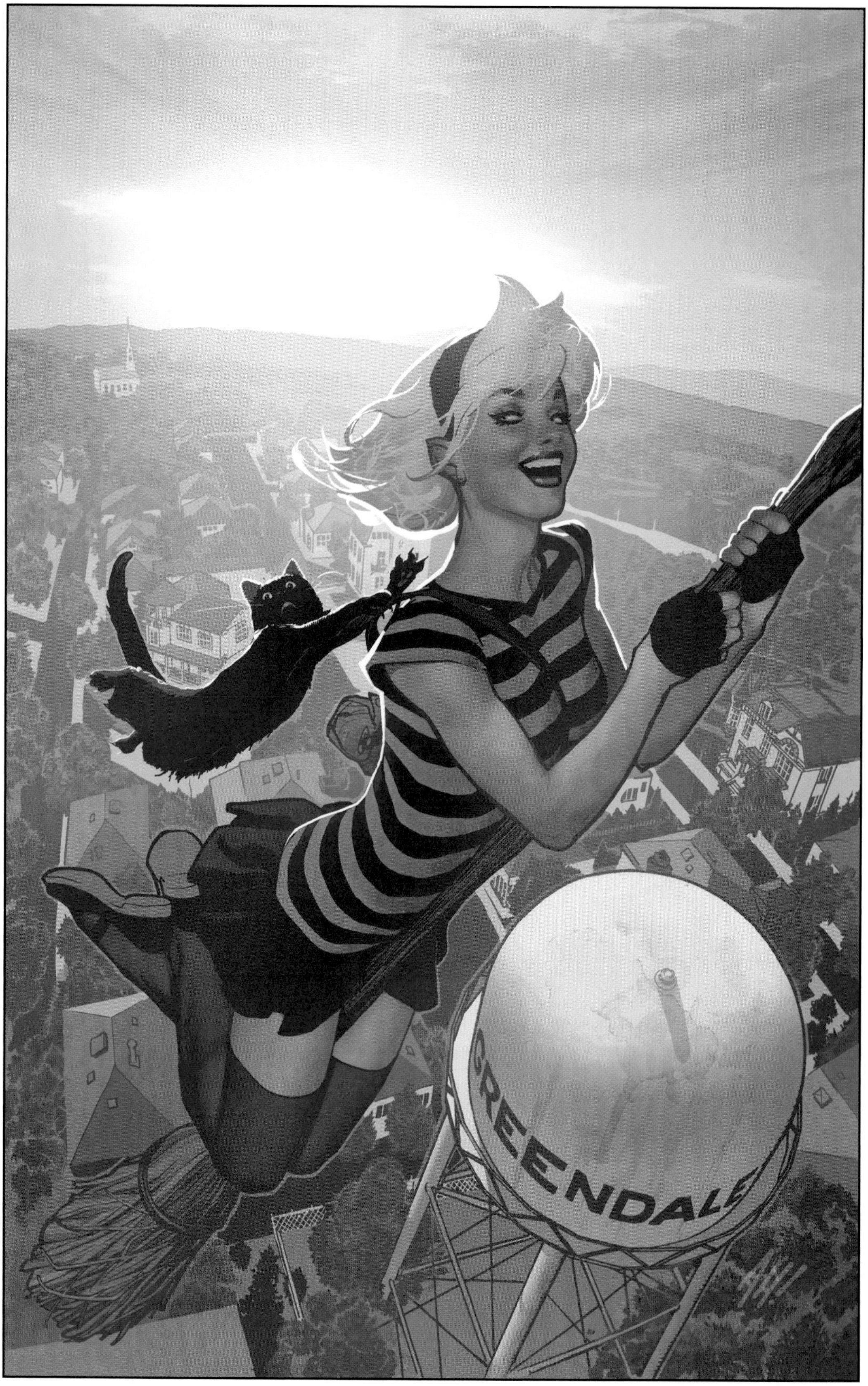
GREENDALE

ADAM HUGHES Previously unprinted *Sabrina The Teenage Witch* cover

Jughead

STORY BY:
RYAN NORTH

ART BY:
DEREK CHARM

LETTERING BY:
JACK MORELLI

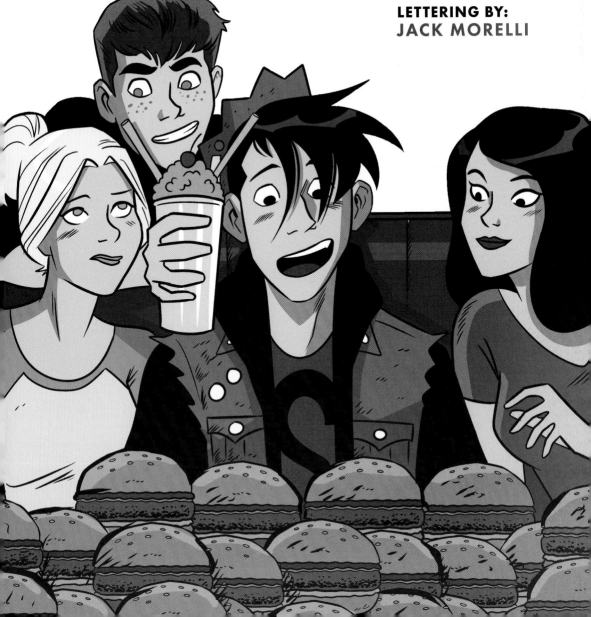

ISSUE TWELVE

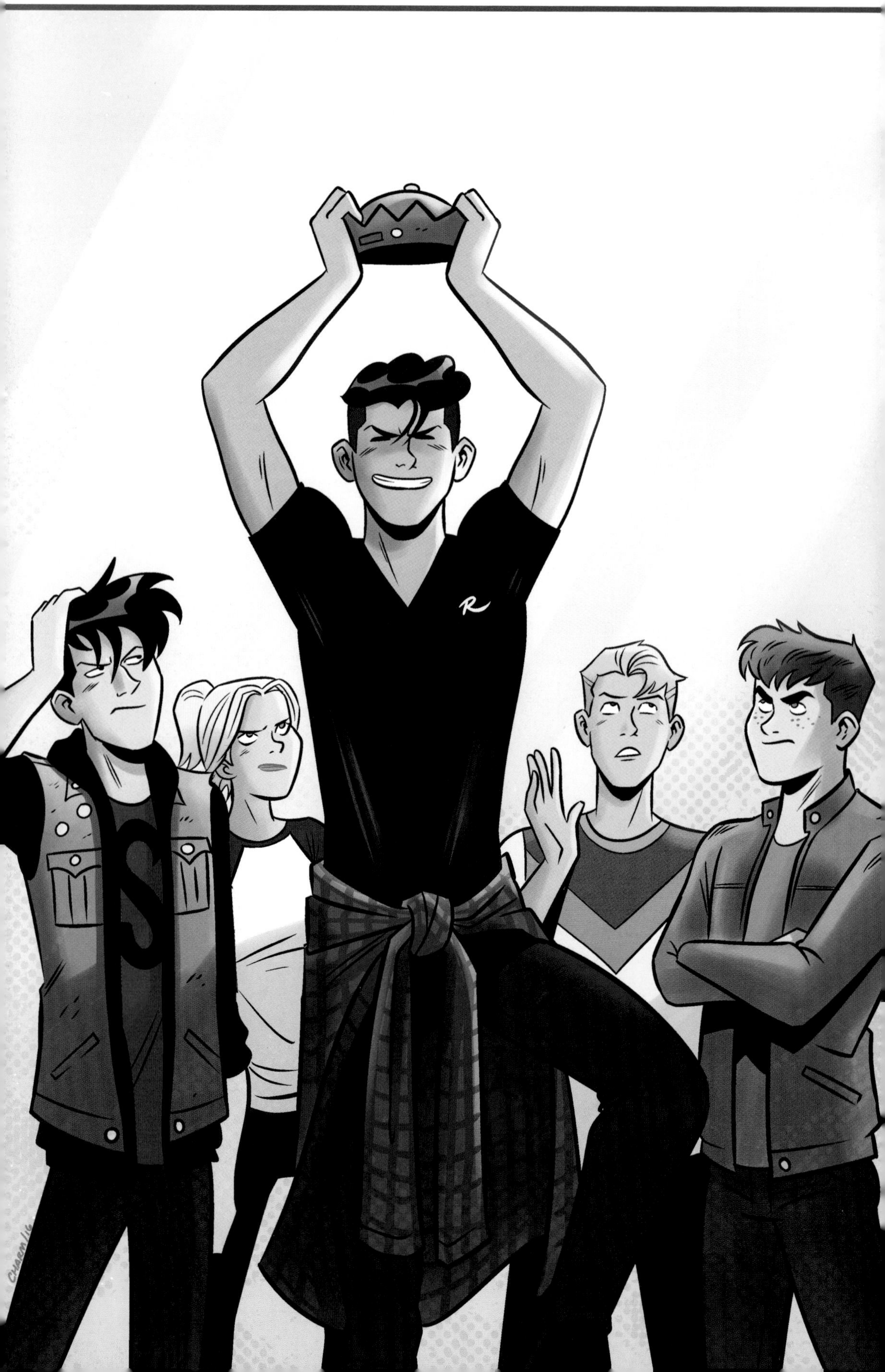

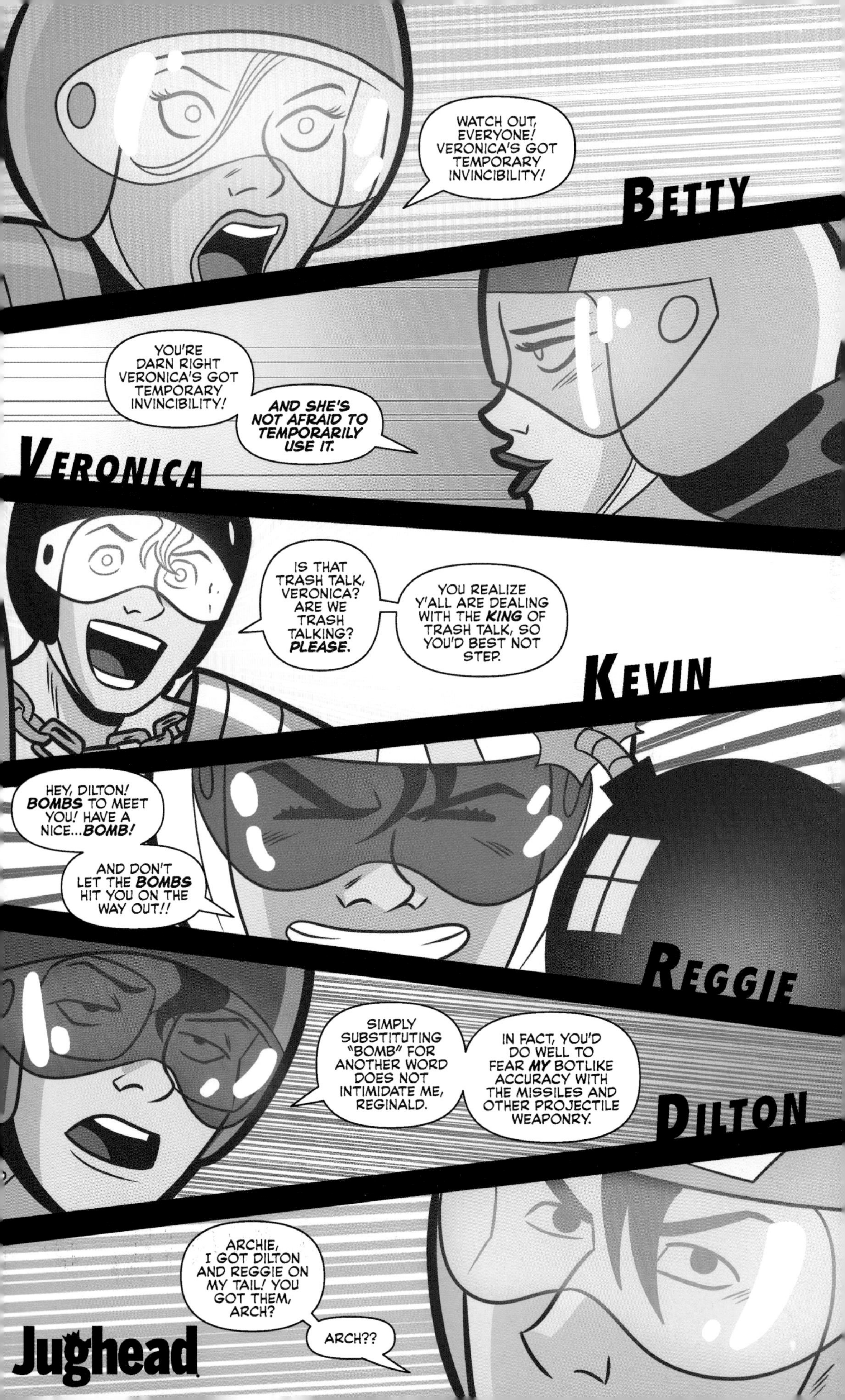

WATCH OUT, EVERYONE! VERONICA'S GOT TEMPORARY INVINCIBILITY!
BETTY
YOU'RE DARN RIGHT VERONICA'S GOT TEMPORARY INVINCIBILITY!
AND SHE'S NOT AFRAID TO TEMPORARILY USE IT.
VERONICA
IS THAT TRASH TALK, VERONICA? ARE WE TRASH TALKING? *PLEASE.*
YOU REALIZE Y'ALL ARE DEALING WITH THE *KING* OF TRASH TALK, SO YOU'D BEST NOT STEP.
KEVIN
HEY, DILTON! *BOMBS* TO MEET YOU! HAVE A NICE...*BOMB!*
AND DON'T LET THE *BOMBS* HIT YOU ON THE WAY OUT!!
REGGIE
SIMPLY SUBSTITUTING "BOMB" FOR ANOTHER WORD DOES NOT INTIMIDATE ME, REGINALD.
IN FACT, YOU'D DO WELL TO FEAR *MY* BOTLIKE ACCURACY WITH THE MISSILES AND OTHER PROJECTILE WEAPONRY.
DILTON
ARCHIE, I GOT DILTON AND REGGIE ON MY TAIL! YOU GOT THEM, ARCH?
ARCH??
Jughead

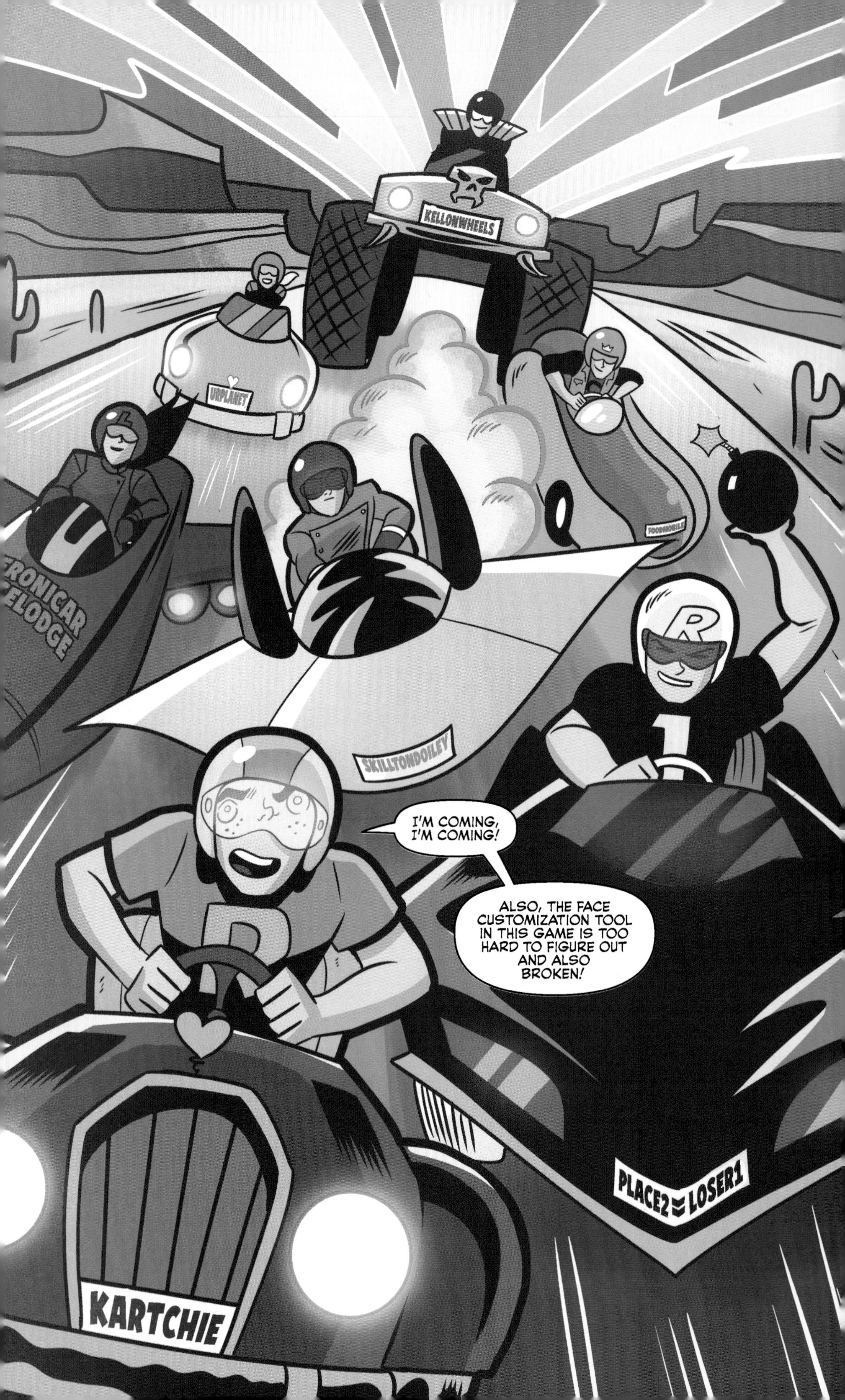
KELLONWHEELS
URPLANET
FOODMOBILE
RONICAR
ELODGE
SKILLTONDOILEY
I'M COMING, I'M COMING!
ALSO, THE FACE CUSTOMIZATION TOOL IN THIS GAME IS TOO HARD TO FIGURE OUT AND ALSO BROKEN!
PLACE2 LOSER1
KARTCHIE

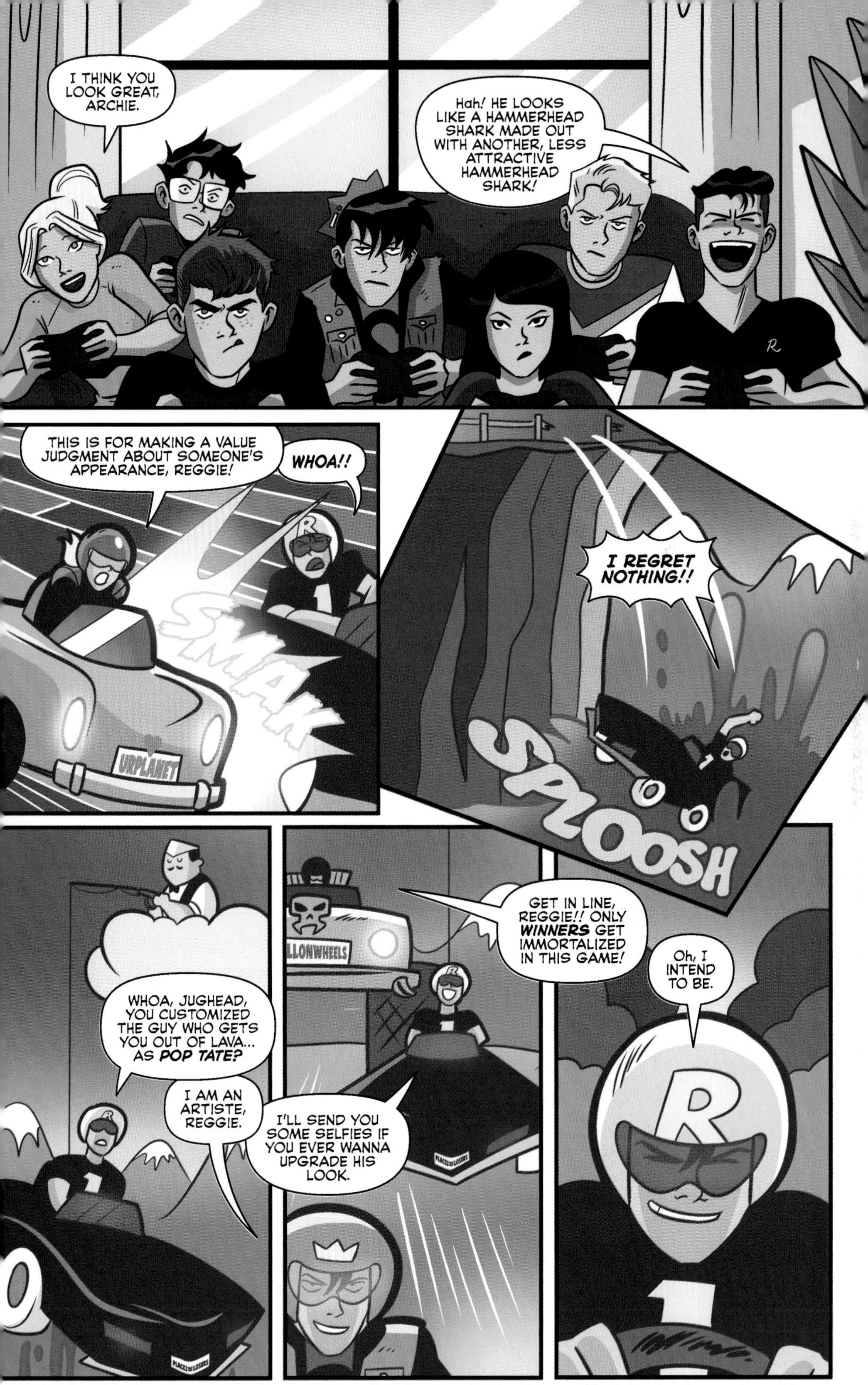
I THINK YOU LOOK GREAT, ARCHIE.
Hah! HE LOOKS LIKE A HAMMERHEAD SHARK MADE OUT WITH ANOTHER, LESS ATTRACTIVE HAMMERHEAD SHARK!
THIS IS FOR MAKING A VALUE JUDGMENT ABOUT SOMEONE'S APPEARANCE, REGGIE!
WHOA!!
SMAK
URPLANET
I REGRET NOTHING!!
SPLOOSH
WHOA, JUGHEAD, YOU CUSTOMIZED THE GUY WHO GETS YOU OUT OF LAVA... AS POP TATE?
I AM AN ARTISTE, REGGIE.
I'LL SEND YOU SOME SELFIES IF YOU EVER WANNA UPGRADE HIS LOOK.
GET IN LINE, REGGIE!! ONLY WINNERS GET IMMORTALIZED IN THIS GAME!
Oh, I INTEND TO BE.

That's right, they were playing a video game those first two pages! Although in real life if Veronica drove a planemobile it would absolutely have the license plate "*VERONICAR FUSELODGE.*" This is canon.

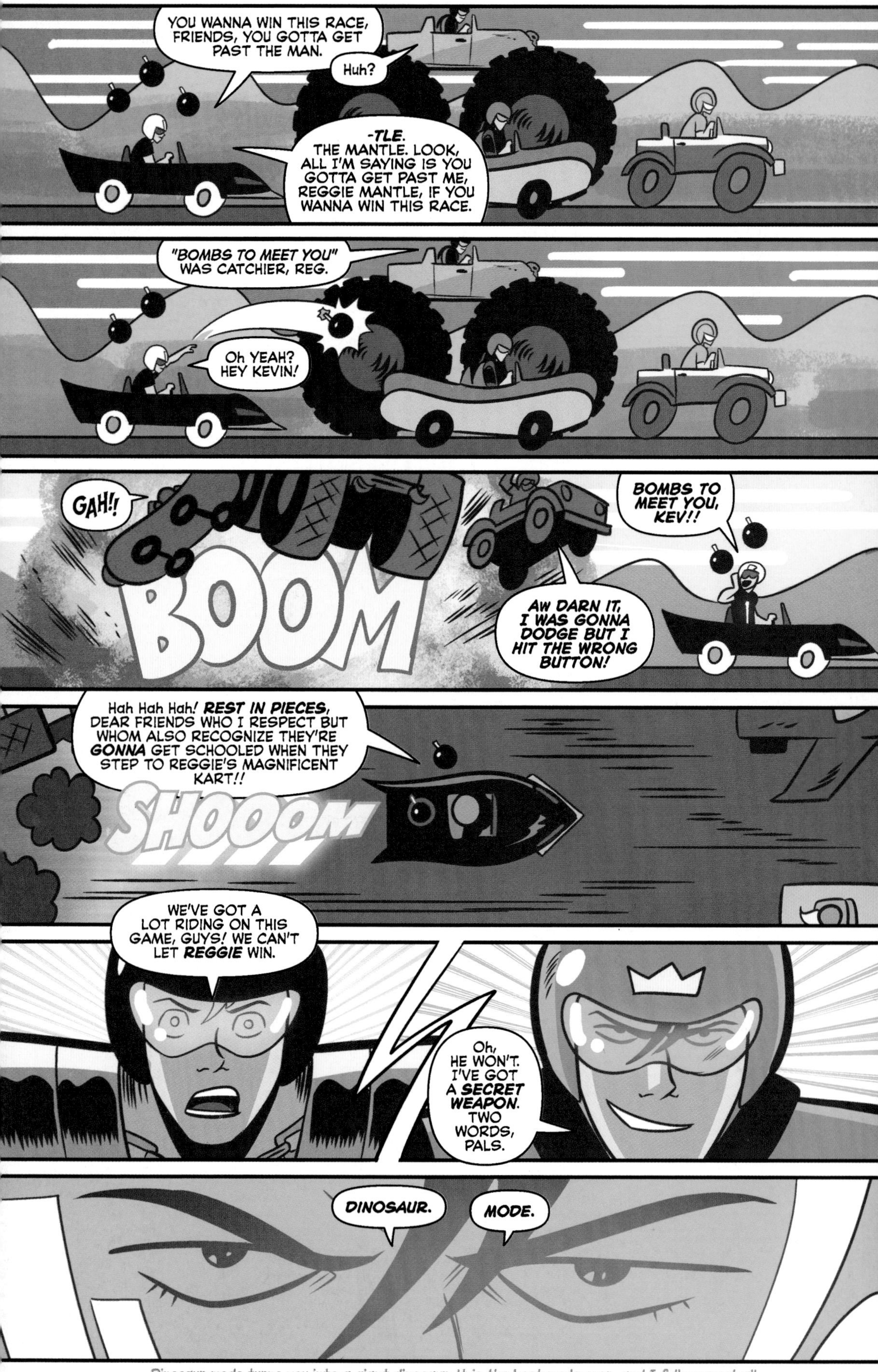
YOU WANNA WIN THIS RACE, FRIENDS, YOU GOTTA GET PAST THE MAN.
Huh?
-TLE. THE MANTLE. LOOK, ALL I'M SAYING IS YOU GOTTA GET PAST ME, REGGIE MANTLE, IF YOU WANNA WIN THIS RACE.
"BOMBS TO MEET YOU" WAS CATCHIER, REG.
Oh YEAH? HEY KEVIN!
GAH!!
BOMBS TO MEET YOU, KEV!!
BOOM
AW DARN IT, I WAS GONNA DODGE BUT I HIT THE WRONG BUTTON!
Hah Hah Hah! REST IN PIECES, DEAR FRIENDS WHO I RESPECT BUT WHOM ALSO RECOGNIZE THEY'RE GONNA GET SCHOOLED WHEN THEY STEP TO REGGIE'S MAGNIFICENT KART!!
SHOOOM
WE'VE GOT A LOT RIDING ON THIS GAME, GUYS! WE CAN'T LET REGGIE WIN.
Oh, HE WON'T. I'VE GOT A SECRET WEAPON. TWO WORDS, PALS.
DINOSAUR.
MODE.

Dinosaur mode turns you into a giant dinosaur. It is the best mode ever, and I fully expect all racing games to steal it in their next releases. Gamers: ***YOU'RE WELCOME.***

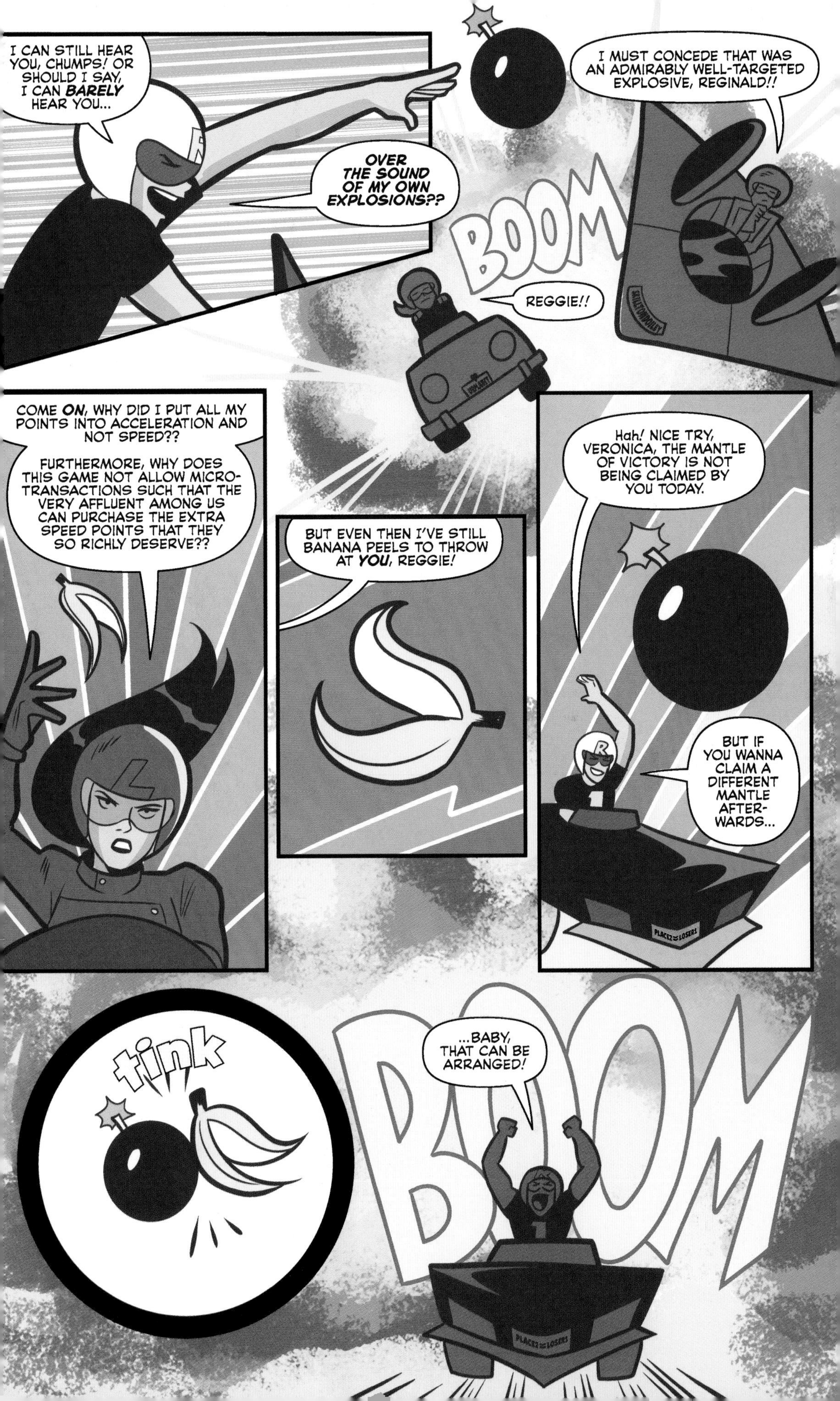

I CAN STILL HEAR YOU, CHUMPS! OR SHOULD I SAY, I CAN *BARELY* HEAR YOU...
OVER THE SOUND OF MY OWN EXPLOSIONS??
I MUST CONCEDE THAT WAS AN ADMIRABLY WELL-TARGETED EXPLOSIVE, REGINALD!!
BOOM
REGGIE!!
COME *ON*, WHY DID I PUT ALL MY POINTS INTO ACCELERATION AND NOT SPEED??
FURTHERMORE, WHY DOES THIS GAME NOT ALLOW MICRO-TRANSACTIONS SUCH THAT THE VERY AFFLUENT AMONG US CAN PURCHASE THE EXTRA SPEED POINTS THAT THEY SO RICHLY DESERVE??
BUT EVEN THEN I'VE STILL BANANA PEELS TO THROW AT *YOU*, REGGIE!
Hah! NICE TRY, VERONICA, THE MANTLE OF VICTORY IS NOT BEING CLAIMED BY YOU TODAY.
BUT IF YOU WANNA CLAIM A DIFFERENT MANTLE AFTER-WARDS...
tink
BOOM
...BABY, THAT CAN BE ARRANGED!

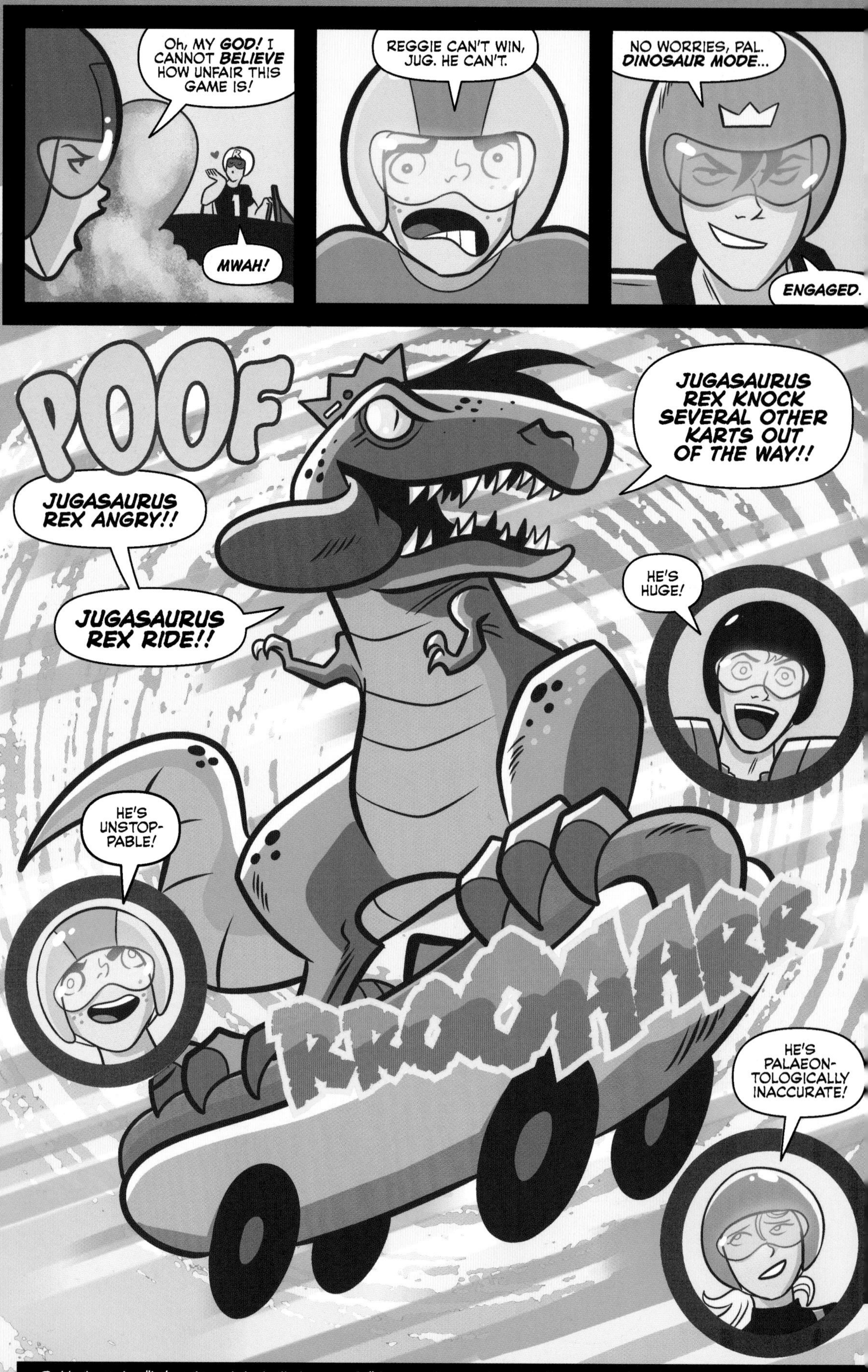
Oh, MY GOD! I CANNOT BELIEVE HOW UNFAIR THIS GAME IS!
MWAH!
REGGIE CAN'T WIN, JUG. HE CAN'T.
NO WORRIES, PAL. DINOSAUR MODE...
ENGAGED.
POOF
JUGASAURUS REX KNOCK SEVERAL OTHER KARTS OUT OF THE WAY!!
JUGASAURUS REX ANGRY!!
JUGASAURUS REX RIDE!!
HE'S HUGE!
HE'S UNSTOP-PABLE!
RROOAARR
HE'S PALAEON-TOLOGICALLY INACCURATE!

Betty is saying "he's palaeontologically inaccurate" because I care about all the paleontologists out there who both like reading comics about a hungry teen **AND** like not being enraged at unexamined inaccuracy in dinosauric representation. Got your back, friends!

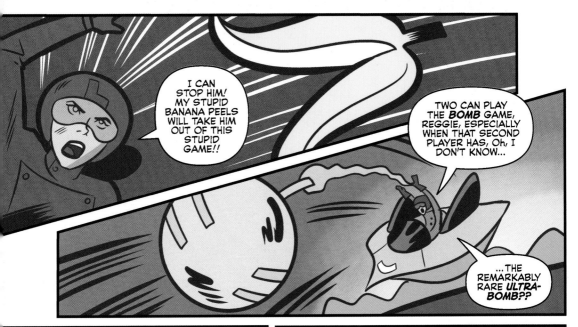

I CAN STOP HIM! MY STUPID BANANA PEELS WILL TAKE HIM OUT OF THIS STUPID GAME!!

TWO CAN PLAY THE *BOMB* GAME, REGGIE, ESPECIALLY WHEN THAT SECOND PLAYER HAS, Oh, I DON'T KNOW...

...THE REMARKABLY RARE *ULTRA-BOMB??*

PLOP

NO NO NO NO NO NO NO!

SCREEEE

NOOOOO!!

DARN IT DARN IT DARN IT!!

JUGASAURUS TAKE FIRST PLACE!! JUGASAURUS HAPPY, WITH ONLY BLOT ON HAPPINESS THAT DINOSAUR MODE MUST EVENTUALLY--

--END!

POOF

AND FRIENDS, WHILE I MAY BE BACK TO BEING A HUMAN BEING, I ASSURE YOU, MY MONSTROUS *APPETITE* IS STILL--

JUGHEAD, MY BOMB!!

tink

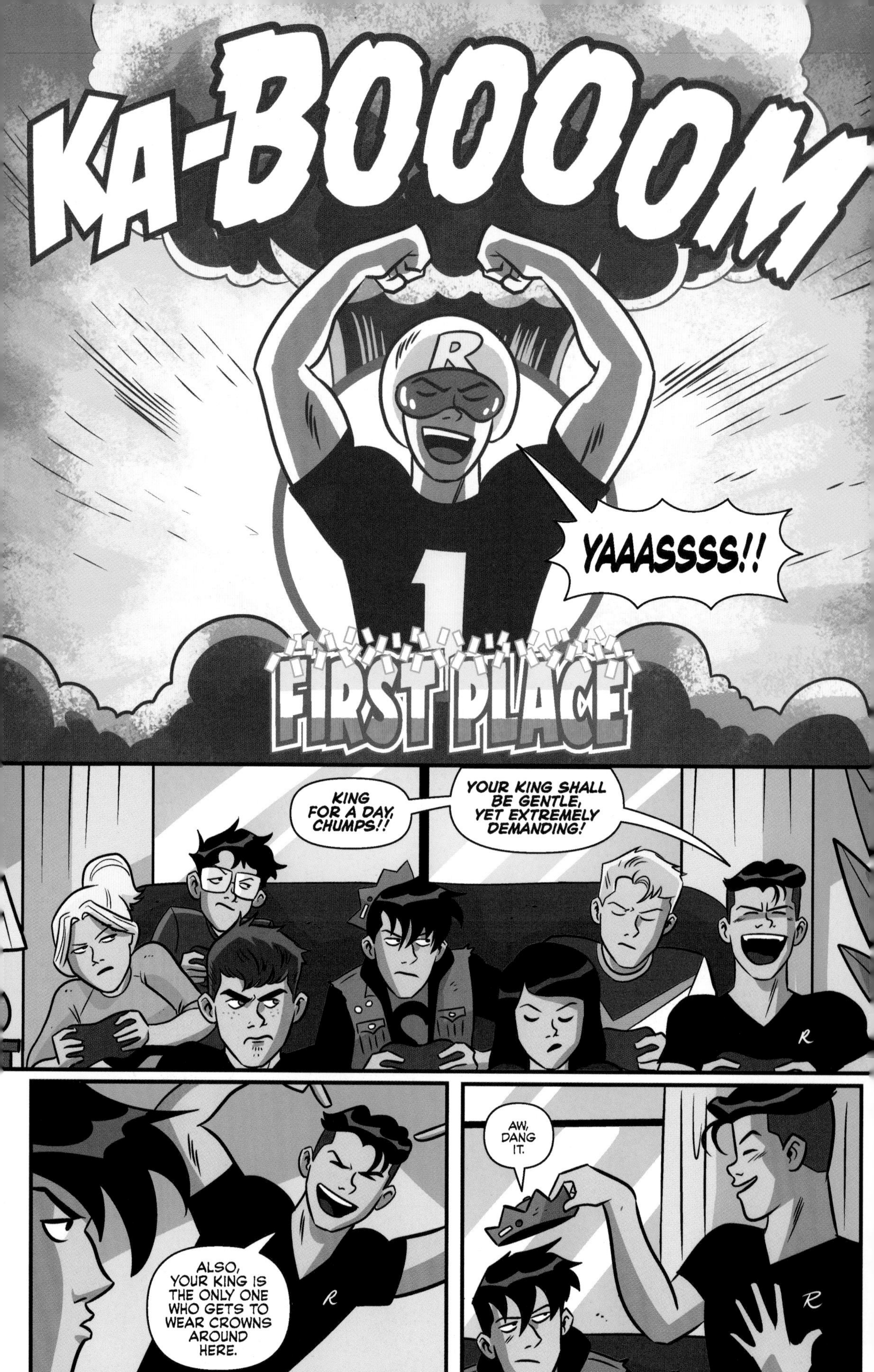
KA-BOOOOM
YAAASSSS!!
FIRST PLACE
KING FOR A DAY, CHUMPS!!
YOUR KING SHALL BE GENTLE, YET EXTREMELY DEMANDING!
ALSO, YOUR KING IS THE ONLY ONE WHO GETS TO WEAR CROWNS AROUND HERE.
AW, DANG IT.

See, this is why you should always be careful about where you toss your implausibly giant bombs. That is the moral of this comic, which technically makes it educational, which means reading this book counts as a school credit. I am almost certain that is the case.

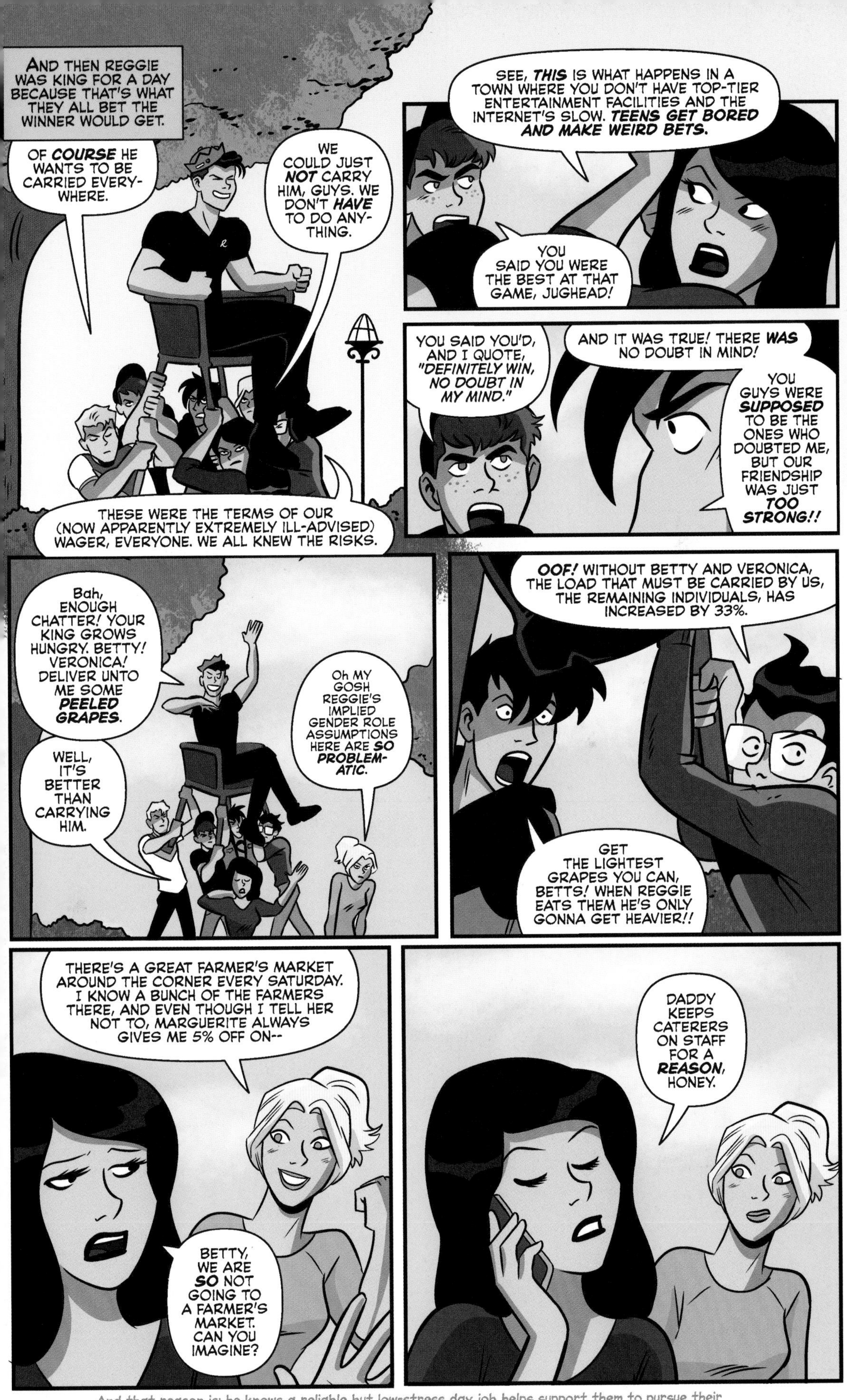
AND THEN REGGIE WAS KING FOR A DAY BECAUSE THAT'S WHAT THEY ALL BET THE WINNER WOULD GET.
OF COURSE HE WANTS TO BE CARRIED EVERY-WHERE.
WE COULD JUST NOT CARRY HIM, GUYS. WE DON'T HAVE TO DO ANY-THING.
THESE WERE THE TERMS OF OUR (NOW APPARENTLY EXTREMELY ILL-ADVISED) WAGER, EVERYONE. WE ALL KNEW THE RISKS.
SEE, THIS IS WHAT HAPPENS IN A TOWN WHERE YOU DON'T HAVE TOP-TIER ENTERTAINMENT FACILITIES AND THE INTERNET'S SLOW. TEENS GET BORED AND MAKE WEIRD BETS.
YOU SAID YOU WERE THE BEST AT THAT GAME, JUGHEAD!
YOU SAID YOU'D, AND I QUOTE, "DEFINITELY WIN, NO DOUBT IN MY MIND."
AND IT WAS TRUE! THERE WAS NO DOUBT IN MIND!
YOU GUYS WERE SUPPOSED TO BE THE ONES WHO DOUBTED ME, BUT OUR FRIENDSHIP WAS JUST TOO STRONG!!
Bah, ENOUGH CHATTER! YOUR KING GROWS HUNGRY. BETTY! VERONICA! DELIVER UNTO ME SOME PEELED GRAPES.
Oh MY GOSH REGGIE'S IMPLIED GENDER ROLE ASSUMPTIONS HERE ARE SO PROBLEM-ATIC.
WELL, IT'S BETTER THAN CARRYING HIM.
OOF! WITHOUT BETTY AND VERONICA, THE LOAD THAT MUST BE CARRIED BY US, THE REMAINING INDIVIDUALS, HAS INCREASED BY 33%.
GET THE LIGHTEST GRAPES YOU CAN, BETTS! WHEN REGGIE EATS THEM HE'S ONLY GONNA GET HEAVIER!!
THERE'S A GREAT FARMER'S MARKET AROUND THE CORNER EVERY SATURDAY. I KNOW A BUNCH OF THE FARMERS THERE, AND EVEN THOUGH I TELL HER NOT TO, MARGUERITE ALWAYS GIVES ME 5% OFF ON--
BETTY, WE ARE SO NOT GOING TO A FARMER'S MARKET. CAN YOU IMAGINE?
DADDY KEEPS CATERERS ON STAFF FOR A REASON, HONEY.

And that reason is: he knows a reliable but low-stress day job helps support them to pursue their artistic careers during their time off. Aw, Mr. Lodge! You're not so bad after all!

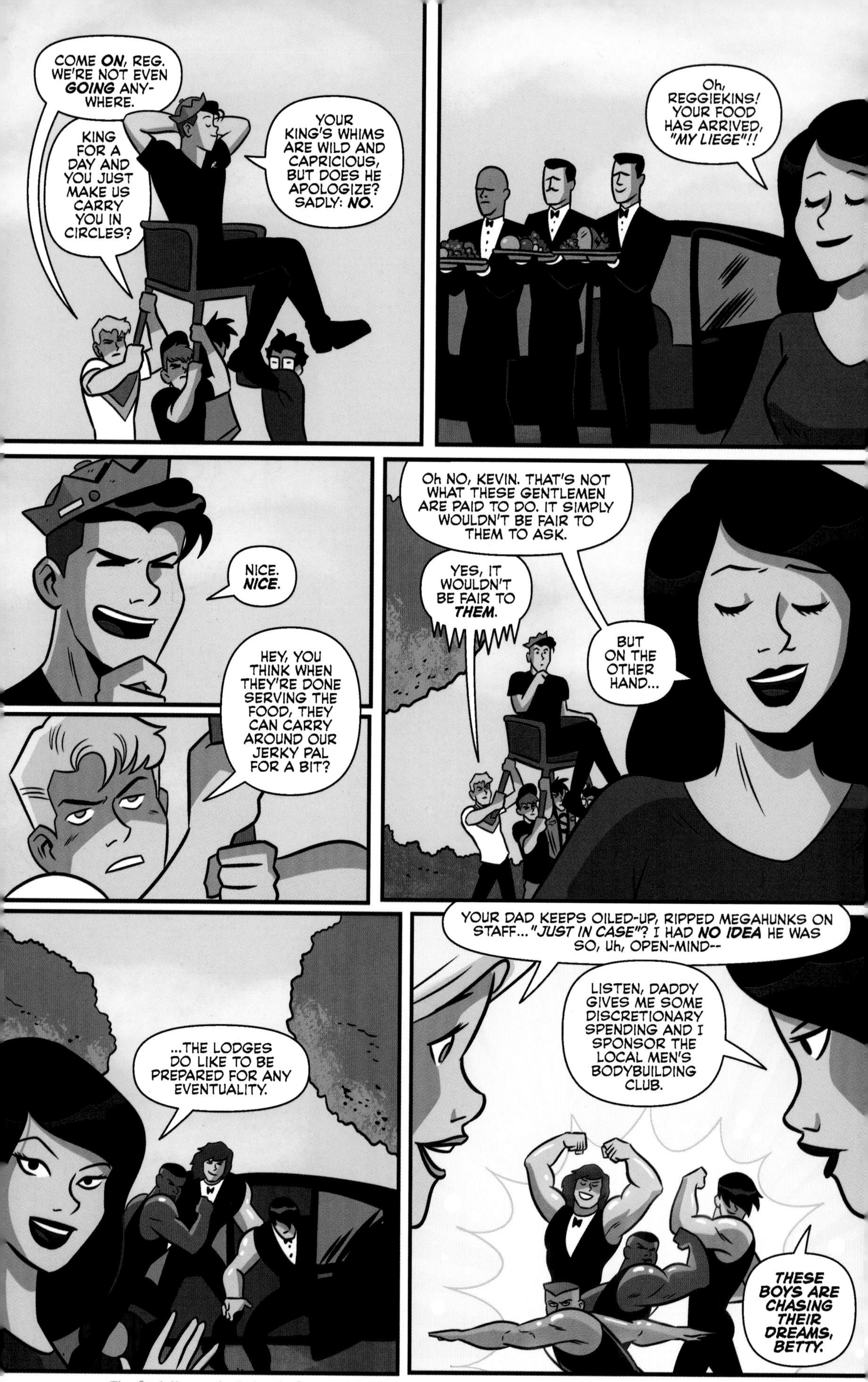
COME *ON*, REG. WE'RE NOT EVEN *GOING* ANYWHERE.
KING FOR A DAY AND YOU JUST MAKE US CARRY YOU IN CIRCLES?
YOUR KING'S WHIMS ARE WILD AND CAPRICIOUS, BUT DOES HE APOLOGIZE? SADLY: *NO*.
Oh, REGGIEKINS! YOUR FOOD HAS ARRIVED, *"MY LIEGE"*!!
NICE. *NICE*.
HEY, YOU THINK WHEN THEY'RE DONE SERVING THE FOOD, THEY CAN CARRY AROUND OUR JERKY PAL FOR A BIT?
Oh NO, KEVIN. THAT'S NOT WHAT THESE GENTLEMEN ARE PAID TO DO. IT SIMPLY WOULDN'T BE FAIR TO THEM TO ASK.
YES, IT WOULDN'T BE FAIR TO *THEM*.
BUT ON THE OTHER HAND...
...THE LODGES DO LIKE TO BE PREPARED FOR ANY EVENTUALITY.
YOUR DAD KEEPS OILED-UP, RIPPED MEGAHUNKS ON STAFF... *"JUST IN CASE"*? I HAD *NO IDEA* HE WAS SO, Uh, OPEN-MIND--
LISTEN, DADDY GIVES ME SOME DISCRETIONARY SPENDING AND I SPONSOR THE LOCAL MEN'S BODYBUILDING CLUB.
THESE BOYS ARE CHASING THEIR DREAMS, BETTY.

The fact they got oiled up before arriving here was a surprise though. They're very complicated hunks with rich inner lives, and it is my privilege to sponsor them.

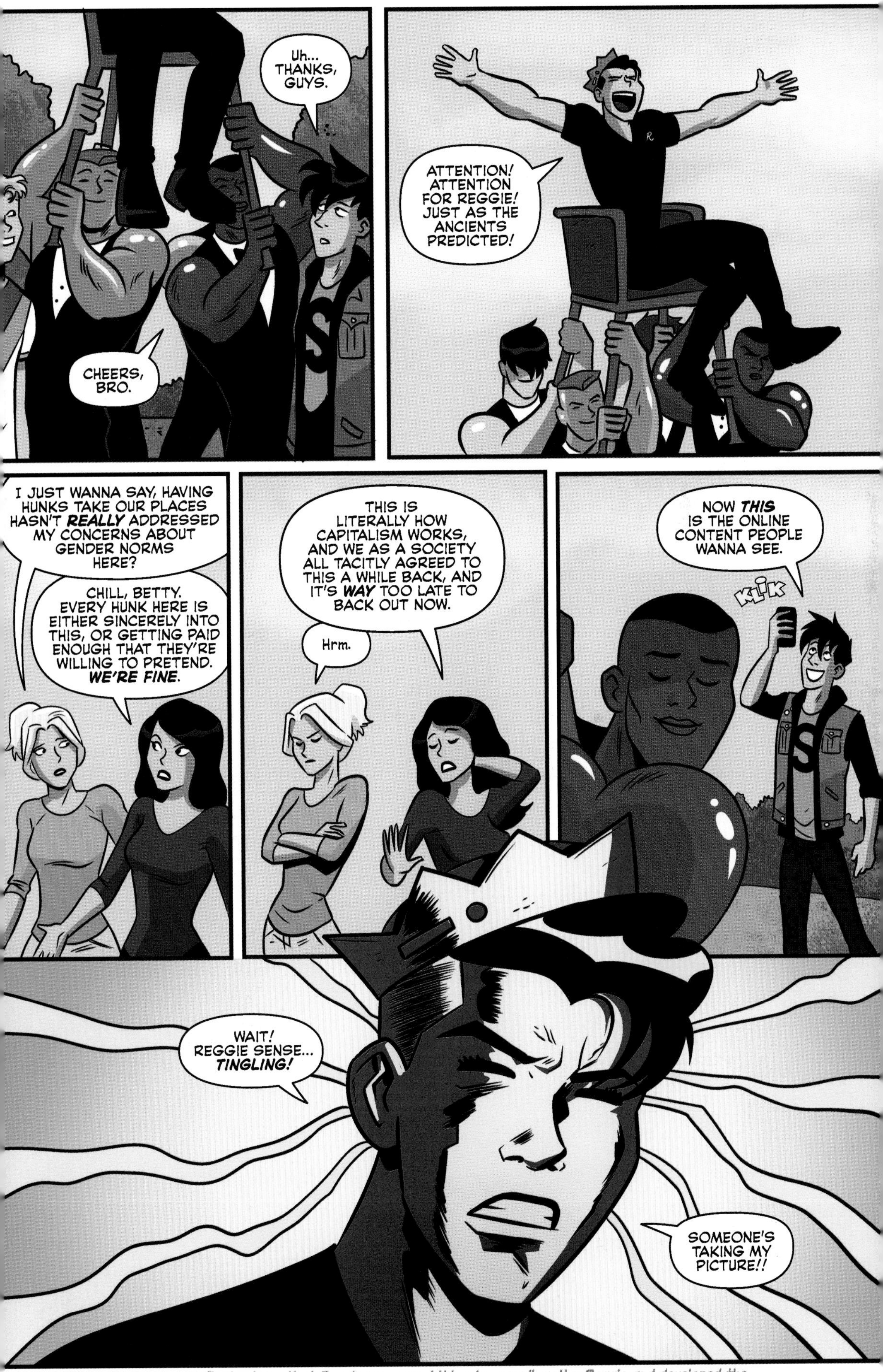
Uh... THANKS, GUYS.
CHEERS, BRO.
ATTENTION! ATTENTION FOR REGGIE! JUST AS THE ANCIENTS PREDICTED!
I JUST WANNA SAY, HAVING HUNKS TAKE OUR PLACES HASN'T REALLY ADDRESSED MY CONCERNS ABOUT GENDER NORMS HERE?
CHILL, BETTY. EVERY HUNK HERE IS EITHER SINCERELY INTO THIS, OR GETTING PAID ENOUGH THAT THEY'RE WILLING TO PRETEND. WE'RE FINE.
THIS IS LITERALLY HOW CAPITALISM WORKS, AND WE AS A SOCIETY ALL TACITLY AGREED TO THIS A WHILE BACK, AND IT'S WAY TOO LATE TO BACK OUT NOW.
Hrm.
NOW THIS IS THE ONLINE CONTENT PEOPLE WANNA SEE.
KLIK
WAIT! REGGIE SENSE... TINGLING!
SOMEONE'S TAKING MY PICTURE!!

Are we confirming here that Reggie was once bitten by a radioactive Reggie and developed the proportional speed and strength of a Reggie?? The answer: **POSSIBLY?**

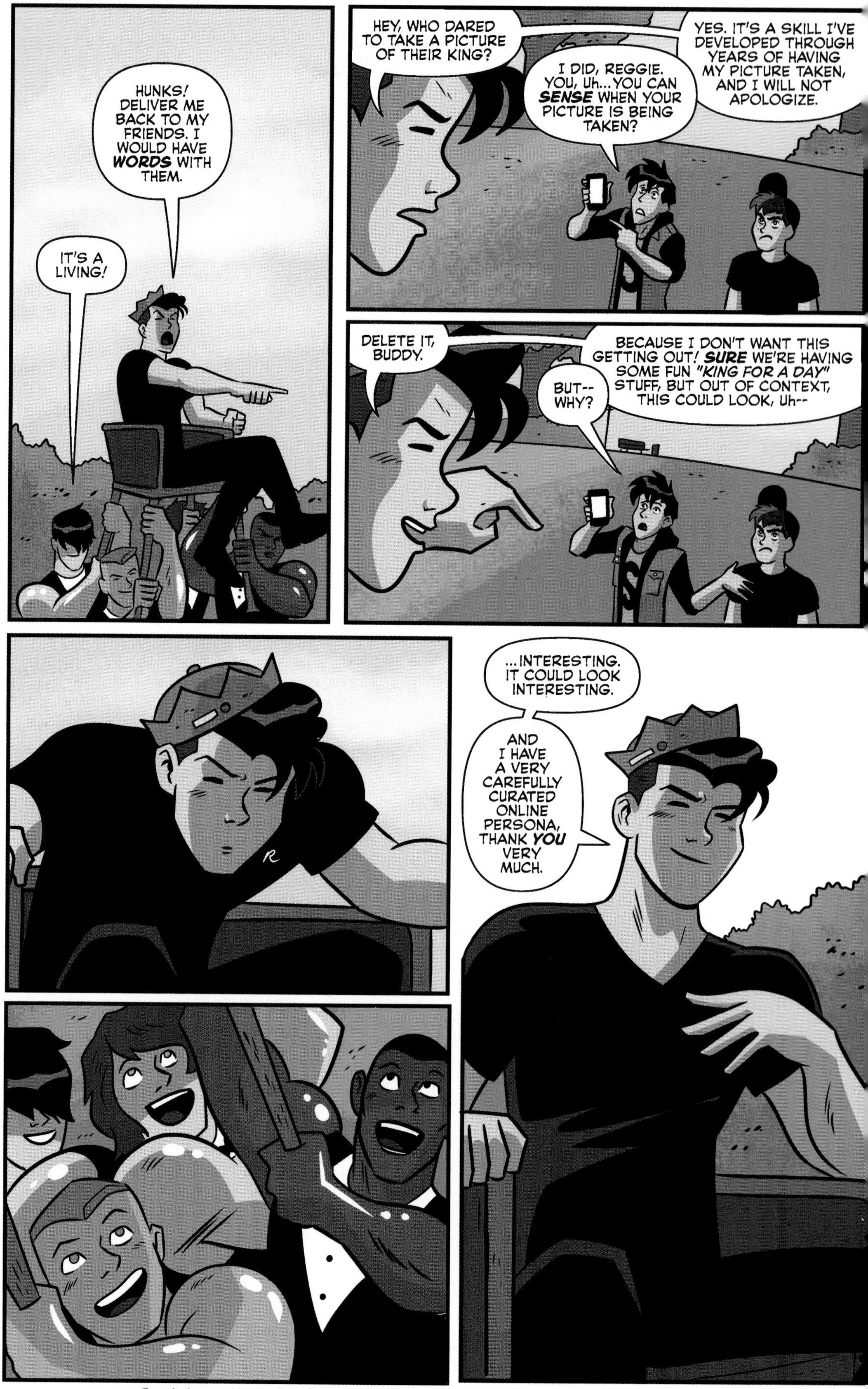
HUNKS! DELIVER ME BACK TO MY FRIENDS. I WOULD HAVE WORDS WITH THEM.
IT'S A LIVING!
HEY, WHO DARED TO TAKE A PICTURE OF THEIR KING?
I DID, REGGIE. YOU, Uh...YOU CAN SENSE WHEN YOUR PICTURE IS BEING TAKEN?
YES. IT'S A SKILL I'VE DEVELOPED THROUGH YEARS OF HAVING MY PICTURE TAKEN, AND I WILL NOT APOLOGIZE.
DELETE IT, BUDDY.
BUT-- WHY?
BECAUSE I DON'T WANT THIS GETTING OUT! SURE WE'RE HAVING SOME FUN "KING FOR A DAY" STUFF, BUT OUT OF CONTEXT, THIS COULD LOOK, Uh--
...INTERESTING. IT COULD LOOK INTERESTING.
AND I HAVE A VERY CAREFULLY CURATED ONLINE PERSONA, THANK YOU VERY MUCH.

Reggie knows his best selfie angles and he's not here to let *AMATEUR* Reggie photographers get them all wrong, thank you very much.

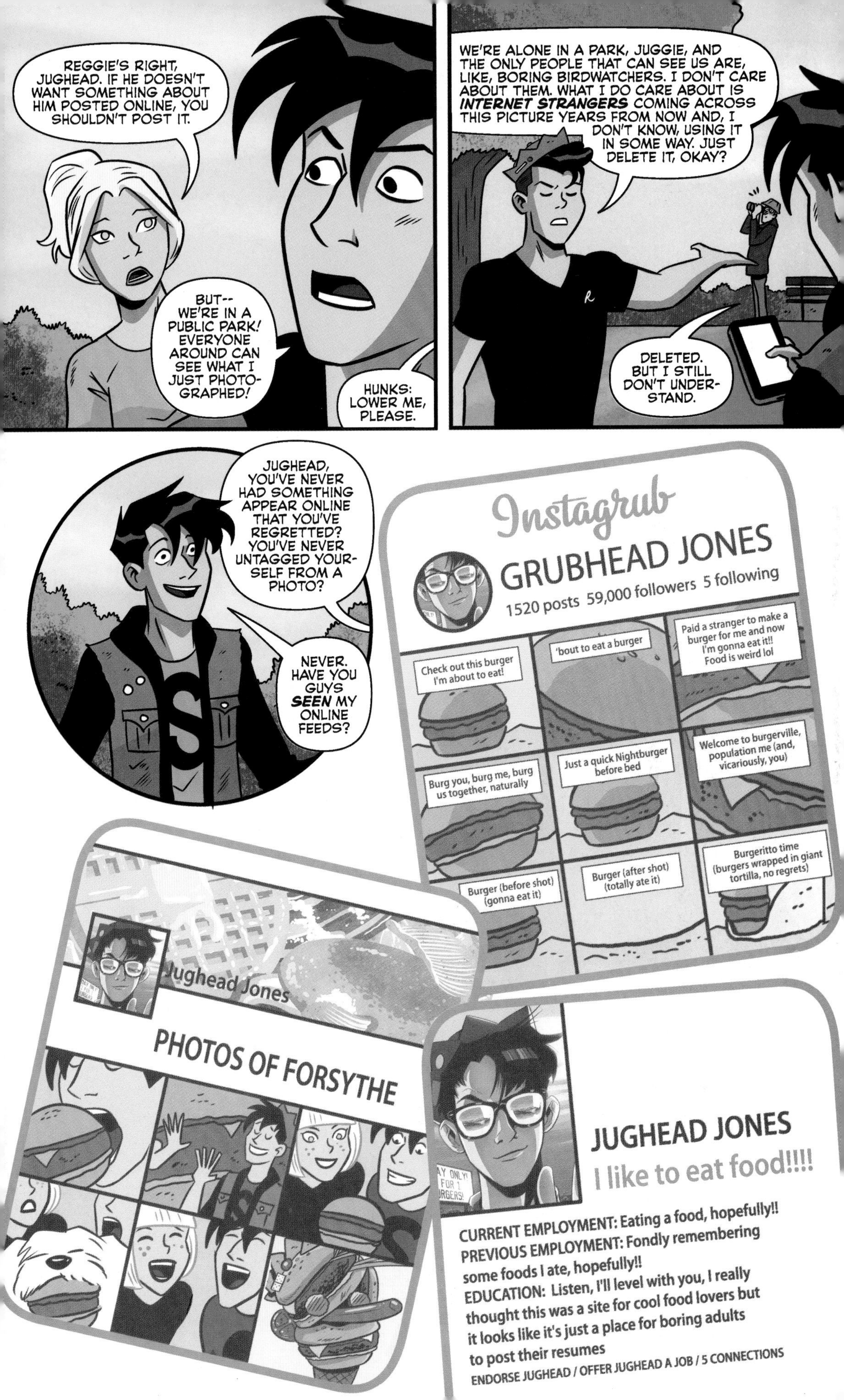

REGGIE'S RIGHT, JUGHEAD. IF HE DOESN'T WANT SOMETHING ABOUT HIM POSTED ONLINE, YOU SHOULDN'T POST IT.
BUT-- WE'RE IN A PUBLIC PARK! EVERYONE AROUND CAN SEE WHAT I JUST PHOTOGRAPHED!
HUNKS: LOWER ME, PLEASE.
WE'RE ALONE IN A PARK, JUGGIE, AND THE ONLY PEOPLE THAT CAN SEE US ARE, LIKE, BORING BIRDWATCHERS. I DON'T CARE ABOUT THEM. WHAT I DO CARE ABOUT IS ***INTERNET STRANGERS*** COMING ACROSS THIS PICTURE YEARS FROM NOW AND, I DON'T KNOW, USING IT IN SOME WAY. JUST DELETE IT, OKAY?
DELETED. BUT I STILL DON'T UNDERSTAND.
JUGHEAD, YOU'VE NEVER HAD SOMETHING APPEAR ONLINE THAT YOU'VE REGRETTED? YOU'VE NEVER UNTAGGED YOURSELF FROM A PHOTO?
NEVER. HAVE YOU GUYS ***SEEN*** MY ONLINE FEEDS?
Instagrub
GRUBHEAD JONES
1520 posts 59,000 followers 5 following
Check out this burger I'm about to eat!
'bout to eat a burger
Paid a stranger to make a burger for me and now I'm gonna eat it!! Food is weird lol
Burg you, burg me, burg us together, naturally
Just a quick Nightburger before bed
Welcome to burgerville, population me (and, vicariously, you)
Burger (before shot) (gonna eat it)
Burger (after shot) (totally ate it)
Burgeritto time (burgers wrapped in giant tortilla, no regrets)
Jughead Jones
PHOTOS OF FORSYTHE
JUGHEAD JONES
I like to eat food!!!!
CURRENT EMPLOYMENT: Eating a food, hopefully!!
PREVIOUS EMPLOYMENT: Fondly remembering some foods I ate, hopefully!!
EDUCATION: Listen, I'll level with you, I really thought this was a site for cool food lovers but it looks like it's just a place for boring adults to post their resumes
ENDORSE JUGHEAD / OFFER JUGHEAD A JOB / 5 CONNECTIONS

AFTER THE 100th BURGER CLOSEUP I MAY HAVE BEEN FORCED TO MUTE YOU, JUGGIE.

LOOK, REGGIE, I'M SORRY. THE PICTURE'S DELETED AND IT WON'T HAPPEN AGAIN.

THANKS, BUD.

SO LISTEN, REGGIE, WE *COULD* SPEND THE REST OF THE DAY WATCHING YOU GET CARRIED AROUND AND FED GRAPES BY HUNKS...

PERFECT, THAT SOUNDS GREAT, LET'S DO THAT RIGHT AWAY--

OR YOU COULD RISK IT ALL AND BATTLE ME ONCE MORE IN A VIRTUAL WORLD INVOLVING BOTH *RACING* AND *KARTS??*

I MEAN...

...I ALREADY WON, SO I THINK I'M GOOD??

Oh SURE, YOU BEAT US. BUT WE WERE LARGELY WORKING INDIVIDUALLY. WE WEREN'T WORKING AS A *TEAM*, ALL TRYING TO DEFEAT YOU.

COME ON, THAT'S IMPOSSIBLE. SIX AGAINST ONE, I'D HAVE TO BE--

--*THE BEST PLAYER OF ALL TIME TO WIN??*

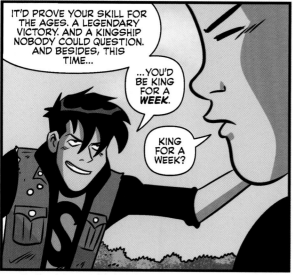

IT'D PROVE YOUR SKILL FOR THE AGES. A LEGENDARY VICTORY. AND A KINGSHIP NOBODY COULD QUESTION. AND BESIDES, THIS TIME...

...YOU'D BE KING FOR A *WEEK.*

KING FOR A WEEK?

WAIT, NO, JUGHEAD! WE DIDN'T AGREE TO THIS!

THIS COULD INTERFERE WITH MY CHESS CLUB MEETINGS, MY AI CLUB MEETINGS, NOT TO MENTION MY AI IN CHESS CLUB MEETINGS!

NO *WAY* AM I RENTING THOSE MEN FOR A *WEEK,* FORSYTHE.

EVEN I HAVE A HUNK BUDGET, EXTRAVAGANT THOUGH IT MAY BE.

I will not have my hunk budget eating into my beefcake and studmuffin and dreamboat budgets, Jughead. *I WILL NOT.*

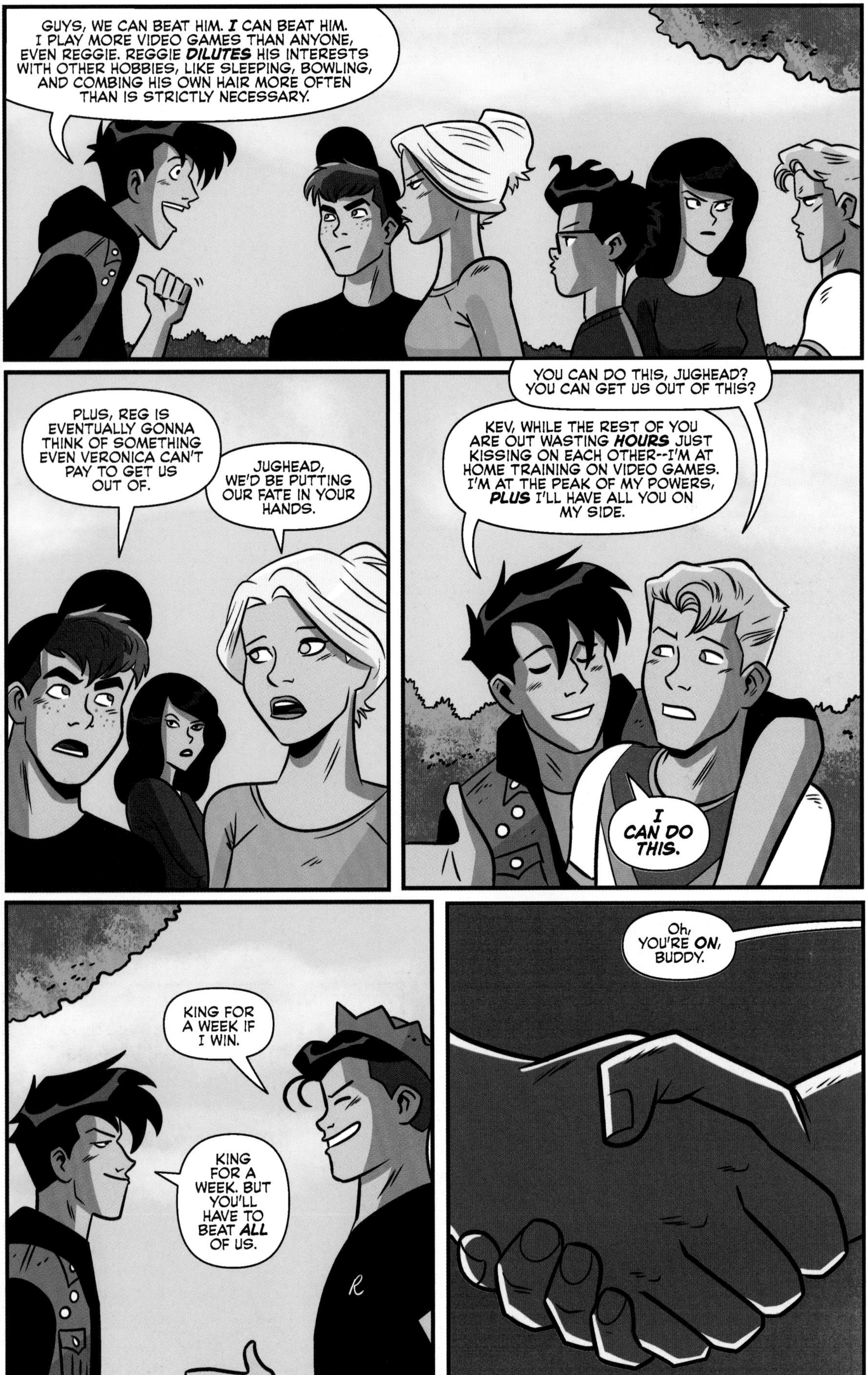
GUYS, WE CAN BEAT HIM. *I* CAN BEAT HIM. I PLAY MORE VIDEO GAMES THAN ANYONE, EVEN REGGIE. REGGIE ***DILUTES*** HIS INTERESTS WITH OTHER HOBBIES, LIKE SLEEPING, BOWLING, AND COMBING HIS OWN HAIR MORE OFTEN THAN IS STRICTLY NECESSARY.
PLUS, REG IS EVENTUALLY GONNA THINK OF SOMETHING EVEN VERONICA CAN'T PAY TO GET US OUT OF.
JUGHEAD, WE'D BE PUTTING OUR FATE IN YOUR HANDS.
YOU CAN DO THIS, JUGHEAD? YOU CAN GET US OUT OF THIS?
KEV, WHILE THE REST OF YOU ARE OUT WASTING ***HOURS*** JUST KISSING ON EACH OTHER--I'M AT HOME TRAINING ON VIDEO GAMES. I'M AT THE PEAK OF MY POWERS, ***PLUS*** I'LL HAVE ALL YOU ON MY SIDE.
I CAN DO THIS.
KING FOR A WEEK IF I WIN.
KING FOR A WEEK. BUT YOU'LL HAVE TO BEAT ***ALL*** OF US.
Oh, YOU'RE ***ON***, BUDDY.

Jughead assumes everyone who wants to kiss on people does actually spend all their time just kissing on people. Hah! I wish, Jughead! I really sincerely wish, Jughead!!

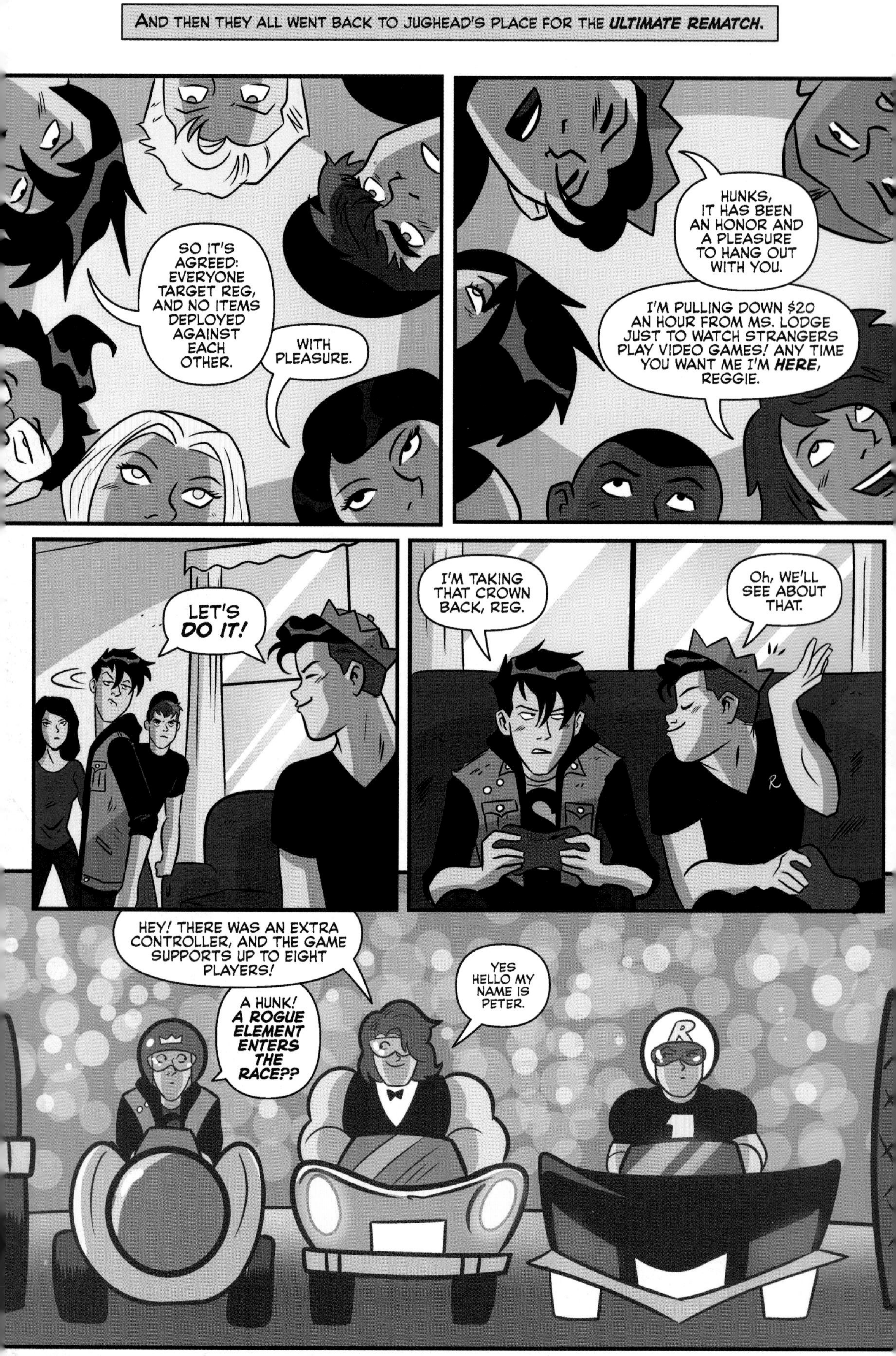
AND THEN THEY ALL WENT BACK TO JUGHEAD'S PLACE FOR THE *ULTIMATE REMATCH.*
SO IT'S AGREED: EVERYONE TARGET REG, AND NO ITEMS DEPLOYED AGAINST EACH OTHER.
WITH PLEASURE.
HUNKS, IT HAS BEEN AN HONOR AND A PLEASURE TO HANG OUT WITH YOU.
I'M PULLING DOWN $20 AN HOUR FROM MS. LODGE JUST TO WATCH STRANGERS PLAY VIDEO GAMES! ANY TIME YOU WANT ME I'M ***HERE,*** REGGIE.
LET'S ***DO IT!***
I'M TAKING THAT CROWN BACK, REG.
Oh, WE'LL SEE ABOUT THAT.
HEY! THERE WAS AN EXTRA CONTROLLER, AND THE GAME SUPPORTS UP TO EIGHT PLAYERS!
A HUNK! ***A ROGUE ELEMENT ENTERS THE RACE??***
YES HELLO MY NAME IS PETER.

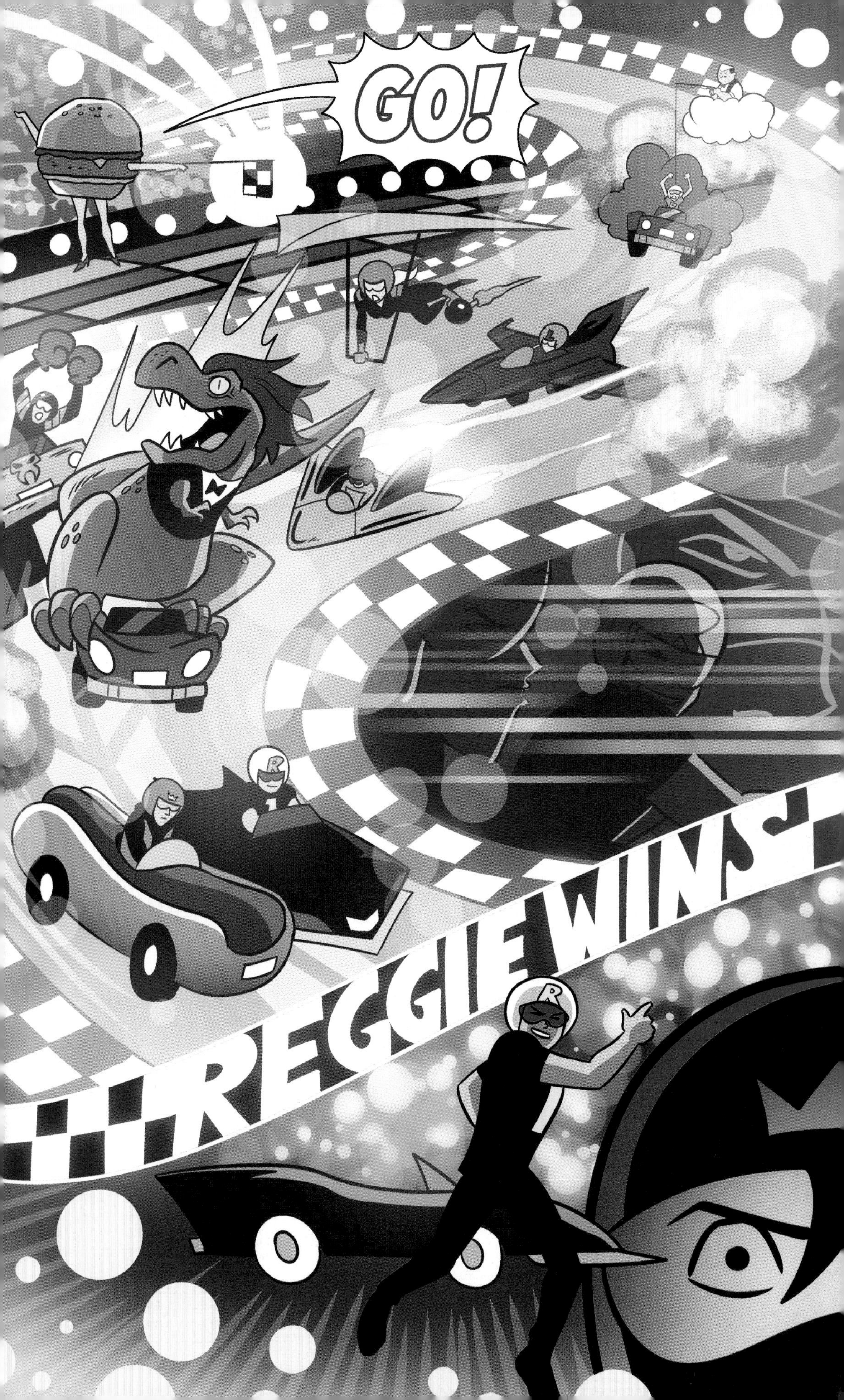
GO!
REGGIE WINS!

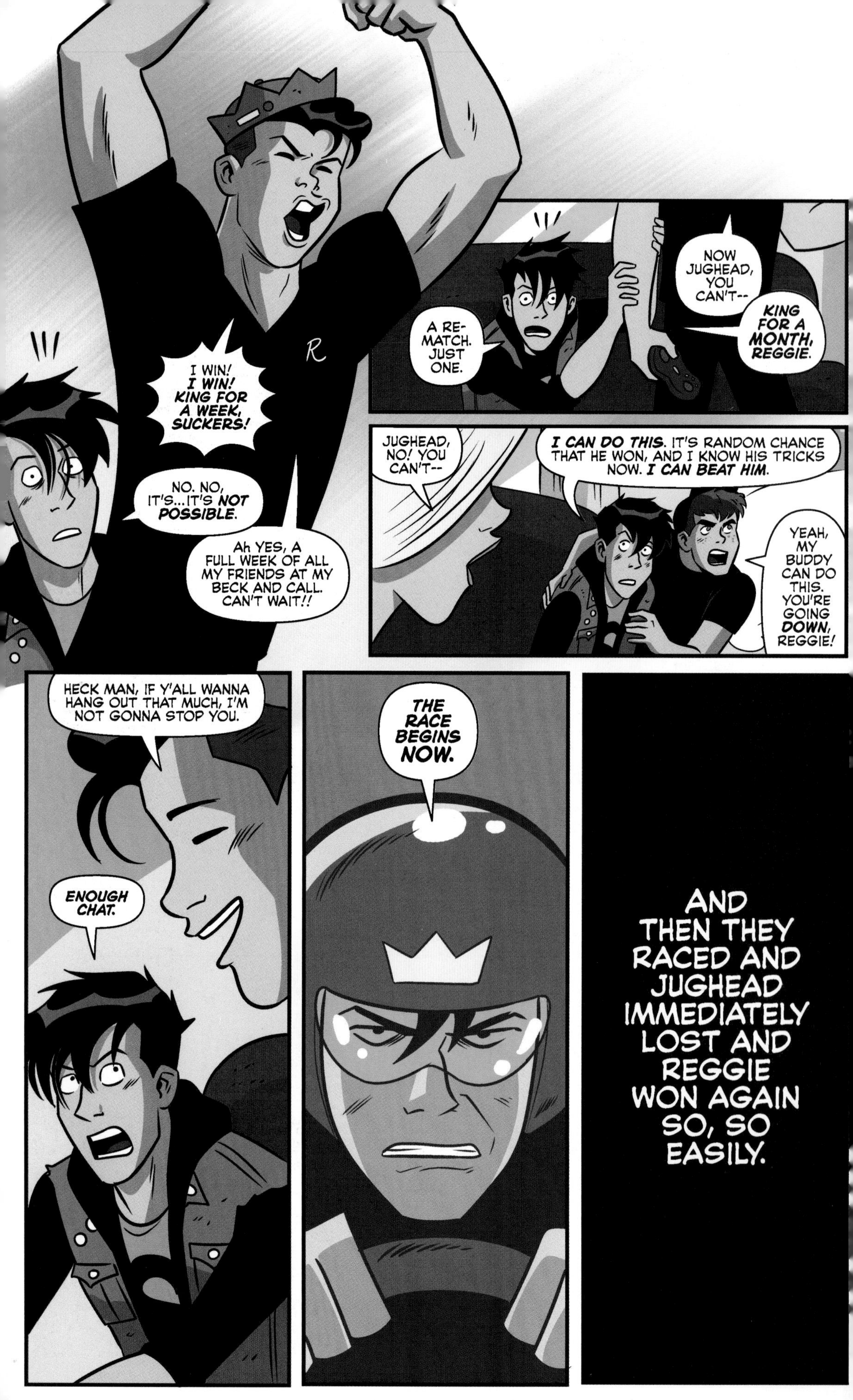
I WIN! I WIN! KING FOR A WEEK, SUCKERS!
NO. NO, IT'S...IT'S NOT POSSIBLE.
Ah YES, A FULL WEEK OF ALL MY FRIENDS AT MY BECK AND CALL. CAN'T WAIT!!
A RE-MATCH. JUST ONE.
NOW JUGHEAD, YOU CAN'T--
KING FOR A MONTH, REGGIE.
JUGHEAD, NO! YOU CAN'T--
I CAN DO THIS. IT'S RANDOM CHANCE THAT HE WON, AND I KNOW HIS TRICKS NOW. I CAN BEAT HIM.
YEAH, MY BUDDY CAN DO THIS. YOU'RE GOING DOWN, REGGIE!
HECK MAN, IF Y'ALL WANNA HANG OUT THAT MUCH, I'M NOT GONNA STOP YOU.
ENOUGH CHAT.
THE RACE BEGINS NOW.
AND THEN THEY RACED AND JUGHEAD IMMEDIATELY LOST AND REGGIE WON AGAIN SO, SO EASILY.

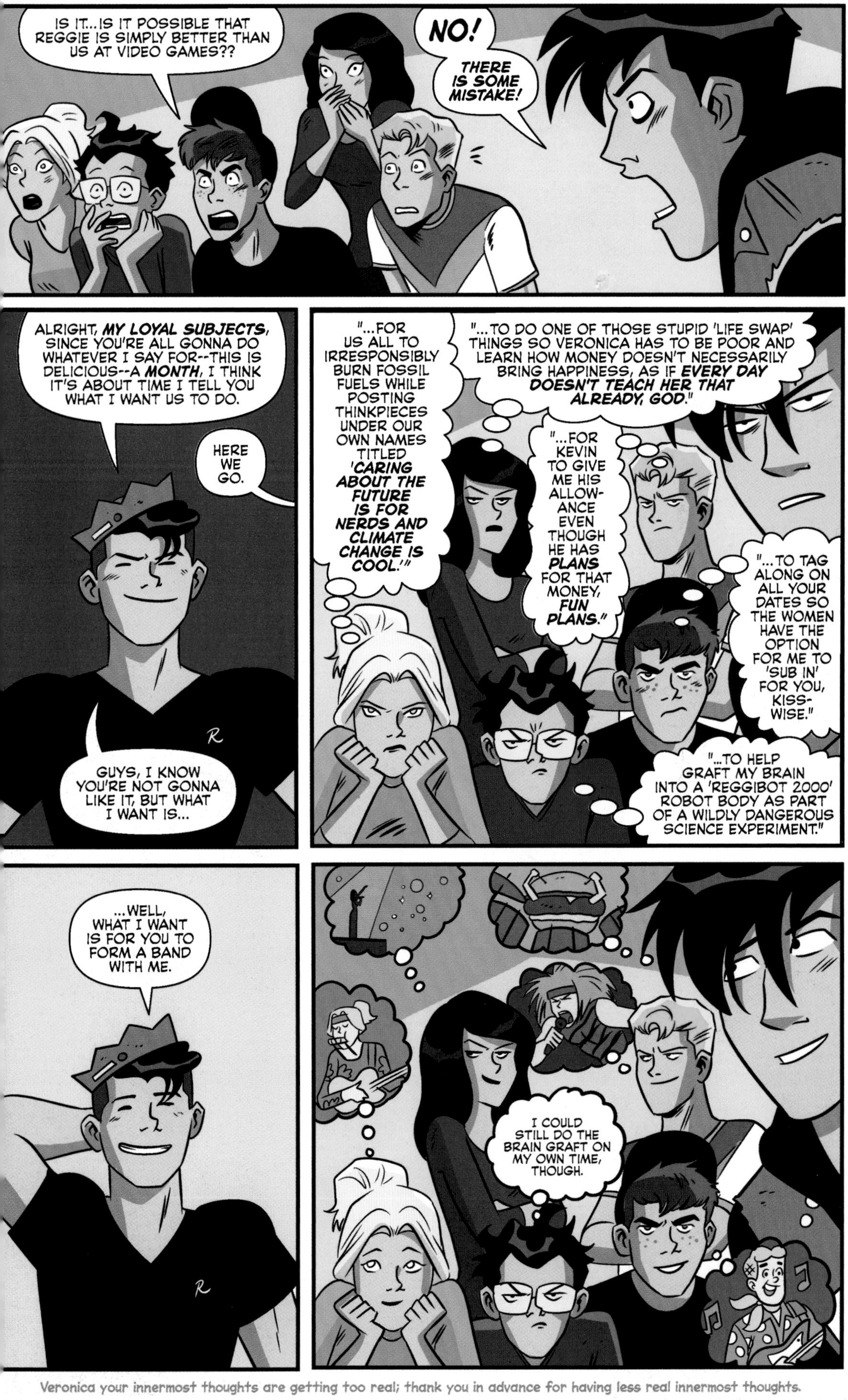
IS IT...IS IT POSSIBLE THAT REGGIE IS SIMPLY BETTER THAN US AT VIDEO GAMES??
NO!
THERE IS SOME MISTAKE!
ALRIGHT, MY LOYAL SUBJECTS, SINCE YOU'RE ALL GONNA DO WHATEVER I SAY FOR--THIS IS DELICIOUS--A MONTH, I THINK IT'S ABOUT TIME I TELL YOU WHAT I WANT US TO DO.
HERE WE GO.
GUYS, I KNOW YOU'RE NOT GONNA LIKE IT, BUT WHAT I WANT IS...
"...FOR US ALL TO IRRESPONSIBLY BURN FOSSIL FUELS WHILE POSTING THINKPIECES UNDER OUR OWN NAMES TITLED 'CARING ABOUT THE FUTURE IS FOR NERDS AND CLIMATE CHANGE IS COOL.'"
"...TO DO ONE OF THOSE STUPID 'LIFE SWAP' THINGS SO VERONICA HAS TO BE POOR AND LEARN HOW MONEY DOESN'T NECESSARILY BRING HAPPINESS, AS IF EVERY DAY DOESN'T TEACH HER THAT ALREADY, GOD."
"...FOR KEVIN TO GIVE ME HIS ALLOWANCE EVEN THOUGH HE HAS PLANS FOR THAT MONEY, FUN PLANS."
"...TO TAG ALONG ON ALL YOUR DATES SO THE WOMEN HAVE THE OPTION FOR ME TO 'SUB IN' FOR YOU, KISS-WISE."
"...TO HELP GRAFT MY BRAIN INTO A 'REGGIBOT 2000' ROBOT BODY AS PART OF A WILDLY DANGEROUS SCIENCE EXPERIMENT."
...WELL, WHAT I WANT IS FOR YOU TO FORM A BAND WITH ME.
I COULD STILL DO THE BRAIN GRAFT ON MY OWN TIME, THOUGH.

Veronica your innermost thoughts are getting too real; thank you in advance for having less real innermost thoughts.

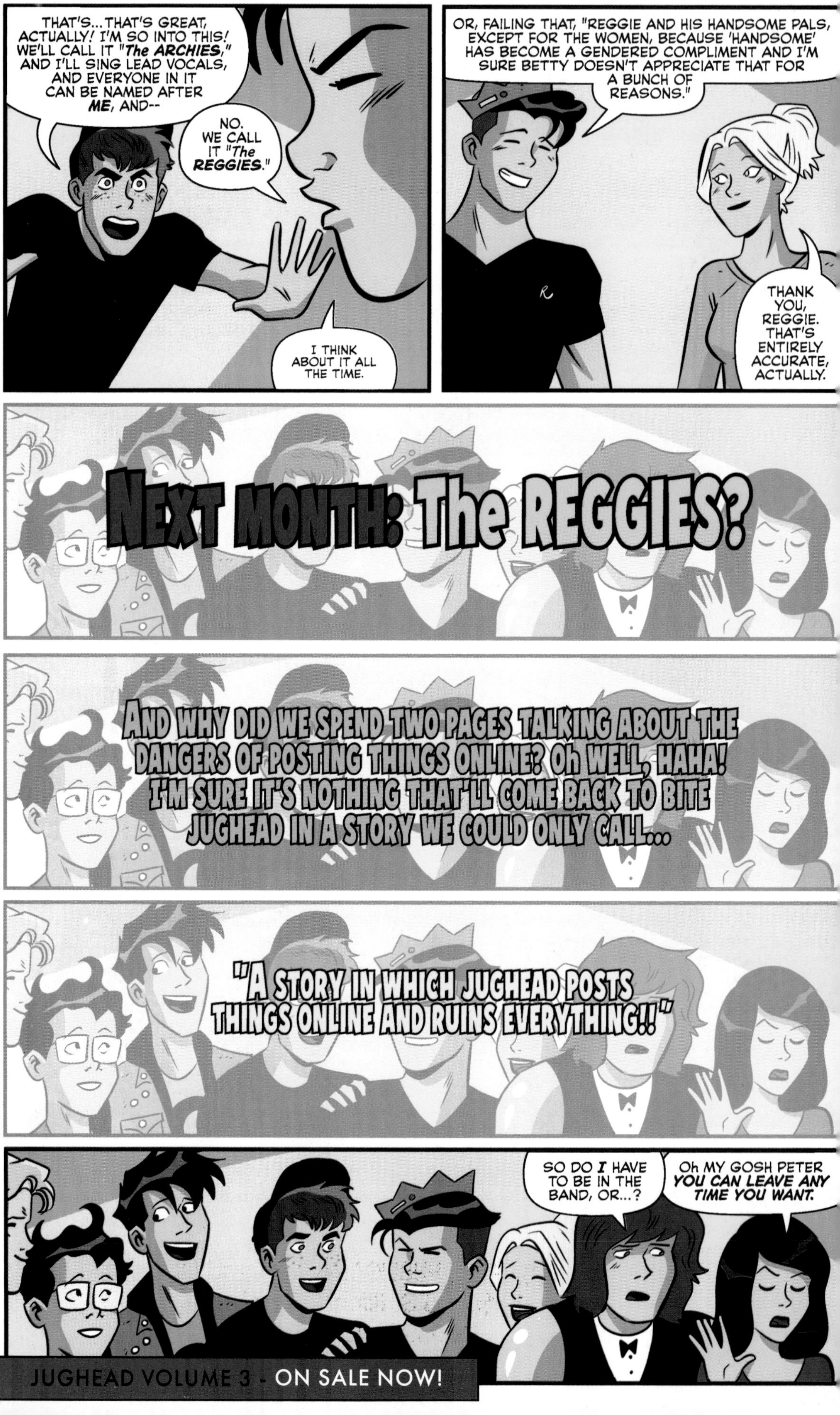
THAT'S...THAT'S GREAT, ACTUALLY! I'M SO INTO THIS! WE'LL CALL IT "*The ARCHIES*," AND I'LL SING LEAD VOCALS, AND EVERYONE IN IT CAN BE NAMED AFTER ***ME***, AND--
NO. WE CALL IT "*The **REGGIES***."
I THINK ABOUT IT ALL THE TIME.
OR, FAILING THAT, "REGGIE AND HIS HANDSOME PALS, EXCEPT FOR THE WOMEN, BECAUSE 'HANDSOME' HAS BECOME A GENDERED COMPLIMENT AND I'M SURE BETTY DOESN'T APPRECIATE THAT FOR A BUNCH OF REASONS."
THANK YOU, REGGIE. THAT'S ENTIRELY ACCURATE, ACTUALLY.
NEXT MONTH: The REGGIES?
AND WHY DID WE SPEND TWO PAGES TALKING ABOUT THE DANGERS OF POSTING THINGS ONLINE? Oh WELL, HAHA! I'M SURE IT'S NOTHING THAT'LL COME BACK TO BITE JUGHEAD IN A STORY WE COULD ONLY CALL...
"A STORY IN WHICH JUGHEAD POSTS THINGS ONLINE AND RUINS EVERYTHING!!"
SO DO ***I*** HAVE TO BE IN THE BAND, OR...?
Oh MY GOSH PETER ***YOU CAN LEAVE ANY TIME YOU WANT.***
JUGHEAD VOLUME 3 - ON SALE NOW!